European Television: Immigrants and Ethnic Minorities

European Television: Immigrants and Ethnic Minorities

Edited by Claire Frachon and Marion Vargaftig

with the assistance of Laurence Briot

John Libbey

JL

LONDON • PARIS • ROME

British Library Cataloguing in Publication in Data

European Television: Immigrants and Ethnic Minorities
I. Frachon, Claire II. Vargaftig, Marion
    302.2345

Translation by Pauline Ridel

Published by

John Libbey & Company Ltd, 13 Smiths Yard, Summerley Street,
London SW18 4HR, England.
Telephone: +44 0181-947 2777: Fax: +44 0181-947 2664
John Libbey Eurotext Ltd, 127 ave de la République, 92120 Montrouge, France.
John Libbey - C.I.C. s.r.l., via Lazzaro Spallanzani 11, 00161 Rome, Italy.

Printed in Great Britain by Biddles Ltd, Guildford, UK

Contents

Acknowledgements   vii

Editors' Note   ix

Preface
Raymond Weber   1

Introduction
Claire Frachon and Marion Vargaftig   3

PART I: ESSAYS

UK TV: A place in the sun?
Trevor Phillips   13

Foreigners on prime time or is television xenophobic?
Jérôme Bourdon   22

Television and racial equality: How the Race Relations Act has helped
Chris Myant   35

Networking for migrant perspectives on television in France and Europe:
the IM'média agency's experience
Mogniss H. Abdallah   45

From Monochrome to Technicolour: The history of PBME (Public Broadcasting
for a Multicultural Europe)
Europe Singh   60

A mirror crack'd from side to side: Black & independent producers and the television industry
Salim Salam 68

The Council of Europe's guidelines 1972–1992
Antonio Perotti 76

PART II: COUNTRIES *by Claire Frachon and Marion Vargaftig*

Austria   91
Belgium   99
Czech Republic & Slovakia   113
Denmark   123
France   135
Germany   159
Hungary   181
Italy   189
The Netherlands   199
Norway   215
Spain   223
Sweden   231
Switzerland   241
United Kingdom   253

PART III: APPENDICES

Sources   281
Festivals   289
Awards   295
Bibliography   297

Acknowledgements

This book could never have been completed without the support, understanding and help of a number of people.

First of all we would like to extend our sincere gratitude to Mogniss H. Abdallah, Jérôme Bourdon, Chris Myant, Antonio Perotti, Trevor Phillips, Salim Salam, Europe Singh for their contributions to the publication.

We would like to thank those organisations who have supported and underwritten this project:

- The Council of Europe
- The British Council
- Channel 4
- The cultural service of the French Embassy in London

Special thanks to: Ritva Mitchell, Elizabeth Rohmer, Caitlin Taylor, Raymond Weber (Council of Europe); Rosemary Hood (British Council); Susan Dunkley (Channel 4); Michel Lummaux (French Embassy in London).

Valuable assistance was provided by:

Austria: Helmut Kletzander (ORF), Inge Landré (French Institut in Vienna).

Belgium: Khiti-Amina Benhachem (RTBF), Mehrdad Tagian (RTBF), Jean-Claude Brodbeck (French Embassy), Philippe Coppieters (Commissariat Royal à la Politique des Immigrés), Marc Dechamps (RTBF), Jacques Gouverneur (RTBF), Anne Remiche-Martynow (director), Miguel Rivière (RTBF), Jos Tuerlinckx (BRTN), Flip Voets (BRTN)).

Czech Republic and Slovakia: Marcela Augustova (CT), Fabienne Drout (French Embassy), Fero Fenic (Febio), Milena Jaresova (CT-Telexport), Damian Kausitz (CT), Ivan Kralik (ST), Ivo Mathe (CT), Petr Sladecek (Nova TV), Jaromir Stvrtna (CT Ostrava), Helena Trestikova (Film and Sociology).

Denmark: Kerstin Hagrup (Filmkontakt Nord), Dino Raymond Hansen (Danish Film Workshop), Esther Heller, Lally Hoffmann (TV2), Filomenita Mongaya-Hogsholm (Worldscan), Annette Olsen (Sfinx TV), Andreas Steinmann (Verden Rundt).

France: Patrice Barrat (Agence Point du Jour), Cati Couteau (INA), Fernanda da Silva (FAS), Claire Doutriaux (La Sept/ARTE), Sylvie Fansten (France 3) Evelyne Georges,

Christiane Herrero (FAS), Catherine Humblot (Le Monde), Marie-Françoise Lévy (CNRS), Antoinette Moreau-Desportes (Ministère des Affaires Sociales), Caroline de Peyster (Librairie Tekhné), Jean-Louis Saporito (Agence Point du Jour).

Germany: Yagmur Atsiz (WDR), Josef Eckhardt (WDR), Bernd Fischer (ZDF), Uli Gondolatsch, Ronald Gräbe (WDR), Claus Josten (ZDF/ARTE), Bärbel Lütz-Saal (ZDF), Hans-Heinz Röll (ZDF), Eckart Stein (ZDF), Martina Schwindenhammer (ZDF), Sophie Truchet, Alke Wierth (Centre for Turkish Studies), Peter Zimmerman (BR).

Hungary: Andrea Borbàs (MTV), Ibolya Fekete, Judit Kele, Judit Safàr, François Truffart (French Embassy).

Italy: Elio Andalo Vimercati, Patricia Baroni (Festival dei Popoli), Massimo Ghirelli (RAI 2), Barbara Capuano (RAI 3), Claudia Origlia (RAI 2).

The Netherlands: Abdeluheb Choho (STOA), Louis Heinsman (NOS), Ed Klute (STOA), Joop Lahaise (ADO), Dick Oosterbaan (NOS), Gerard Reteig (Migranten TV Amsterdam), Huub Spall (NOS).

Norway: Caroline Babayan (Kaleidoscope), Hildur Ferskaug (Kaleidoscope), Ada Haug (NRK), Toril Simonsen (Film Kontakt Nord), Egil Teige (NRK), Tonje Tunold (NRK Sami).

Spain: Lola Alvarez (Canal Sur), Jaume Vilalta (TVE), Alina Iraizoz (TVE).

Sweden: Märten Andersson (SVT, Kanal 1), Antonia Carnerud (ADC Sweet Movie), Goran Guner (Film Kontakt Nord), PeA Holmquist, Lars Lindberg (SVT Lulea).

Switzerland: Tina Boillat (Rencontres Medias Nord-Sud), Anne Bouvrot (TSR), Helga Duschek (TSR) Ruth Gibellini (TSI), Edith Hossle (DRS), Jean-Bernard Neuenschwander (Office Fédéral des Etrangers), Lorena Pianezza (TSI), Claude Torracinta (TSR).

United Kingdom: Tariq Ali (Bandung Production), Manuel Alvarado (John Libbey & Company), Rena Bhagrath (British Council), Barbara Dent (British Council Paris), Farrukh Dhondy (Channel 4), June Givanni (British Film Institute), Alec Hargreaves (University of Loughborough), Simone Mondesir (Channel 4), Narendhra Morar (BBC in the Midlands), Geoffrey Morris (BBC), Colin Prescod, John Twitchin.

In particular, we would like to thank the Publications and Documentation Service at the Institut National de l'Audiovisuel (INA), the Association Dialogue entre les Cultures (ADEC) and the Centre d'Information et d'Etudes sur les Migrations Internationales (CIEMI), especially Myrna Giovanella, for their unfailing aid and advice for the French version of the book.

Warmest thanks are also due to Charles Brown, Ed Girardet and Peter Newborne for their constant support and attention.

And, to all those, too numerous to mention, who joined us in this undertaking, a heartfelt thank you.

Editors' Note

The first European Television and Immigration Conference/Festival was held at the Arche de la Fraternité Foundation in Paris in June 1992.

We had undertaken this project for several reasons: to try to escape from an insular French exploration of these problems by looking at what was being done elsewhere; to enable media professionals – writers, film makers, producers, heads of programme units – from all over Europe working with these themes to meet and compare experiences; to lay the groundwork for a debate on the role of television in handling immigration themes in the face of growing intolerance.

We wanted this debate to be based on a concrete body of evidence: the programmes produced during the 1990s. Some were actually made for immigrants or ethnic minorities, but there were also mainstream programmes – magazines, serials, documentaries and children's programmes – that shared a common aim of making viewers more aware of the truth about immigration.

This necessarily practical research was launched in about 15 countries: the traditional countries of immigration, such as Germany, Belgium, France, the United Kingdom, the Netherlands, the new countries of immigration that used to export labour, like Spain and Italy, the Scandinavian countries with their legendary tolerance (Denmark, Sweden, Norway) and two countries from the former Eastern bloc (Hungary and the former Czechoslovakia) confronted with problems concerning minorities and refugees.

Leaving aside newscasts, too heavily dependent on current events, we collected information on approximately 200 programmes, produced by 28 European channels, which were presented, examined and compared by genre at the June 1992 conference.

We felt it was essential to go further because behind the images lay the policies of the various channels, sometimes set out in their charters, sometimes reflecting the determination of individuals struggling within the system to make their ideas heard. Meanwhile, in the background, the history of immigration and current political policies shed a different light on each country's particular set of circumstances.

In the book published in France in April 1993 under the title *Télévisions d'Europe et Immigration*, we reported on the outcomes of the conference and grouped the information collected into chapters covering 14 European countries. This new edition in English has been completely revised and updated.

The book is still divided into two separate and complementary parts. The first section presents new interpretations and perspectives by researchers and producers. The second gives a non-exhaustive inventory of recent television programmes produced and broadcast by channels in 15 European countries. It also provides a thumbnail sketch of immigration in each country, with a glance at the general broadcasting scene and the policies of the individual channels. New initiatives and festivals are listed at the end of each chapter. The presentation of the chapters varies slightly because of the diversity of situations.

Generally speaking, we have put more emphasis on material provided directly by the channels themselves. It was sometimes difficult to obtain up-to-date information: the broadcasting scene is constantly changing as new channels emerge and others disappear, and in some countries schedules are continually being reshuffled. We thought it was important to provide the full background and history of some magazines made for immigrants or ethnic minorities,[1] showing how their content and format has changed over the years, because these changes also reflect shifting attitudes, demands and policies.

This book represents an initial attempt at an overview of the 1990s, providing the facts needed for a better understanding of what is happening in Europe now.

---

1 The terminology varies from country to country: immigrants in France, guest workers then foreigners in Germany, blacks or ethnic minorities in the UK. These differences have been retained in our descriptions.

Preface

Raymond Weber

Director of Education, Culture and Sport, Council of Europe

Television has once more reached a historic crossroads. For one thing, the GATT trade negotiations have put the contested notion of 'cultural exception' back in the headlines. And the technologies that we hardly dare to call new any more because they become obsolete so quickly have given us a glimpse of a type of television so radically different that today's problems may soon appear equally out of date.

First, let us look at 'cultural exception'. Everyone agrees nowadays that broadcasting comes under the heading of culture, but a quick look through this book will shed new light on what this really means. If broadcasting is not just a commodity like any other, why is it that all television channels – whether public or private – necessarily define their policies in terms of commercial competition, and why should there be this eternal debate about audience figures and market share? Admittedly, companies have to secure financing and advertising revenue, but are we not the heirs to cultural democratization theories precisely because of that most influential of mass media, television? If we look at it this way, it is not the viewing figures that matter, but the quality and diversity of the programmes. Concern for those who are the most culturally deprived and for whom television is the sole source of knowledge should be a major objective for television.

In this respect, immigrants are the most culturally deprived of all. They have a culture – their own, that of their country and their ancestors – but they have very little of the culture of the country in which they have to live. It is this gap that creates an awareness of something missing and gives immigrants the feeling of exclusion which so many observers have described. This book also reminds us that while some countries are more attentive than others to what we at the Council of Europe call 'cultural rights', not one of them devotes prime time to specific audiences.

1

Faced with this gap – and this discrimination – some people think that the solution lies in new technology; a television system based on theme channels, with pay-per-view, is one of the most frequently quoted options. Digital compression will allow an increasingly large supply of different programmes. Transmitting thousands of channels through one cable is no longer just a fantasy, and it is true that these channels could answer the wishes and requirements of many different types of viewer. The role of new technologies, as mentioned earlier, is to stay ahead of the field in order to expand the industries that manufacture them. They are supposed to launch new services and create new demands. The viewer already has available catalogues full of programmes that can be ordered using the remote control and a credit card. So here we are again, back in a consumer cycle of creating and fulfilling demand, and there is no guarantee that these new hypermarkets being built along the information highway will prove capable of breaking out of the mindset of 'everyone for themselves'.

What can be done? Where can we find solutions that are not simply thought up by some people and imposed on others? The education programmes that the Council of Europe has offered the European media for about ten years now are an attempt to answer these questions. We emphasize that these programmes should be incorporated into the primary school curriculum. Shaping a critical and intelligent attitude towards the media and developing pupils' sense of responsibility from an early age seem to us to be essential lessons in today's multicultural societies. But convinced as we are of the primordial and irreplaceable role of these lessons, we also know that it cannot be the only answer to the question, which is ultimately one of reducing and if possible eliminating the inequalities in gaining access to the media. A form of television devised by and for minorities: this is what everyone should be concerned about. This is exactly the idea that is supported in this book, and that is why it is a particular pleasure for me to introduce it to you. The black producers in the United Kingdom described by Salim Salam, well-known programmes such as *Birthrights*, or the analysis of the remarkable job being done by the Commission for Racial Equality, which has used more than one programme in its struggle against racism and inequality – all these contributions are signs of the emergence of a different kind of television. Not only would this new television foster the sociocultural integration of immigrants, it would give all those from the dominant culture something to think about – those who are little inclined to make new contacts and to seek personal fulfilment in the discovery of difference and diversity. 'Culture covers both living and doing', Antonio Perotti writes in his book *Plaidoyer pour l'interculturel* (The case for intercultural education).[1] This book invites us to do both.

---

1   Perotti, Antonio, *The case for intercultural education*, Council of Europe Press, 1994.

Introduction

Claire Frachon and Marion Vargaftig

Everyone now agrees that television is a powerful medium. 'The box', as fascinating as it is disturbing, absorbs and reflects the various concerns of a society in search of its identity at the dawn of 'Greater Europe', with its outbreaks of racism and nationalism. While instances of racism on television are more rare than is widely supposed,[1] it seems that television in general does not anticipate changes in society – even though it does keep a watchful eye on prejudice and reactionary tendencies. Television is mostly content to follow and assimilate social trends but sometimes influences them; treatment of minorities is no exception and their relations with television are often stormy. This reinforces our view that television is like a cracked mirror: while it reflects society, it often does so imperfectly, distorting or fracturing reality to a greater or lesser degree. The mirror may reflect the history, attitudes and politics of a given period but not always in a way that is simple or direct.

It is a sign of the times that the views of the researchers and producers in the first part of this book concentrate on warning against oversights, on the need to portray minorities fairly, and on recent initiatives. Although they acknowledge the pioneering role played by the United Kingdom, they also warn against any easy or uncritical endorsement of the 'British model' which has been so highly praised by other European countries. The danger that they highlight is that of mistaking first, faltering steps for great strides thereby underestimating the scale of the task facing those who would wish to see radio and television fulfil its obligations in a diverse, pluralistic and democratic society.

The second section provides a survey of the differing national responses within Europe to issues of ethnicity, cultural diversity and migration, placing the media's handling of such matters within their broad political and historical concept. Al-

---

1 See Jérôme Bourdon's article, 'Foreigners on prime time or Is television xenophobic?' in this volume.

though these chapters do not purport to be exhaustive or critical analyses, they do highlight the similarities and differences between different European responses and their juxtaposition in this volume, in itself is very revealing. They show not only the slow pace of change but also the uneven progress that has been made to date and the scale of the challenges that remain ahead.

European television channels are starting to consider it their duty to take account of ethnic minorities, but minorities are still a long way from being part of daily life on television, of being accepted as totally ordinary while having the chance to make their voices heard. Let us look first at how programmes have changed over the years. Comparing those made since the 1960s up to the present highlights the transformations that have been made, not just in terms of content and target audience but also in the type of programmes produced.

In the 1960s, when large numbers of immigrant workers started arriving from the Third World, television magazines were made specifically for them. Although the public channels' charters often do not mention any obligation to take account of this sector of the population (who pay their licence fees like anyone else), it is the public channels which took up the task of broadcasting programmes for immigrants – except in France.

These magazines, which were usually produced by the news departments and were always broadcast in immigrants' own languages, were intended first of all to respond to the newcomers' specific needs. The programmes provided practical information about life in the host country while maintaining a link with the country of origin – because at that time immigrants were expected to return home when their labour was no longer required. Germany's *Gastarbeiter* (guest workers) were the first to have their own television programmes. *Nachbarn, unsere Nachbarn* (Neighbours, Our Neighbours) was launched on ZDF in 1963, followed by *Ihre Heimat, unsere Heimat* (Your Homeland, Our Homeland) on WDR. The titles speak for themselves: the aim was to combat homesickness with features often produced by Greek, Italian, Polish or Yugoslav television. Each community had its own slot, in its own language, with German subtitles.

In 1965 Belgium's French-language public channel, RTBF, launched its first magazine for immigrants and by the 1970s practically every immigrant community – Italian, Spanish, Portuguese, North African – had its own programme. The formula remained more or less unchanged until 1987, when cable broadcasts of Italy's public channel, RAI 1, and Spain's RTE 1 led to the magazines for immigrants from these countries being taken off the air. It was argued that there was no need for such programmes when immigrants could receive broadcasts from their home countries. We return to this point below.

The first French magazine, *Mosaïques*, broadcast on the state-owned FR3, only in 1976, took by and large the same editorial line and adopted a similarly patronising tone. But there was one major difference: unlike its cousins in other countries, *Mosaïques*, then *Rencontres*, were financed directly by the Fonds d'Action Sociale (FAS – Social Action Fund), a public body answerable to the Ministry of Social Affairs; the FAS even had to buy airtime for the programme until 1990. The idea was to address individuals rather than communities with a view to helping them integrate - or rather to assimilate them – into French society. So it was the same magazine for everyone, leading some communities to complain that they were being completely ignored while the North Africans got all the airtime. The most recent one, *Premier Service*, launched in 1993, broadcast every morning at 7.00 am, stopped production in 1994 and will not be replaced in 1995.

In the United Kingdom, the BBC launched its first magazines for Indians and Pakistanis in 1965. The aim was above all to help immigrants learn English, while teaching them about the British way of life by providing practical solutions to everyday problems. The BBC quickly opted for a variety of concepts and approaches by creating, producing or buying documentaries, fiction series, cultural magazines and educational broadcasts. The arrival of the privately owned Channel 4, set up in 1982 to meet the needs of all minorities in Britain, gave fresh impetus to this trend. Whether as players in the social debate or characters in fiction, minorities are increasingly a part of the British broadcasting scene.

Other countries, having to cope with immigration at a later period, made different choices – Italy, for instance. The magazine *Nonsolonero*, launched on RAI 2 in 1988, aimed to get as many viewers as possible involved in thinking about inter-ethnic coexistence by taking up themes that television news tended to neglect or even distort. Rather than targeting immigrant groups, the magazine's prime objective was to make Italians aware of these newcomers. One might think that Italians – many of whom had to emigrate after the Second World War for economic reasons – would be more understanding about immigrants to their own country, but this is not the case. *Nonsolonero* was unfortunately taken off the air in 1994 as a result of political upheavals and their repercussions on the public channels.

It is also interesting that Hungary only started producing magazine programmes for minorities, in their own languages, in the 1990s, although these minorities had been in the country since the redrawing of Central and Eastern Europe's boundaries at the end of the First World War. Slovakia, on the other hand, has been broadcasting a magazine for the Hungarian minority there since 1983. What the Hungarian, Czech and Slovak public channels have in common is that in 1991 all of them launched regular magazines for Romanies in response to concern about growing hostility towards this community.

During the 1980s, as immigrant workers were joined by their wives and families, it became clear that they would be staying in the host countries and were set to become part of everyday life there. A second generation was born and grew up there. Broadcasters began to wonder whether they should continue making programmes in Arabic, Turkish or Portuguese, and whether they should even continue what detractors described as 'ghetto magazines' – maybe also because they were not shown at peak viewing times. Would it be better to concentrate on major documentary series about immigration and factual programmes aimed at a wider audience? Was it even necessary to make a choice between these types of programme, which could be regarded as complementary? At the same time, minorities' political activism and the fight of leading producers with roots in the communities, started to give them a voice and coincide with a shift in portrayal of minorities and helped bring about the emergence of programmes representing their own interest.

In the Netherlands, the NOS tried to maintain a balance between magazines for immigrants and programmes of more general interest, in line with the Dutch tradition of respect for people's origins and cultural difference. In 1993 on Sunday afternoons the third channel shows programmes made specifically for the Turkish, Moroccan and Chinese communities, including children's programmes, news magazines and music broadcasts. Documentaries and magazines intended for a wider audience go out on the same channel during prime time. It should be emphasised that the NOS charter clearly defines the fundamental role and responsibilities of television. The tendency in 1995 is to have less and less programmes in Turkish or Arabic.

Sweden is the only Scandinavian country with a public television department specifically for minorities. It was set up in 1975. STV has been producing *Mosaik*, a weekly magazine in Turkish, Greek, Serbian and Croatian, since 1987. Made up of short features on cultural and social topics, *Mosaik* can be picked up in all Scandinavian countries but it has retained a neutral tone. Denmark's TV2 prefers to provide quite provocative programmes about minorities for a wide audience in the form of documentary series or good investigative reporting. The Norwegians, like the Germans, have made a special effort with their programmes for children and young people, stressing tolerance and a receptive outlook on other cultures and languages. This could provide others with food for thought.

Switzerland, with three official languages and three public television channels, has tackled the issue from another angle. The French-language TSR has decided to emphasise topical broadcasts for a wide audience rather than producing magazines for foreign workers. TSR informs viewers about the circumstances in which immigrants live and work, and its news magazines *Temps Présent* and *Tell Quel*, launched in 1969, have made their mark worldwide. These programmes frequently feature items about refugees, illegal immigration and asylum-seekers. Their hard-hitting investigations do not hesitate to show the dark side of Switzerland's famous prosperity, even going so far as to point out embarrassing facts. TSI, the Italian-language channel, has taken a different approach, producing four programmes especially for Italian and Spanish immigrants.

While magazines are undeniably useful when they respond to a specific need, documentaries enable broadcasters to reach, inform and educate a wider audience, especially by revealing matters that are too often ignored. But the role that fiction can play in this respect should not be underestimated; using immigrants as characters in fiction gives ordinary members of the public the chance to identify with them. Soaps, sitcoms and television films can help to portray minorities in everyday life and thus break the vicious circle that tends to associate them with crime, clandestinity and all sorts of other problems. British television has understood this. But even when minorities have access to television, they are too often portrayed as the British public expects to see them. Most of the time, members of ethnic minorities are not involved in conceiving programmes or writing scripts and there is a tendency to fall back on stereotypes. Even when minorities do get a look-in, the restrictions imposed by broadcasters often mean their ideas have to be watered down. This is what happened in France when the two Algerian-origin authors of the series *La famille Ramdan*[1] were forced by the channel M6 to make major alterations to their script.

The 1990s saw the emergence of cable and satellite broadcasting all over Europe, and the beginning of access to foreign television. They also made it easier to set up theme-based and local channels. This caused a major shake-up on the broadcasting scene in each country and led to audiences being defined differently. The new channels were usually targeted at sectors of the population who felt they had been neglected or ignored by traditional broadcasters; ethnic minorities were an obvious example. Foreign channels, including those from immigrants' countries of origin, arrived in force and are now widely available in the host countries. But it would be wrong to think that just because immigrants have welcomed foreign channels enthusiastically and have been among the first to buy satellite dishes, this releases the public channels from their duty to serve the whole population. It is true, though, that public service television increasingly has a tendency to take a commercial approach rather than trying to provide 'citizens' television'.

In France, for example, one-sided or superficial reporting of the Gulf War led to a massive increase in sales of satellite dishes. Ethnic minorities were thus able to pick

---

1   See the chapter on France.

up dozens of channels that gave them an alternative view of what was going on. This was most noticeable in the poorer suburbs, where people watch a lot of television. Twelve Turkish channels can now be received in Western Europe, covering a wide spectrum of political and religious views. Since September 1994 the Algerian government has been broadcasting its national public television service via the Eutelsat satellite – without attempting to conceal its political motives. Minorities' enthusiasm for satellite only serves to highlight the underdevelopment of cable in France, where the few community projects for cable channels have never got off the ground. As for the short-lived multicultural channel TV Mondes, which offered ample airtime to second-generation immigrants, it was forced to stop broadcasting in 1991. The French view that immigrants should be 'integrated' probably explains the failure of cable channels aimed at minorities. The development of satellite television – impossible to regulate or control – could backfire because it keeps immigrant communities inward-looking and tends to cut them off from the host country.

The 13 million or so people of foreign origin living in Europe represent a valuable potential audience for the new theme-based channels. High production costs mean that these channels operate mainly by repeating the same programmes in different time slots. What they want is ready-to-broadcast programmes that can be acquired cheaply. These so-called ethnic channels – and especially those based in Britain – are fortunate in that huge stocks of films and programmes are available from Hong Kong and India. However, although these channels are popular with first-generation immigrants eager to watch programmes in their own languages, subsequent generations do not necessarily share their enthusiasm.

The Netherlands, which has one of the highest rates of cable penetration in the world, introduced local channels for immigrants, known as Migranten TV, in major cities in 1984. These channels proposed a range of programmes devised and produced especially for immigrant communities, but only in 1994 the one launched in Amsterdam, which offers a mix of news, culture and entertainment, has managed to secure the necessary financing to continue. The Dutch are currently seeking less costly ways of providing local television.

Immigration again became a hot political issue in the 1990s and the influx of illegal immigrants and increasing racism have hoisted immigrants into the headlines of Europe's newscasts and news magazines. Spain, for instance, confronted by large numbers of immigrants arriving from Africa via the Straits of Gibraltar, too often tackles the issue in terms of illegal immigration and black market labour. It is high time that all television programmes reflected the presence of minorities in Europe in a natural and unprejudiced way, but this has not happened yet. This makes it even more important to give minorities the chance to express their own views so that television shows the subject from all angles. Although few immigrants appear in front of the cameras, there are even fewer behind the cameras, and this situation also has to improve if we want to change what we see on our television screens. This requires a new policy that would ensure fair representation of minorities among television staff and enable people from an immigrant background to make programmes. The Council of Europe has long supported this view and has come up with various initiatives and recommendations, but only very recently have a few European channels started to take notice. The most forceful have got together to try to persuade the European Broadcasting Union (EBU) to adopt a code of conduct on the subject.

Although this book makes it clear that there is no such thing as an ideal programme, it does highlight the many projects now being organised in the name of multiculturalism. This single concept which has become significant, covers a multitude of ideas, some of them contradictory: from respect for difference to the struggle against racism, from the integration of foreigners to the discovery of different lifestyles, from the battle for social justice to portayal of the Third World. Multiculturalism draws together somewhat haphazardly broad and important ideas of tolerance and openness to others, and mixes them up with a generous dollop of political correctness. It is to be hoped that European broadcasters will soon reach agreement on a set of guidelines that will enable our television screens to provide a true reflection of the diversity of our societies. It will be an important test for our democracies.

Part I
Essays

UK TV: A place in the sun?

Trevor Phillips

Head of Current Affairs, London Weekend Television

There was a time in British life when the appearance of a dark face on a TV screen would provoke peculiarly unBritish reactions: that is to say, strong and passionate responses. White viewers would reach for the phone to object. Hundreds would bombard the TV stations' switchboards with complaints that 'niggers' could not speak the Queen's English, or that they did not understand the British way. Black viewers would reach for their telephones too. But in their case it was to call relatives and friends to tell them to turn on their TV sets straight away or else they might miss the sight of a black face on the nation's most popular medium. It was rather like birdwatchers being called to see a particularly rare species before it disappeared.

Today, things are different – on the surface, at least. As I write, the BBC's national news is being read by a black woman, Moira Stuart. When she finishes, the local news, in the UK's biggest region, the Southeast, will be read by another black woman, Jacqui Harper. Over on the main commercial channel, ITV, the day's top news bulletin will be read by a black man, Trevor McDonald. On Channel 4, Zeinab Badawi and Shahnaz Pakhravan will be doing the same for Channel 4's cerebral evening news programme.

It's not just in journalism that British TV is moving into colour. The top children's TV show, *Gladiators*, is hosted by a black man, John Fashanu, and a white woman with a foreign name, Ulrika Jonsson. The BBC's top entertainer for some seasons has been the Birmingham-born black comedian Lenny Henry. In an area increasingly important to TV – sport – the faces both on the field and on the pundits' bench

13

are more often than not a mixture of colours.

We are a long way from where we started, in the days when black people appeared only as extras, or as the objects of nature documentaries. We are told frequently by industry bosses that all Britain's peoples have a place in the TV sun. It's just a matter of time and training. I am not so sure.

Some months ago, I was invited to see a senior BBC executive, who hoped to tempt me to join the Corporation. I arrived at TV Centre in a new – large – car, dressed smartly, but casually. I told the gateman why I was there. My name was on the list of expected visitors, I pointed out. He disappeared for a few moments to check, and returned to direct me to the car parking space that had been reserved for me. Just as I was about to pull off, he leaned forward over his clipboard, with a puzzled frown, and said ' Sorry – who did you say you'd come to pick up?' Evidently, in spite of all the preparations and fuss, a black man in a Jaguar could mean only one thing at TV Centre – a chauffeur come to pick up a BBC bigwig.

Sadly this attitude is still all too prevalent throughout the British media. Black and Asian people are visitors, not part of the national fabric. And in this, of course, what the media village is doing is simply reflecting the attitudes of the society as a whole. In Britain today, ethnic minorities account for some six per cent of the population as a whole. The bulk of these are people whose families came originally from Africa, the Asian subcontinent or the Caribbean. Most of them are either of African origin or of Asian origin – though it's a complex group, not easy to define simply. It is frequently forgotten that many of those who think of themselves as Asian came from the Caribbean or Africa. A quarter of those who define themselves as Afro-Caribbean have non-black partners, and their children will be what is currently described as 'mixed-race'. Our minority communities have produced writers, artists, musicians and performers who are talented and successful both here and abroad in their own right. Yet to watch British TV you would imagine that these are monochrome, grey, marginal, irrelevant communities which occasionally produce outstanding individuals.

Does it matter? After all this is just TV we're talking about – not manufacturing industry, not brain surgery, not even the higher reaches of leading edge science. It is essentially ephemeral and passing. But it is increasingly the place where the nation invents itself. If you're not there, you don't exist. We may not be invisible but we are insignificant in our presence. And this isn't just abstraction. Perhaps the most substantial fear of many black and Asian people in the UK is that of racially motivated attack. There is some anecdotal evidence that many of these attacks occur because the attackers believe that no-one cares what happens to black or Asian people. The result is all too graphically charted by Professor Bhikhu Parekh in a paper prepared for the All-Party Parliamentary Group on Race and Community. He points out that:

> ... the carefully researched British Crime Survey estimated that 130,000 racially motivated incidents occurred in 1991. Of these, about a quarter were assaults, a fifth cases of vandalism, and two fifths those of threats ... The last two years also saw fourteen racially motivated murders of Afro-Caribbeans and Asians, some particularly vicious ... It would hardly be an exaggeration to say that one in every two Afro-Caribbean and Asian families directly or indirectly suffered from the effects of racial incidents in 1991.

Set alongside that the levels of achievement of minorities in schools, their relative poverty, and historic high levels of unemployment, especially among the young and you draw a picture of distressingly marginalized set of communities – both in the mirror of TV and in the real world.

But when I entered TV in 1980 it looked as though it could be different. In the two years that followed one of ITV's leading commercial companies transmitted no less than 60 editions of a half-hour documentary programme called *Skin*, about and for the capital's ethnic minority viewers. As it turned out others watched avidly. The standards of journalism were high. The team – mostly though not exclusively black and Asian – built up reputations as being tough and professional. This was followed by two series made by LWT for Channel 4 – *Black On Black* and *Eastern Eye* – aimed at, respectively, black and Asian viewers. These were targetted series, and the research showed that they hit up to 90 per cent of their target audiences regularly. But they succeeded in drawing an audience which was neither black nor Asian. And they created new names for British TV – for example the rastafarian poet Benjamin Zephaniah, as well as showcasing the resurgent British gospel movement, and in the case of *Eastern Eye*, virtually inventing the bhangra sound.

On the face of it, even when these series were controversially ended in 1985, it was thought they would simply provide the platform for more and better interventions by minorities in British TV. There would be new programmes aimed at the minorities; and many of those who had worked in those specialist programmes would find their ways into so-called mainstream programming. It should have happened – but it didn't.

So far there is little evidence that the minority programme makers who came from this stable have found their way into important positions in the industry. In this respect too, television simply reflects what is happening elsewhere. When it comes to corporate Britain, there are limits to equality it seems. And the limits seem to coincide with the point in any organization or profession where real power is exercised.

Take, for example, the civil service: we serve in the lower reaches of the civil service, but there are few black faces amongst senior ranks except where the jobs are concerned with ethnic minority affairs. 2.1 per cent of top staff are minorities as opposed to three times that proportion in the population; only 50 per cent of whites are in lower administrative grades compared to 71 per cent of blacks.

Similarly, though there are many black and Asian lawyers, and have been for many years, none has been judged suitable for the higher levels of the judiciary. For example there are only 4 minority circuit judges out of 510, 11 out of 866 recorders.

A cursory look at the *Financial Times* 100 produces some executives from companies set up on their own – principally by Asian businesspeople. But minorities are absent at the top levels of the great Plcs or the public sector monopolies.

White South Africa has taken down the 'whites only' signs. But they could usefully be redeployed in Britain, to be put on the boardrooms and executive offices of corporate Britain. Even where minorities succeed, for example in sports, or entertainment, few make the transition to management. Black footballers have been present in the professional game for years – yet football league chairmen seem unable to see their merits as coaches.

Of all industries, television should be able to overcome this sort of problem. It is an industry where things move quickly, where the average age is young, where there's been expansion in the past and where there is constant movement of people, where the turnover of staff should allow for change to take place quickly. I am not one of those who believes that people are led by what they see on TV. But I do believe that what happens in this industry is indicative of what is happening elsewhere.

There are researchers and producers and even directors in British TV. But on the executive floors – where real decisions about scheduling, programme style and tone are taken – there are virtually no black faces. Despite the growing number of black faces on screen, amongst the hundreds of TV programme executives who wield power in the BBC, ITV and Channel 4, there are only four non-whites – and two of those executives deal exclusively with programmes for minorities.

Neatly, in the so-called mainstream there is one of us for each major channel – the head of politics for the BBC, and the head of current affairs for LWT, in ITV. I wish I could say it was tokenism. But one executive out of two hundred feels less like tokenism and more like an accident.

By the way all four of the non-white executives I've referred to started in the same place – making *Black On Black* and *Eastern Eye* for London Weekend in the early

1980s. It is a damning indictment that in more than a decade the industry has not moved on, and that no other company has taken the initiative to build a more representative management. Though the four of us are friends, we, like American Presidents and their Vice Presidents avoid travelling together for the sake of the industry; were we to be involved in an accident the power structure of British TV would be whiter than that of South Africa.

Minorities, it seems, are welcome as long as they don't expect to have any influence. But British TV may be losing out by failing to remedy such bias. Recently a friend who had been negotiating with a large American company told me that when the negotiations collapsed and the deal fell through, one of the Americans took him to one side to commiserate. The American then said 'Of course some of it is down to the way you guys handled it'. My friend said ' What do you mean?'. 'Well', said the American 'For a start you looked a bit old fashioned'. My friend, who wears Armani and carries a Psion organizer couldn't believe it and told the American so. The American shifted uneasily and said 'Look, here's one thing: in North America no-one would go into a negotiation like this with an all-white team'.

So much for the penetration of the mainstream. On the existence of specialist programmes there has been more progress. After London Weekend's magazine programmes ended in 1985, Channel 4 commissioned the black entertainment series *Club Mix* and the comedy *No Problem*. There were also further specialist factual programmes, especially on the BBC. The Corporation screened the black magazine *Ebony*, as a response to the commercial sector's *Black On Black*, later followed by *Network East* aimed at South Asian viewers. But over time the commercial sector has fragmented its multicultural programming to such an extent that it has had little presence in the schedule. Channel 4 succeeded to some extent with its comedy *Desmond's*, but in reality this programme, outstanding as it was, is yet another variant on an old British format – the workplace-based sitcom, made familiar by shows in factories, department stores, bus stations and so forth. Only the advent of a free-wheeling discussion programme hosted by the journalist Darcus Howe, the award-winning *Devil's Advocate* has put Channel 4 back on track with a programme with an original format based on authentically black ways of debating big issues. The programme, controversial as it is has now won a secure place in Channel 4's schedules.

Over on the BBC, after a period of uncertainty, the multicultural programmes unit has made substantial strides. *Network East* and *East* are now regular slots. *All Black* is a series aimed at Africans and Afro-Caribbeans, yet to find its feet but promising much. And recently the broken comedy series *The Real McCoy* has been supported into a third series by the BBC.

But there are many who now argue that all such series are diversions that allow the broadcasting establishments off the hook. Are these limited interventions allowing the TV establishment to, once again, marginalize the interests and priorities of minorities, by effectively saying to producers and directors from those minorities ' Don't bother us – you've got a slot, and that's where you belong'. Thus aspiring drama writers are sent to black comedy, game show directors told to apply to *The Real McCoy*, the potential *Panorama* producer diverted to *All Black* or *East*. There are increasingly those, including influential writers like Trix Worrell and Mike Phillips who argue that these ghetto programmes should be mothballed and that minority artists should compete – and be judged – on the same basis as everyone else.

I sympathize with the argument, but don't support it. Whatever the shortcomings of the 'specialist' strategy it is true that many young programme makers who would not otherwise have made any productions had the opportunity to learn their craft on the so-called 'ghetto' shows. The way to solve the diversion of talent is not to get rid of the only proven access for minority talent – it is to make sure that the other routes open up.

On both 'mainstream' and 'ghetto' fronts, however, the broadcasting environment is not favourable. On the commercial channels, the reform of the broadcasting acts has made the pressure on revenue greater than ever before; ITV companies are having to give greater sums to the government, and their airtime sales departments are being forced to compete ever more fiercely for revenue with the new channels. For programme makers the need to gain large and valuable audiences is stressed time and again by the men who now run the commercial TV business – and that means satisfying the need of minorities will take a lower profile than ever. More-over, commissioning executives and schedulers know what sells – safety first. Tried and trusted faces, familiar formats and middle of the road sentiments rule out the prospects of new voices from other places finding an airing.

Channel 4, the channel charged with the responsibility of catering for minority interests including those of the ethnic minority communities, is changing too. The new Broacasting Act gave it the responsibility of raising its own revenue from advertising, a job which had previously been left to the ITV companies, who paid a levy to fund Channel 4. The evidence is that Channel 4 is succeeding triumphantly in raising revenue – but principally with a diet of films and imported US product which features black stars, but could hardly be described as British multicultu-ralism in action. Most of the output of its multicultural programmes unit is poorly funded and largely consigned to the outer reaches of the schedule. It is, of course perfectly consistent with this approach for Channel 4 executives to point out that without that revenue they probably would never have the money to fund lossmak-ing minority shows; but even this rebuttal demonstrates the extent to which it is revenue considerations rather than those of the remit that are increasingly calling the tune at Channel 4.

Over at the BBC, the high-minded and determined Director-General, John Birt, has described a vision of the Corporation's future which projects a viewing experience that serves and includes all Britons. This in theory should safeguard a place for the specialist programmes; it should also mean a tough policy on training and promotion. Indeed the BBC recently stood up courageously in defence of a decision to award half of its regional traineeships to people from ethnic minorities. That's a good signal, but recent decisions which suggest that the Corporation plans to mount a ratings assault on ITV imply that the overall aims of the BBC may work against any commitment to minorities. For example the Corporation's drama department has, against its own staff's wishes brought in one of ITV's popular drama chiefs, Nick Elliott to shore up its peak time performances. Elliott to his credit, was responsible for ensuring that there were leading and substantial black characters in LWT's drama hit *London's Burning*, and even tried an (unsuccessful) action fomat with a black/white hero pairing. But there is little doubt that neither he nor his colleagues will hesitate to go for the jugular if necessary – even if it means putting a hold on the apirations of those who want the BBC's face to resemble that of its viewing population more closely.

From the BBC, ITV and Channel 4 there seems little to hope for by way of concern for the interests of minorities. Even the highly regulated system of broadcasting that survives in the UK cannot guarantee equal treatment. Oddly enough however it may be the forces that normally work against minorities that we may have to look towards to find new opportunities. The two most important influences shaping the future of the British broadcasting scene are new technology – especially new modes of distribution – and the free market.

Broadcasters looking for new streams of income are turning to satellite and to cable for expansion. It is becoming clearer that such channels will have to be funded by subscription and pay per view. It is predicted that though satellite may curently take only six per cent or so of the viewing audiences, it will grow to the end of the century; and when satellite's share flattens out, cable will go on growing to the point where satellite and cable between them may take up to a third of the viewing audience. The shock troops of the new channels will undoubtedly be movies and sport. But there is only a limited number of times that any audience will switch on to see *Terminator 1, 2* or *X*; and there must be only so many oddly named football tournaments that will attract fans to pay.

So in order to persuade new viewers to sign up, the cable and satellite operators are looking for more and more niche channels. Ethnic minorities are evidently such a group. Already there are two Asian cable channels and one black channel. The latter, significantly is American-owned, ultimately by the hugely successful Home Box Office. HBO saw the need to colonize minority viewing early when they bought up the lossmaking Black Entertainment TV organization. What HBO grasped was that minorities, partly because of low incomes and unemployment tend to have disproportionately high levels of TV viewing. For a movie based channel, such an audience is extraordinarily valuable, and any marginal marketing advantage – such as a black channel – would repay the marginal cost. HBO clearly believe that the same applies in the UK.

It is true that the economics of cable mean that such channels have to be low-cost. That means little original programming, long runs of repeats from other channels and poor presentation. Yet, for many minorities this may, increasingly, be the only way that they get a voice in the broadcasting world. And as the minority communities themselves become less poor they may have the funds to support better programming. Asian communities in particular find themselves able to support both a Hindi-movie channel plus a channel based on news and speech.

There is one other development that may bode well for a minority presence on the cable and satellite systems. The key point for producers in the media is that they sell their products several times – and in several countries. In some respects Britain's minority communities have as much in common with their cousins abroad, as they do with their white neighbours. Smart producers are now beginning to see that they can produce programmes for which can be aired in several countries, and the costs of which can then be shared.

For example, a TV producer who buys the rights to a major Hindi movie could find outlets for it in London, Toronto, New York, Nairobi and Johannesburg. Until satellite and cable, there weren't the broadcasting opportunities to take advantage of his property; with a broadcasting environment desperate for product he can do business. This is not yet true for original programming – but it will be.

The greatest irony in the TV landscape may well be this: the paternalistic, regulated environment of the terrestrial channels may increasingly force minorities off their agenda, whilst the buccaneering free marketeers of the cable and satellite channels could well begin to offer the chance of a presence hitherto undreamt of. And with the voracious appetite of the new channels, we could soon see more minority talk shows, quizzes, daytime soaps, viewer access programmes and entertainment extravaganzas. Black and Asian people will begin to see themselves, where they want, when they want and speaking in their own terms.

The political effect of such a separate existence on TV has yet to be seen. But one thing is sure: few black people will need to ring Granny to tell her that there's a black face on the telly in future. If she's not watching the programme, it'll probably only be because she's appearing on the show herself.

Foreigners on prime time or is television xenophobic?

Jérôme Bourdon[1]

Historian, Researcher at the Institut National de l'Audiovisuel

The rise of various forms of racism[2] in Europe has called the role of the media – and particularly television – into question. From its early days, television has been regarded as a source of immense power. The debate on racism is no exception to this rule: while some observers hope that intelligent programme planning can be used as a weapon in the fight against racism, others have attacked media professionals for allowing people to express openly racist views during TV broadcasts, alleging that this has contributed to the resurgence of racism. Thus a lengthy survey of how 'ethnic prejudices' are passed on in everyday conversation has no hesitation in concluding that the media and the élites who have access to them play a basic part in '*the production*' (my italics) of racial prejudice (Van Dijk, 1987, p. 359).[3]

---

1   This essay was written in 1992 for the French version of this book.

2   As Marletti (1991) points out, it is misleading to speak of only one kind of racism.

3   This author does take most of his examples from the press, but he does not hesitate to extend his theories to include the media as a whole.

Before considering the effects of racism, it is important to define what we mean by 'the presence of racism' on television.[1] What categories of programme may help to shape public opinion on ethnic minorities? And, more fundamentally, how does television categorize 'outsiders'? In order to speak well or ill of other people, in order even to talk about 'other people', we first need to know who they are.

The latter question is crucial because television, despite many predictions to the contrary since the 1970s, is not a segmented medium but a mass medium, and to most intents and purposes a national one. Like the modern press, it has developed in a national framework which it may itself have helped to shape. 'Newspapers, which certainly do not include the best of literary culture, act as cement for the masses', Max Weber wrote in 1924, defining the masses – in other words the modern nation – as having 'a particular feeling of group solidarity in the face of other groups' (Gerth & Mills, 1958, pp. 174–178). Since then, as Schlesinger (1991) has pointed out, most theorists on nationalism, especially Benedict Anderson, have linked it in varying degrees to the emergence of the mass media.

Like the mass circulation press before it, television reaches a wide variety of different audiences, but it is constantly constructing an image of this audience by stressing certain ways of speaking, by showing certain customs, aspects of history, colours of skin, religious practices. Every day, television sketches out a 'we', a collective identity with shifting borders. It chooses, rejects, excludes, welcomes, praises or makes fun of its subjects. This 'TV nation' has its stars, its regular spokesmen, its supporting actors, extras, spoilsports and scapegoats. Not all viewers belong to the communities represented (and they probably all feel, at some time or other, that television is excluding them).

It is against the background of this dense flow of TV programmes that we have to judge the task of defining a nation. The praiseworthy approach of pointing out 'incidents' and 'excesses' of all kinds – in other words, overt and avowed racism – is bound to be insufficient. Virtuous indignation about a joke is pointless because a racist joke can only be understood against a broad background and to criticize it presupposes that a whole set of questions have been resolved: is the joke symptomatic of a dominant trend in the programming? Is it aimed at a community which is generally unfairly treated in the media? Isn't it better to make a joke now and again than to systematically portray a foreign community as a victim?

In order to handle the issue of 'the image of the foreigner' on TV properly, we have to put the monster of television as a whole in the dock. This is why, just as I did not

---

1   The ideas expressed here owe much to Ara (1991), Marletti (1991), Twitchin (1988), as well as to questions put to Joop Lahaise (ADO, Amsterdam) and Claudia Origlia (Nonsolonero, RAI), with the help of Laurence Briot.

dwell on explicit cases of overstepping the mark, I have not mentioned broadcasts aimed specifically at immigrant communities, which usually only reach a small audience, or the few documentaries devoted to the subject of immigration. These broadcasts are only a drop in the ocean of the thousands of hours of TV schedules, and do little to shape the image of immigrants and foreigners in a country.

By this I mean to suggest that this phenomenon should be observed primarily through prime time and mass-audience programmes. Such broadcasts reach the entire population: their audiences include all those who make up the nation, all age groups, all nationalities, all cultures. These are the programmes from which viewers from ethnic minorities may – or may not – get the impression of being constantly excluded. These are the programmes from which viewers from cultural majorities construct their images of the 'outside' world in the broadest sense of the term: not just foreign countries but also regions, neighbourhoods or social circles which they do not know or frequent. The media have a considerable – and hard to define – social responsibility in producing these programmes. After looking at cases where programme presenters have 'overstepped the mark', I shall look at the main types of broadcast, the ones that are talked about – and those that are sometimes forgotten.

Racist 'excesses'?

In France the term 'racist excesses' became fashionable among journalists after the regulatory body for broadcasting, the Conseil supérieur de l'audiovisuel (CSA), issued a statement on the subject in November 1991.[1] In particular, the statement criticized a remark made by a football commentator during a match between Lens and Nantes on 15 September: 'Thirteen coloured players out of 26, that's a lot'. The CSA also criticized a sketch that made fun of sex education in a class composed mainly of North African pupils (part of the variety show *Sébastien, c'est fou* broadcast on 19 October 1991 by TF1). On 28 November, shortly after the statement was released, the chat show *Mardi Soir* on Antenne 2 caused an outcry because of fiercely racist comments made by a skinhead during a report. A year and a half earlier, on 6 February 1990, *Ciel Mon Mardi* on TF1 had included anti-Semitic comments and denials that the Holocaust had taken place. *Mardi Soir* and *Ciel Mon Mardi*, which are no longer on the air, were described by the CSA as French-style 'trash TV' – although they are models of discretion compared to the more outrageous American chat shows.

All these cases have various characteristics: indeed, it is difficult to know how to describe them. If we say that the people concerned 'went too far', does this mean that they got carried away, that when racism is not being discussed television stays

---

1   *Le Monde*, 9 November 1991, p. 13.

within its bounds and that foreigners should be pleased with their image (or lack of one) as portrayed by broadcasters? This metaphor suggests another: the ratings war, in other words the search for images that satisfy the instant tastes of most viewers. Humour that makes fun of foreigners, xenophobia that causes an outcry are examples of racism that commercial television may see as recipes for boosting their viewing figures.

The ensuing wave of indignation, as well as being fleeting, comes from outside the world of television. In most European countries, the comment or joke is mentioned or criticized after the programme, not on the air, by another organization or group, and then quoted in the press. One direct consequence of this is that, given newspaper readership figures, these incidents go unnoticed by the many people whose only source of news is television. The only exception to this is the BBC, which has produced a series of three documentaries devoted to how racism is expressed on television.[1]

A third point: whereas it is often newspapers which criticize television, in many countries the press itself is the main primary source of views hostile to foreigners. Countries with a tradition of popular newspapers relying heavily on scandal (like the British gutter press, which also exists in Germany) are familiar with the kind of stories in which the foreign origin of the individuals in question is emphasized and people are attacked because of their nationality or ethnic origin. According to Claudia Origlia, Italy also has more overt racism in the press than on television. In France, careful reading of the more popular dailies reveals an undercurrent of racism in many news items.[2]

The role of journalists: newscasts and debates

Debates on the ethics of communication, which have been in vogue since 1990, have focused mainly on journalists, but in many countries, especially Britain, France and Italy, TV news programmes are not where racist opinions or remarks against foreigners are most likely to be heard. Journalists – because of the way they are recruited and because of the general ideology of the profession, which supports democracy and integration – are opposed to overt racism and are usually anxious to draw attention to it. In France they may have given airtime to the extreme-right National Front and its leader Jean-Marie Le Pen, but they have made it clear that they do not support the party's views. It should be pointed out that French politi-

---

1 *The Black and White Media Show*, which I will return to later. See also the book published to accompany the series (Twitchin, 1988). The Netherlands is planning to carry out a similar project in the near future.

2 Hargreaves (1992) backs up this statement by quoting Pierre Seguret's thesis on the image of immigrants and immigration in the French press (Université Paul Valéry, Montpellier, 1991).

cians in general have an increasing tendency to colour their speech with racist overtones.

Some prominent journalists are inclined to highlight anti-racist opinions when dealing specifically with the subject of racism. One example was TF1's Anne Sinclair, in a noted debate after the Dreux by-election in 1983; ten years later Christine Ockrent took a similar stand in *Direct*, a programme on Antenne 2 devoted to the topic of racism. Both debates followed the same format: people with racist views were shown in prerecorded reports but only those who opposed racism were actually in the studio and able to explain and develop their arguments. It still causes an outcry when someone expresses racist views live on TV – an example was given earlier under the heading Racist 'excesses'.

In addition, whatever their faults, journalists are more closely monitored than people in other professions (or they monitor themselves more closely). Witness what happened to the presenters of the programmes *Mardi Soir* and *Ciel Mon Mardi*, which were criticized for much the same motives, as described above. *Mardi Soir*, presented by journalist Daniel Bilalian, was taken off the air by the channel's bosses, whereas *Ciel Mon Mardi*, a showcase for star presenter Christophe Dechavanne, was allowed to carry on as if nothing had happened.

Immigrants in television news: criminals and claimants

However, this attitude on the part of journalists does not give cause for optimism. In the Netherlands, precise information is available about the way foreigners are portrayed in news broadcasts. Like newspapers, television news has no hesitation in taking up the worrying theme of an 'invasion' of the country by refugees, as happened during the first four months of 1985 when a group of about 3,000 young Tamils fleeing the civil war in Sri Lanka were described as a 'wave of illegal immigrants'. The 'political' reasons for their flight were rapidly called into question; it was hinted that, like many others, they had left their country for 'economic' reasons. In the spring of 1992, the 'invasion' angle was widely taken up following a massive police raid on Ghanaian drug dealers in the Bijlmermeer, south-east Amsterdam. According to Joop Lahaise, most of the media had no hesitation in using the information as given to them by the police, which implied that the majority of people in the neighbourhood were involved in drug dealing.

This example leads us to the heart of the problem raised by television news: whatever tone is used, there is no doubt that the link between 'immigration' and 'crime' arises frequently. In this respect, television is no different from the press. More generally, although it is hard to catch TV news programmes red-handed making racist comments, immigrants are systematically portrayed in a poor light and nothing is done to counterbalance this image. 'Ten people arrested, including three Moroccans' the Piedmont regional news programme announced on 3 February 1990 (Marletti, 1991, p. 77). Television is not immune from such explicit remarks, although it refrains from making them more often than the press. A person's ethnic origin, whether specifically mentioned or merely shown on the screen, is usually associated with a conflict, problem or difficulty. As one Swedish media professional pointed out: 'Immigrants appear most often in stories about refugees, conflicts and crime. But the media give little or no background information that might allow the facts reported to be better understood.'[1]

The reverse side of this 'criminal' image is the view of the immigrant as victim. This is the second classic stereotype of the 'prime time immigrant', which has the advantage of not exposing programme makers to accusations of racism and which may offer considerable dramatic value. It is not surprising, therefore, that in Italy 'slice of life' TV programmes portray immigrants as victims – women more often than not – and lapse easily into simplistic scenes of abject poverty (Marletti, 1991, p. 95). The danger of this is obvious: it continues to link immigrants with the idea of problems and complications.

Another pitfall is that the image of victim may again be turned on its head to become 'quasi-criminal'. For the victims of injustice have only to assert their rights rather than passively hoping they will be treated correctly and they take on a worrying aspect. Two examples can be used to illustrate this. In the autumn of 1992, French television news gave massive coverage to the 'Malians of Vincennes': Malian immigrant workers and their families were camping out in the middle-class Parisian suburb to demand proper housing. The reports usually said nothing about where the families came from, how long they had been in France and how serious the problem was. On the other hand, their negotiations with the authorities were described in detail and it was reported that they had turned down some offers of accommodation – suddenly the 'victims' became claimants driving a hard bargain. In the Netherlands, immigrants were the main victims when an El Al Boeing crashed into apartment buildings in the Amsterdam suburbs. Dutch television started out by treating the victims sympathetically, but it later questioned the legal status of some families who were asking for compensation.

Immigrants may also be victims of the image of their homeland. Very broadly speaking, third-world countries are represented in the media as places of war, famine and, politically speaking, of intolerance, as an Italian study shows in detail (De Marchi & Ercolessi, 1991). When a war breaks out involving the homeland of

---

1 Survey quoted in the introductory paper to the conference 'Public Broadcasting for a Multicultural Society: A Report on the Present Situation in Seven European Countries', held in Noordwijkerhout, Netherlands, from 15 to 17 October 1992.

an ethnic minority, the way the conflict is reported by the media is bound to have repercussions on the image of that minority. The portrayal of Islam, Islamic nations and Moslem immigrants warrants systematic study, because this is an issue that concerns all European countries. 'Everyday' Islam is only seen on television in special broadcasts put out at off-peak times. Immigrants' Islam is almost systematically presented as a source of difficulties linked to 'integration problems'.

Moreover, the link between 'dangerous' Islam abroad and immigrants' Islam is often made quite explicitly. The Salman Rushdie affair, the Gulf War and the case of 'Islamic scarves' in French schools[1] are good examples of how this more or less controlled 'contamination' of the image of immigrants works.[2] Similarly, in February 1989 a demonstration staged in Paris by several hundred people (mostly Pakistanis and therefore unrepresentative of French immigrants as a whole) calling for the death of Rushdie received extensive TV coverage – without being balanced by the views of the Moslem community or communities in France.

On anti-racism

The portrayal of immigrants as victims may satisfy what Joop Lahaise, talking about Dutch society, calls 'the anti-racist consensus' among the media and other élite groups, a consensus which in the case of journalists is 'an obstacle that prevents media professionals from realizing how they portray minorities'. The same observation has been made in Italy (Marletti, 1991); in the absence of a detailed examination of immigrants' living conditions, journalists – who have only recently started to pay real attention to the presence of immigrant communities – quickly adopted the same style of presentation as their European neighbours. Despite the democratic goodwill shown towards them, 'TV immigrants' are still 'problem' groups, victims who have to be protected (once they stop being criminals).

Even when it is done with the best of intentions, portraying the immigrant as a victim may produce a backlash – especially against a background of economic recession – that may be summarized as follows: 'They always talk about *them* and never about us' ('us' could mean non-immigrant job seekers, for instance).[3] This backlash, frequently presumed to occur, has been clearly shown to exist in a

---

1   In 1989, two Moslem schoolgirls were sent home because they insisted on wearing 'Islamic scarves', thus contravening the principle that French state schools are secular. The connection between education and religion, a sensitive subject in France, has come up on several occasions since.

2   For France, see Hargreaves (1993), Perotti & Thépaut (1991).

3   The portrayal of Jewish minorities in the media (they are systematically linked to anti-Semitism or the Holocaust) raises very similar problems.

German qualitative survey carried out in 1986 (Eckart, 1990), which concludes that it is difficult to effectively convey anti-racist attitudes to viewers unless they are already converted to the cause. In particular the survey warns journalists against using emotion or pathos to dramatize the situation of immigrants.

Fiction: where are the ordinary immigrants?

Most of the fiction watched by European viewers is of American origin, cinema films included, which raises another problem in the portrayal of immigrants or foreigners on television: lack of realism. The main 'ethnic' issue dealt with by American TV is that of relations between blacks and whites – in circumstances that bear very little relation to those in Europe. The Hollywood tradition of series has gradually sought to incorporate 'positive' black heroes into police drama or to deal directly with the problems faced by mixed couples. More recently, series like the Cosby Show have shown middle-class blacks being socially successful. Whatever the merits or otherwise of these programmes, European viewers of diverse origins do not see their situation reflected in them.

What about the fiction programmes produced by European TV companies? Except in the United Kingdom, they only began to portray ethnic minorities in fiction at a very late stage. French TV series, in particular, are still strangely dominated by the white middle class, much as American TV fiction was in the 1950s. In this respect social exclusion is mixed in with ethnic exclusion. The rare exceptions noted recently show what a difficult task this is, because the ideology of integration prevents authors from making too much of the distinctiveness of foreign cultures. Even so, it is hard to see why it is so difficult for French scriptwriters to integrate (in the strictest sense of the word) people of foreign origin into their story lines – without making them criminals or victims, but simply showing them leading ordinary lives.[1]

The United Kingdom introduced ethnic minorities, especially blacks, into crime series much earlier than other countries. The soap opera *EastEnders* is one of the few instances of European TV fiction to show 'non-problematic' relations between blacks and whites. I wish to examine here a particular variety of fiction, the situation comedy. From the 1960s onwards British sitcoms such as *Till Death Us Do Part* (1964–74) portrayed a white, racist, right-wing Briton, with the aim of making him look ridiculous. This initial series, a great success, was followed by *Love Thy Neighbour* (Thames Television, 1971), in which the main – white – character is always having rows with his black neighbour. Programmes like these led pro-

---

1 See the exceptions quoted by Hargreaves (1993), including the sitcom *La Famille Ramdan* on M6.

ducers and commentators to wonder about the effects of sitcoms: were they really making fun of negative feelings towards foreigners, or were they providing a legitimate outlet for such feelings? 'Some black actors refuse to appear in these programmes because of the stress they put on insulting racist jokes' (Pines, 1986). It is true that the expression of nationalist or community feelings is often linked to humour.

Games, quizzes and variety shows, humour and racism

These types of programme also deserve a closer look because they are the scene of conversations studded with jokes, quite apart from the comedy sketches they sometimes contain. They attract large numbers of viewers and occupy an important place in programme planning. They provide an outlet for the emotions of viewers (who may identify with those taking part and with the players chosen for the games) and a snapshot of typical TV viewers (through the choice of guests and participants).

Are any foreigners seen in these programmes? No systematic studies have been done that might answer this question. One American researcher (Samuelson, forthcoming) investigating French game shows took part in a number of such programmes. In his own words, he felt like a 'good foreigner' (slightly eccentric but not threatening). But what about non-western minorities, such as North Africans in France, Asians in the United Kingdom, Turks in Germany? They appear much less frequently in these types of programme. Again, the United Kingdom is the exception to the rule: ethnic minorities there are 'better represented in the studio and in programme credits' (Hargreaves, 1992, p. 19).

How are foreigners spoken about in these programmes? I am thinking first of all of variety shows, but also of quiz and game shows. In everyday conversation as in TV conversation, humour and jokes often take foreigners as their target, and humour does have its advantages. As the *Black and White Media Show* points out, it often goes unnoticed. It can be hard to criticize, such as when immigrants are portrayed as victims, and it is deeply ambivalent: a racist joke may well make a racist and an anti-racist laugh together, each recognizing in it a separate target and a different fear.

The examples available to the attentive TV viewer are legion, and may sometimes give rise to indignation, as shown by viewers' letters. During the programme *Kiosque à musique* in October 1986, well-known French presenter Jacques Martin came out with 'Telemann, who was German, it wasn't his fault, you can't help where you're born'. During the same month the variety show *Champs-Elysées* included a whole string of jokes about the Japanese.[1] These two relatively old

French examples concerned citizens of developed countries, who may be considered more socially acceptable as victims. But xenophobia is still with us, as in the successful British sitcom (*Allo, Allo*, still on the air at the time of writing, December 1992), in which British actors make fun of the French during the Resistance and imitate French accents.

Non-western immigrants may also become the targets of humour. Claudia Origlia quotes several examples of Italian variety shows (*Drive In* and *L'Araba Fenice* on Italia Uno and *Quelli della Note*, in 1984–85 on the RAI) in which Arab characters were made fun of. The racist jokes were supposed to be deriding racism via a sort of 'very conscious self-mockery', but a sense of ambivalence and unease was often the result. Italian sitcoms have used immigrant characters in a similar way: *Zanzibar*, a successful series that lasted for more than six years, was about a street trader – an archetypal immigrant character in the minds of Italians.

The *Black and White Media Show* also picks up humorous extracts from quiz shows like *Every Second Counts* and *A Question of Sport*, and sometimes even from the news, about the difficulty of pronouncing names of Indian origin. Humorous, but heavy with significance: it sets communities speaking different languages against each other while challenging the identity of the person whose name is made fun of at the most basic social level.

The clearest example available comes from France: in October 1991 a French 'comic' scored a great success – and provoked a minor scandal – with a song broadcast several times on radio and TV telling the story of an 'Arab riding a camel in Algiers and stealing scooters in Paris'.[1] More recently, on 2 November 1992, a popular variety show (*Les Inconnus*, France 2) included a comedy sketch showing three Caribbean women working in a hospital, careless and lazy to the point of caricature.

When criticized, the comics concerned often plead that they too are of foreign origin and cannot therefore be accused of racism – but do they know how their jokes are interpreted? It is as if they wanted to prove their ability to fit into society by showing that they are capable of laughing at themselves, thus reinforcing the main stereotypes instead of trying to break with them. This tendency may be further strengthened by the professional environment in which they work. In the United Kingdom successful black comic Lenny Henry, interviewed on the *Black and White Media Show*, recalled that at the start of his career he was often under pressure to make fun of African stereotypes.

---

4   Reported by *Télérama*, 29 October 1986.

1   It was sung, for instance, on *Club Dorothée*, a TF1 children's show, at 4.40 pm on 18 October 1991, according to the ARA & CIEMI study (1991, p. 17).

Sport, music, advertising: neo-racism or the 'Benetton effect'

In conclusion, let us take a look at those aspects of television which do not fit into a specific category but which often feature people of non-European (extra-Community, to borrow the Italians' term) ethnic origin. One Swedish observer has described this as the 'Benetton effect',[1] a sort of made-for-television exoticism: 'Blacks and immigrants appear as singers, dancers and sportspeople'. It could be added that they are also seen as models – but they are restricted to these roles. During a test week in France, 'there were no immigrants or blacks in quiz shows but they often appeared in variety shows as singers and dancers' (ARA & CIEMI, 1991, p. 12).

Can these be called positive images? Above all they present a distant, exotic picture, not unconnected with neo-colonialist fantasies about 'the beauty of the natives'. The positive image of foreign sportspeople fits in perfectly with the chauvinism of sports commentaries, one of the few cases in which overtly nationalist and racist remarks are made. Carlo Marletti (1991) describes such remarks as 'post-racist do-it-yourself': 'post-racist' because they are never explicit, sound very up-to-date and are impossible to contest openly. But they are still racist, contributing to ignorance, to the idea of foreigners as far-off and different, and thus reinforcing stereotypes.[2]

What, if anything, can be done?

Let us return to our point of departure. Keeping count of instances of racism doesn't mean much compared to the scale of the problem. On the whole, fiction, quiz and variety shows and news magazines on European television show middle-class whites typical of the consumer society – a world in which immigrants are condemned to crime, poverty or showbusiness with the three corresponding typical characters of the troublemaker, the dependant or the entertainer (Barry, 1988). French integration ideology may work as an obstacle here: by trying at all costs to show only immigrants who have adopted a totally French lifestyle, the many who have retained a culture of their own but who still wish to be integrated into French society are forgotten.

What can be done to correct distorted impressions such as these? This overview has shown at least that the answer does not lie in professional codes of conduct or sets of rules. The tendency to play on national identity – even in a chauvinistic and

1   A reference to the international advertising campaign 'United Colors of Benetton', which showed people of different ethnic origins – but leaning towards stereotyping and not without a measure of provocation.

2   Similarly, John Twitchin (BBC Education) said at the Grande Arche conference: 'The more racist society becomes, the more popular Blacks are.'

sometimes racist way – in order to attract viewers is inevitable against this background of intense competition, in which the ratings war has become institutionalized 'demagogy' in the literal sense. Careful reading of professional codes of conduct shows that they strongly condemn racism and extol respect for others;[1] the trouble is that these codes are not being implemented.

If any control *can* be exerted, it is probably on two levels. Firstly – the one that comes to mind most often – is at government level. Correct choice of those in charge of public broadcasting and a regulatory framework that does not encourage competition and chasing advertising revenue can do more than any number of statements of good intent, which may conceal a lack of long-term policy. The second level, less frequently mentioned, is that of the TV companies themselves. Real 'professional' authority comes nowadays from the heads of channels, and it is their management that can introduce monitoring systems (which must be expensive if they are to work) and punishment for infractions.

In any event, an effective incentives policy has to operate at all levels. For to give a fairer and more accurate view of ethnic minorities on television, to climb the slippery slope of prejudice and competition (with the latter feeding the former), sufficient time must be taken at every stage of the production and monitoring process (organizing training, hiring staff, scriptwriting, choosing guests). With a commercial system in which speed is everything, monitoring and public service bodies can only play their part if the government gives them room to manœuvre in the long term and if it shares the view that television has real social responsibility.

Sources

ARA (Associations Rencontres Audiovisuelles) and CIEMI (Centre d'Information et d'Etudes sur les Migrations Internationales), *Présence et représentation des immigrés et des minorités ethniques à la télévision française*, report, available in photocopied form, 1991.

Barry, Angela, 'Black Mythologies: the Representation of Black People on British Television', In *The Black and White Media Book*, ed. Twitchin, John. Hanley, Trentham Books, 1988 (reprinted 1990).

Bourdon, Jérôme, 'Le Programme de télévision et l'identité nationale', *MédiasPouvoirs*, 28 October 1992.

Eckart, Josef, 'Audiences' Reactions to Television Programmes about Foreigners in West Germany', *Media Perspektiven*, 10/90.

Gerth, H. & Mills, C.W., *From Max Weber, Essays in Sociology*, Galaxy, New York, 1958.

Hargreaves, Alec, 'Ethnic Minorities and the Mass Media in France', In: *Popular Culture and Mass Communication in Twentieth Century France*, eds. Chapman, R. & Hewitt, N. Lewison/Mellen, in press.

Hargreaves, Alec,' L'immigration au prisme de la télévision en France et en Grande Bretagne', *Migrations-Société*, 4 (21), May–June 1992.

---

1   Edouard Guibert emphasized this point at the Grande Arche conference.

Hargreaves, Alec, 'Les immigrés dans les soaps et les sitcom de fabrication européenne' in *Télévisions d'Europe et Immigration*, Paris, Institut National de l'Audiovisuel et Association Dialogue entre les Cultures, Paris, 1993.

Marletti, Carlo, *Extracomunitari, Dall'immaginario collettivo al vissuto quotidiano del razzismo*, RAI-VPQT, Milan, Eri, 1991.

Perotti, Antonio, & Thépaut, France, 'Les Répercussions de la guerre du golfe sur les arabes et les juifs de France', *Migrations-Société*, 3 (14), March–April 1991, pp. 65-82.

Pines, Jim, *Black & White in Colour: Black People in British Television since 1936*, London, British Film Institute, 1992 (see especially the introduction).

Samuelson, Edward, Les jeux à la télévision française (thesis), University of New York, 1993.

Schlesinger, Philip, *Media, State and Nation*, London, Sage, 1991.

Twitchin, John, (editor) *The Black and White Media Book*, Hanley, Trentham Books, 1988 (reprinted 1990).

Van Dijk, Teun A., *Communicating Racism*, London, Sage, 1987.

Television and racial equality: How the Race Relations Act has helped

Chris Myant

Senior Information Officer, Commission for Racial Equality

Laughing at yourself is never easy. For black or Asian people in Britain today to do so in the most public and yet most intimate of all mediums, television, is a sign of their growing self-confidence. When the black and Asian comedy series, *The Real McCoy* won the Commission for Racial Equality's 1993 Race in the Media Award for television the confidence was there for all to see. The awards were established by the Commission to highlight what should be an increasingly important dimension of today's media: material that reflects Britain's diverse society in way that positively helps people understand each across the various ethnic fault lines which can so easily becomes frontiers of hate, prejudice and division.

Television in Britain today can produce comedy which uses those differences positively because it takes itself so seriously. This type of programme is not an accident of creative talent, but the culmination of much debate, soul searching and public pressure in the particular context of regulation, social responsibility and accountability in which British television exists. It is also a result of the rather unique positive legal environment in which race relations in Britain have been placed.

It has not been easy getting to this point. Twenty years ago the first academic study of the impact of the media on attitudes towards race in Britain concluded that:

> At present the news media, like the British white population still have to accept that Britain is a multiracial society. For this reason they have been able to give emphasis to 'immigration' and 'immigrants' while ignoring the fact that increasingly the people characteristically labelled 'immigrants' are in fact British.[1]

The judgement was fair enough in its day. It is still a valid criticism of significant parts of the printed media. But for television it is becoming out of date.

The *BBC Producer's Guidelines* contain a short sentence which puts the modern approach in a nutshell. Speaking of ethnic minority people in Britain, it says:

> Few are immigrants and many have known no other home. They are an integral part of British society.[2]

Making them an integral part of British television has been the means by which the visible face to television *is* now being rapidly changed. The change is there in news programmes, it is there in drama and in the advertising on commercial channels. Products, which only a couple of years ago companies and agencies would have considered unsellable if accompanied by a black or Asian face, are now marketed in television commercials with black and Asian actors or personalities. Among the most prominent broadcasters now are figures like Trevor McDonald, who began his career as a journalist in Trinidad and, still with some of the Caribbean lilt in his voice, has for two years held the position of the main newscaster in the most popular news programme on British television, ITN's *News at Ten*. He has become as much a part of British life as tea and toast. There is a fair chance that if you ask any young person who their most popular comedian is, the answer would be the black television star Lenny Henry. The list of such stars is growing year by year.

Perhaps a certain Rubicon was passed in 1993 when Cilla Black's *Blind Date*, a popular commercial channel show in which a young man or woman chooses a

---

1   Hartman, Paul & Husband, Charles. *Racism and the Mass Media: A study of the role of the mass media in the formation of white beliefs and attitudes in Britain.* Pavis Poynter, London, 1974, p. 211.

2   BBC Producers' Guidelines, BBC 1993, p. 94.

partner for a date from three hidden behind a screen, showed Cilla asking a young woman about to choose her man who would be her ideal male. There was no gasp from the audience, not a flicker on anyone's face when she answered eagerly and happily: Lenny Henry. Indeed, *Blind Date* now has had black men choosing a partner from among three white women.

A question of immigration or of race relations?

Though the idea of a multiracial society as something to be welcomed and valued in its own right is far from universally accepted in Britain (various opinion polls show that a deep seated prejudice remains strong among a significant minority within the white majority), it has been officially supported since 1965 when the first Race Relations Act was passed. Under successive Race Relations Acts, Britain acquired both a law which made racial discrimination unlawful and a body, independent from Government though publicly financed, which was charged with helping individuals take complaints of racial discrimination to courts and with promoting equality of opportunity.

No one would claim that racial discrimination has been eliminated in Britain. Quite the contrary. But there is now in place a complex system of law, institutions and practices which seeks to promote equality of opportunity based on the assumption that Britain is a multi-racial society with a diverse cultural inheritance that is to be valued and not smothered.

At the heart of this system is the Commission for Racial Equality. Appointed by the Home Secretary under general requirements laid down by the Race Relations Act, the members of the Commission have to reflect the general range of interests and communities in Britain. There are Commissioners from the trade unions and business, Commissioners from different ethnic minorities, and Commissioners from different political viewpoints. The Commission's money all comes out of the public purse, but Government cannot intervene to tell it what to do. Several hundred people a year get free legal help from the Commission to take cases of discrimination to courts. At the same time the Commission can set about its own inquiries using powers rather like those of an investigating magistrate. If it finds there was racial discrimination by an employer or by someone providing a service it can enforce new practices to ensure equality of opportunity. At the time of writing, for instance, the Commission is investigating why several regiments in the British army are all-white. Since the investigation got underway at the end of 1993 the Ministry of Defence has announced several new measures to encourage ethnic minority youngsters to join the armed forces.

Working for equality opportunity

Much of the Commission's effort also goes into promoting good practice: devising equal opportunity programmes and persuading employers and service providers to follow them. Unlike anti-discrimination laws in some societies, the Race Relations Act in Britain rules out so called positive discrimination. Employers and service providers cannot give special favours to particular ethnic or racial groups. But they can adopt wide ranging equal opportunity programmes to ensure that members of all racial groups have an equal chance in getting jobs or availing themselves of services. Monitoring the ethnic or racial origins of employees, for instance, is now becoming an accepted practice. It takes place in much of public sector and public utility employment though it is nowhere near as common in the private sector.

Some employers have now moved on to using the information the monitoring reveals about the under-representation of particular groups to guide programmes of action to encourage more people from ethnic minorities to apply for jobs, to make the appointment and promotion systems truly fair and to eliminate racial harassment and abuse at work. In service delivery ethnic monitoring is now getting established. Hospitals in the health service are due to monitor the ethnic origins of all their patients from April 1995 and the criminal justice system is in the process of setting up systems which, by 1998, should give a general picture of how the police, the prosecution services, courts and prisons treat different ethnic and racial groups.

Against this general background, television in Britain is among the most visible of those implementing equal opportunity programmes in employment and, at least in terms of policy statements, is taking seriously the need to make sure that the images and programming on the small screen also reflect the ethnic diversity of British society.

The regulatory environment

All British terrestrial broadcasting takes place within a code-based and regulated environment which stresses the need to achieve certain standards in output. This is obvious and widely understood in the case of the publicly owned BBC governed as it is by the provisions of a Charter which place a direct responsibility of public service on the Corporation. But in the commercial television sector as well, the 1990 Broadcasting Act requires television licence holders to detail the arrangements they will implement for 'promoting equality of opportunity between persons of different racial groups'.

Special training courses for young people from ethnic minorities wanting to go into television are now available. A significant number of young journalists who have developed their skills in ethnic minority community papers have now been recruited to television. And some of the new independent production companies have a specifically ethnic minority workforce or community base. Under government requirements, the BBC must now put out much of its programme production to these independents. At one level this has helped to free up programming choice but at another it has broken up the centralized production system within which equality of opportunity programmes in employment can gain real bite. The BBC has set itself the target of 8 per cent of its employees coming from the ethnic minorities by the year 2000. The last comprehensive survey of employment in broadcasting revealed that in 1989 the proportion across the whole of the BBC and the commercial sector was only 0.9 per cent. Clearly there is still a long way to go as indeed the Independent Television Commission (ITC), set up under the Broadcasting Act, has accepted. It requires each licence holder to meet up to performance standards in employment with racial equality measures a part of that process. Reviewing the performance of the first year of the new Channel 3 licensees for 1993, the ITC concluded:

> Considerable scope exists for further progress in terms of the employment of women, ethnic minorities and disabled people, both overall and at different levels within ITV ...

The percentage of their employees coming from ethnic minorities for the two commercial television companies serving London, Carlton and LWT, was 5.5 per cent and 6 per cent respectively. The ethnic minority percentage in the London population as a whole is over 20 per cent.

Progress in terms of employment at the higher reaches of television is even slower. Out of hundreds of programme executives in television only four are non-white and two of these deal with ethnic minority programming, not general programming.

Alongside the requirements on employment, there are codes on programme content and on advertising. Viewers can complain against these codes to bodies within the television power structure and outside it. There is now a strong and lively tradition of public complaints against media institutions to which television is no exception. In several instances these codes make reference to the issue of race. The second edition of the Broadcasting Standards Council code of practice published in February 1994 says for instance:

> The Council's research in 1991 showed how racist terms continued to be regarded more and more as deeply offensive, outpacing some traditional terms of abuse. Britain is a multiracial society and constant awareness of the deep cultural, religious and economic gulfs existing between the races is needed if they are to be successfully bridged. The wrong choice of language has the ability to divide rather than to unite.[1]

---

1   *A Code of Practice*, page 44. The Broadcasting Standards Council, 1994.

The Council was set up under the Broadcasting Act to offer advice and hear complaints over the standards achieved by broadcast materials. A similar wording appears in the ITC's Programme Code and in its Code of Advertising Standards and Practice. Significantly the Advertising Standards Authority, the advertising industry's self regulatory body, inserted a specific clause mentioning race in its own code which, up to 1994, had avoided any such reference.[1]

All the regulatory and complaints bodies issue regular public reports on their findings and programmers and advertisers use these to guide their practices. The ITC for instance in February 1994 criticized a television advertisement run for Carling Black Label lager which played on British-German rivalries in a triumphalist manner using as its usual theme the Dambusters Raid on German dams during World War Two music. The ITC did not ask for the advertisement to be withdrawn but responded to viewers' complaints about it by saying:

> The ITC believes there is room in television advertising for a degree of good natured humour about differing national characteristic provided it is not off-ensive or likely to be seen as condoning hostile attitudes.

There is a fine line between humour and causing offence. An advertisement featuring a white actor blacked up to look like an Indian chef and saying in a fake Indian accent 'Most goody goody' as he warms up a precooked Chicken Korma Kiev was dropped in April 1994 after one Asian viewer protested that he had been taunted by white youths using the catchphrase. Popular game show host Des O'Connor was criticized by the Broadcasting Standards Council when he remarked before 11 million viewers that playing his records (his singing is notoriously lampooned by other comics) 'got rid of all the cockroaches and the Gypsies parked down the lane'. He apologized. But on other occasions when sensitivities are touched, the broadcasters have not accepted the legitimacy of the attack. Many Greek Cypriots living in Britain have been offended by a character in a popular BBC sitcom series *Birds of a Feather*. A Greek Cypriot cafe owner was shown in prison. Greek Cypriot community papers campaigned for a change in the comedy in the early months of 1994 but without success.

Taking television into a multiracial society

For the Commission for Racial Equality the media has always been a priority in working for change. Soon after it was formed in 1977, the Commission issued a broad strategy statement outlining how it saw its work. The statement committed the Commission to use:

---

1   The ASA's Code clause 14 reads: 'Advertisements should contain nothing that is likely to cause serious or widespread offence. Particular care should be taken to avoid causing offence on the grounds of race, religion, sex, sexual orientation or disability'.

> ... the media and all other channels of communication not just to counter the racialist doctrines of various extremists but also to stimulate more serious public discussion of the issues and problems associated with the development of a multiracial community and to widen public understanding of the contribution made by ethnic minorities to the economic and cultural life of the nation.

For the Commission, seeking to achieve such a priority has not been a task it has tried to keep just to itself. It set about showing how the media did not meet up to the needs of a multiracial society.[1] And it then sought to use the evidence of bias to secure change on the part of the media and to get the media to take responsibility for driving that change through itself. At first there was great resistance – from all parts of the media. As one of the leading academics involved in media studies at the time commented:

> Perhaps surprisingly on the surface, but more understandably in view of the prevailing professional values and practices, those same people who justifiably claim the right to probe into all corners of society appear to be somewhat reluctant to be investigated themselves.[2]

The Commission proposed action across a broad front: equal opportunity programmes for employment, special training, special projects for ethnic minority actors, monitoring of output, integrated casting. The first half of the 1980s was dominated by the drive by the Commission, actors organizations, ethnic minority pressure groups and others to get broadcasting institutions to accept the basic validity of the argument and their need to act. The second half of the decade saw the start to the implementation of practical programmes involving equality measures both on the screen and behind the camera. Only in the first half of the 1990s has this work really begun to see fruit with formal requirements in employment clearly laid down, equal opportunity departments established and operating.

Television for the young has perhaps moved furthest in terms of onscreen portrayal. Monitoring of this was introduced in children's BBC programming in 1992, but the issue had been at the forefront of concerns for many years and black and Asian presenters have played a significant role in children's BBC TV for a decade and a half as well as in the BBC schools and education programming.

This type of initiative has also been combined with an active anti-racist content to

---

1 See for instance the CRE research publications *Public Awareness and the Media: A study of reporting on race* by Barry Troyna, CRE 1981; *Television in a Multiracial Society: A research report* by Muhammad Anwar, CRE 1983.

2 Professor James D Halloran, Director of the Centre for Mass Communication Research at the University of Leicester in his preface to *Public Awareness and the Media*.

special series of programmes. Which has the most impact is, perhaps hard to tell. The committed programmes, like the *Dynamite* series on BBC Children's TV in the summer of 1994 have a more restricted audience and one in which many of the viewers will already be committed to the cause, while the general programming projecting positive images of black and Asian people has the larger audience but an indirect impact. Both approaches have a part to play in breaking down prejudices, generating positive images in the minds of white and non-white alike.

Hard though the task might have appeared to be in broadcasting (and the same advances seen in television have been experienced in radio), the state of play in the printed media is far worse. In the newspaper trade there is no culture of public service and accountability. There is not even an acceptance at the formal level in some major newspaper institutions of the justice of the equal opportunity argument when it comes to race. The mass tabloid national newspaper press in Britain – virtually none of which have taken on board the detailed equal opportunity practices that television now has at the heart of its employment policies – has often made fun of the reforms in content that television has implemented in the 1990s. Such things form part of the long-running debate around issues of so called 'political correctness' that have featured strongly in their columns. They can only be news because they touch on that reservoir of prejudice. So when the BBC announced in the autumn of 1993 that it was going to repeat the puppet sci-fi series, *Captain Scarlet*, a freelance journalist invented the tale that the Commission for Racial Equality was complaining to the BBC over the fact that the villain of the tale was called Captain Black while the hero's commander was a Colonel White. No such complaint had been made – though it is the case that were the BBC to remake such a series today it would probably not choose such names – but the story was repeated in every large circulation newspaper and ran for days despite repeated denials from the Commission. What is perhaps significant is that, despite these often quite determined press campaigns, television has continued to improve its content.

The way ahead

Regulation is a back stop and a standard setter, it does not ensure a better service. It can prevent the broadcasting of offensive programmes, it cannot ensure the production of positive images offering a truer reflection of a multiracial audience. That depends on the creative involvement of programme makers. Much has been achieved, but much still needs to be done by broadcasters. They have perhaps established the framework, they still have to furnish the house.

Attempting to encourage that process the Commission is now seeking to positively encourage excellence in broadcasting on race issues. It launched a Race in the Media Award in 1992 designed to get all broadcasters to think positively about race and to produce programmes which improve understanding by all.

Importantly a winner of the first year's award was not a programme which just challenged white racism but one which tackled problems *within* Britain's black communities. *The Violence Must Cease* in the BBC's *Open Space* community access series looked at black on black violence. *Open Space* executive producer Giles Oakley said of the programme: 'We looked at an issue which could be seen as critical of the black community, but allowed them to open up the debate in their own terms'. One of the 1993 awards went to the BBC TV comedy series, *The Real McCoy* produced by a non-white team. Again this series is not 'anti-racist' but is a hard hitting, honest set of programmes in which people from ethnic minorities can laugh at themselves in a way which constructively undermines racism.

The Race in the Media Awards are now an established part of the media scene in Britain and will play a part in encouraging the development of a television service which meets the needs of all. Interestingly a majority of the commercial television broadcasters are now offering sponsorship money in one way or another to this project.

Using television more directly against racist prejudices is something the Commission took up in 1994. Linking with the largest advertising agency in the country, Saatchi and Saatchi, the Commission launched a three year public education campaign which will use television as well as newspaper and cinema advertising. Funded by corporate and individual donations the campaign is expected to run into the many millions before it is concluded. The first TV advert featured the theme that babies have no racial prejudice, it is something we *learn*.

There are those who argue that such advertising will have little effect. That 1974 study of the media and racism argued: 'Advertising campaigns to promote racial tolerance do not necessarily challenge the basic social injustices, and, to the extent that they confuse tolerance with justice, they will pursuing the wrong goal ... Prejudiced attitudes cannot be changed significantly independently of the structural relationships to which they relate.'[1] If the only thing happening in television were to be a few CRE advertisements, that criticism might still be valid. Instead it now forms part of a wide ranging programme of work in employment, on content and in social action coverage either in programmes or advertisements. As the convener of the judges for the Institute of Practrices in Advertising's Advertising Effectiveness Awards, Chris Baker, commented when the campaign started: 'The CRE's campaign is social engineering. It can create an atmosphere intolerant of prejudice'. Particularly so, one might add, when the images appearing on British TV screens are now ones of successful black and Asian sports stars as well as

1   Hartman and Husband, *ibid* p. 213.

musicians, or presenters with a familiar and friendly presence right in your own home, or comedians and actors who make you laugh or cry, touching emotions at the heart of your personal identity.

Of course there is still a long way to go. Though change is fast it has not gone far enough. The highly popular game shows are still overwhelming white. 'Genera-sian Game: Ethnic search by BBC Chiefs', the *Daily Star* quipped in a headline when it claimed to have discovered that only one family in the game show *The Generation Game* had been Asian during its 1992 season.[1] Equally overwhelmingly white are the popular TV soaps. Some of the most popular are made in Australia – *Neighbours* on BBC and *Home and Away* on ITV – which reflect the white image of society most British people would hold of that country. Black and Asian actors do not get leading roles in any of the main soaps though all of them have begun to respond to criticisms and sought to feature different ethnic minorities and covers themes of prejudice. When the Australian TV executive Bruce Gyngell denounced the popu-larity of the Australian soap as a sign of continuing prejudice in Britain he touched on a raw nerve and was denounced by both BBC and ITV programming bosses.[2] But then the fact that the nerve is raw is a good sign. The complacency of the past has to an extent gone.

---

1 *Daily Star*, 3 June 1993. The *Star* is the most right wing of the mass circulation tabloids and regularly runs stories with a barely concealed racist content to them. It sells around three quarters of a million copies each day.

2 See the reports in the *Guardian* 2 November 1993 and *Daily Mirror* 3 November 1993. Gyngell was head of the failed breakfast TV on the commercial side, TV-AM, which featured an Asian newscaster, Lisa Aziz, though it had few other non-white faces.

Networking for migrant perspectives on television in France and Europe

The IM'média Agency's experience

Mogniss H. Abdallah

Head of the IM'média agency

I M'média is a multimedia news agency set up in 1983 in the wake of the movement arising from immigration and the working class. The agency produces material for news and documentary television programmes, in France and elsewhere, as well as for the non-commercial sector (non-profit organizations, institutions, etc.). It co-produced the weekly broadcast *Rencontres* (Encounters) shown on the French public channel FR 3 in 1989, and a European window within *Rencontres* in 1990.

IM'média is working to establish a European network of independent producers whose aim is to put current events and history, seen from the viewpoint of immigrant communities, back into their own hands, especially on television. The people running the agency take their cue from the black studies movement in the United States and Britain and look for ways of bringing different communities together to form new kinds of urban culture.

After launching a documentary series on immigrants' reactions to the rising tide of racism in Europe, IM'média co-produced a 52-minute programme called *Douce France* (Sweet France) for Britain's Channel 4 in 1992, as well as several features on black society in England and Germany reeling with shock at the return of old demons. It also encourages broadcasting groups in Italy, Spain and Portugal to tackle the recent phenomenon of increasing immigration across Europe's southern borders.

In the summer of 1981, the French media discovered the existence of second generation children of immigrants through what became known as 'rodeos', a form of joy-riding, in Les Minguettes, a working-class suburb of Lyon. Initially a common form of protest that involved stealing BMWs and other luxury cars in the city centre, then setting fire to them in the suburbs after a chase with the police, these 'rodeos' were later set up from start to finish by sensation-seeking journalists who paid youngsters to provide them with good pictures. It was no coincidence that this new portrayal of the typical immigrant – young, at a loose end and involved in petty crime – came just as the French Right had decided to use the contentious issue of immigration to go back on the offensive after its presidential election defeat on 10 May 1981. An important part of the politicians' strategy was to prevent young immigrants from asserting their new legitimacy, acquired after the deportation of young people and immigrants who had permanently settled in France was abolished and after foreigners were granted freedom of association in October 1981. The issue remained central to relations between Right and Left throughout the 1980s, with the Left becoming increasingly indecisive as the years went by, both in power and when it went into opposition (1986–1988).

This new image of the young immigrant as yobbo also stood out as a modern contrast to the traditional portrayal of the immigrant worker as submissive and poverty-stricken, weighed down with longing for his home village with its out-moded traditions and mint tea, and with his old Peugeot 404 kept covered ready for an unlikely return home. The young immigrant movement that emerged in the late 1970s came to represent an independent voice, a sort of counter-culture born of the struggle against deportation of foreigners and racist or 'security-motivated' crimes and against police harassment on run-down housing estates.

At first, what was known as *'beur'* culture (from the French backslang for 'Arab') was a symbol of open revolt, often borrowing from the black American example but also incorporating aspects of cultural experiments by immigrant factory workers in the 1970s. Groups of young immigrants seeking to make their voices heard sprang up spontaneously in major cities, becoming involved in amateur drama groups, photography, super-8 film, militant newspapers and magazines, free radio and especially music. Nonetheless, their work remained restricted to a local audience and received little media coverage (the daily *Libération* was virtually the only newspaper that attempted to analyse the phenomenon). Although these groups at first had no idea that they might constitute a new social movement that could change people's ideas about immigration and the struggle against racism, a sort of informal coordination soon spread, starting with the anti-deportation networks and propelled by the youngsters' eagerness to satisfy their thirst for culture and to see what was going on elsewhere. Young immigrants from all over France flocked to the Rock Against Police concerts held near Paris and relayed to Lyon and Marseille.

Meanwhile some groups, in the course of their struggle against police violence and racist crime, learned how to negotiate with the media – and television in particular – to secure a different portrayal of themselves. In Vitry-sur-Seine, near Paris, a group of young immigrants stopped a television crew from the public channel Antenne 2 from filming on their high-rise estate after a 15-year-old boy was killed by a caretaker. The youngsters accused the media of pandering to people's fears about security in their coverage of such estates and pointed out that the murder had been committed shortly after the caretaker had seen the film *Death Wish*, with Charles Bronson, on television. Rather than issuing yet another statement denouncing the media, the group suggested putting over their own view of events by broadcasting excerpts from their super-8 films *Zone immigrée* and *Ils ont tué Kader* (They killed Kader). They agreed to appear on television on one condition – that the programme would be shown live. It was a case of take-it-or-leave-it, and the channel finally accepted, buying several minutes of footage and organizing a studio debate. The young members of the Mohamed group were subsequently much sought after by the press and by other broadcasters. Gradually they became experts, a compulsory point of call for those journalists bold enough to venture across the Paris ring road to confront the urban jungle beyond.

In *Mosaïques*, a magazine broadcast by FR3 on Sunday mornings, aimed at immigrant families and produced by Algerian film maker Tewfik Farès, coverage of the *beur* movement was conspicuous by its absence. Young immigrants became exasperated by the image of the immigrant-as-victim put over by the programme, which always seemed to lag behind what was going on in the real world. In particular, they criticized Tewfik Farès and his team for being too close to the embassies of the immigrants' home countries and to the French government, and for keeping off the programme people who wanted to start producing their own material rather than simply being interviewed. After *Mosaïques* was lambasted by the Gaspard Report – which was financed and ghost-written by the ministry of social affairs in 1983 – its producers did try to cram as many *beurs* as possible into the programme. But the *beurs* had already moved on...

It was against this backdrop that IM'média was founded in Lyon in 1983 following a training course for about 20 young people from immigrant families, most of them children of North Africans or with one North African and one French parent. The course was held in May and June 1983, at the height of a protest movement by immigrants in temporary housing and of the troubles in Les Minguettes (clashes between young people and the police, a hunger strike, the shooting of Toumi Djaïdja, preliminary plans for the March For Equality that was to mark a turning point in the *beur* movement, and the first demolition of high-rise apartment blocks). It also happened during the French Open tennis tournament, in which two top French players of immigrant origin made their mark – Tarik Benhabilès and Yannick Noah (who won the men's singles title). 'Noah is beautiful', one headline read, sparking what was to become the black and *beur* fashion movement.

Among the IM'média trainees were Djida Tazdaït and Farida Belghoul, who were to become leading figures in the *beur* movement, and up-and-coming journalists such as Paulo Moreira. Other participants in this practical and theoretical course – the importance of which was probably underestimated by those charting the emergence of the *beur* movement – included Ahmed Boubeker, later a sociologist and journalist, and Rachid Taha of the Arab rock group Carte de séjour (Residence Permit).

The IM'média agency was registered as a non-profit organization after drawing up a list of the factors that deprived young immigrants of a collective voice in society. Aiming to cover the whole of France, it had branches in Paris, Lyon, Saint-Etienne and Marseille. The original idea was to form a team of professionals to act as the central node of a network of immigration-oriented organizations and groups with a view to negotiating better representation in the media. The agency wanted to have done with portrayals of the 'noble savage', commented on by so-called experts who took it upon themselves to think for others. IM'média planned to have its own editorial line and to come up with finished products. From the start, the agency took a multimedia approach, with the emphasis on news and current affairs, using copy submitted to the daily press, photo-features and video film.

The news agency formula gave IM'média plenty of scope to combine its own material (supplied to the media in kit or ready-to-broadcast form) with reports and film tailored to meet individual demands. It also sought to provide an alternative to the kind of interpersonal quarrels and power struggles between cliques that are typical of the sort of post-Left organizations whose members have crept into the media and which undermine both the *beur* movement and the French style of fighting against racism.

The obvious questions that arise concern quality, technical competence and resources. With this in mind, IM'média put the emphasis on individual professional training as an essential stage in each person's involvement with the agency. There were members who enrolled in further education institutions, sometimes for two or three years. Some of them – probably the majority – went on to become broadcasting technicians at the end of their studies because of the job security offered by this profession. Others, anxious to earn a living and freaked out by the idea of a string of temporary contracts in an organization perceived as hostile to the mass media, got stuck in run-of-the-mill jobs with, for instance, the newspaper *Libération* in Lyon, Radio France Internationale or the public television channel FR3. Too frequently, they were assigned to covering North African and religious affairs with a dash of social comment thrown in. Some cut the umbilical cord with IM'média (although it is too early to say whether this is a good idea), while others, in regular jobs with the mass media, work for the agency now and again on specific projects.

Unlike other national organizations arising from the *beur* movement, IM'média received no government subsidy when it was launched. Paradoxically, it was not until Gaullist Jacques Chirac returned as prime minister in 1986 (first 'co-habitation' with President Mitterrand) that the Fonds d'action sociale (FAS - Social Action Fund) deigned to give grants and loans to IM'média.

The agency's improved finances enabled it to buy BVU and high-band equipment and to provide more systematic coverage of current events. Meanwhile, the agency had been concentrating on producing independent material, including a quarterly magazine and *Vidéo-news*, a package of short social and cultural items. Part of the second edition of *Vidéo-news* was taken from *52 minutes pour le câble*, which was made for a competition organized in 1985-1986 by the future Mission câble to encourage independent programme production. Foreign television channels have often used film from IM'média's archives; French channels, on the other hand, are still bogged down in a corporatism aggravated by their journalists' fears that upstart *beurs* are about to take over their jobs. There have been examples of some original forms of cooperation, from advisory roles to co-productions, enabling IM'média to get involved, for instance, in supervising *Licence to Kill*, a 35-minute film shown on prime time by Britain's Channel 4 in 1985 and 1987. Cooperation between IM'média and the *Race Today* group in Brixton was behind this film. Leading members of *Race Today* such as Darcus Howe and Tariq Ali went on to form Bandung Productions, a black production company, while Farrukh Dhondy became the multicultural commissioning editor of Channel 4.

For an audiovisual record of immigration

In late 1983, IM'média made a 26-minute documentary called *Minguettes 83: paix sociale ou pacification?* for the exhibition 'Les Enfants de l'immigration' held at the Georges Pompidou Centre in Paris. It was filmed during a training course in Lyon by a group of youngsters from one of the government-declared 'priority urban development areas' that symbolize the 'problem suburbs'. Two years later the documentary was shown in Lyon to those same youngsters, who in the meantime had slipped back from being enthusiastic participants in breaking news to being passive spectators of an urban renovation programme beyond their control. 'Did we really do all that?' was their astonished reaction as they were reminded of what their movement had achieved. This story serves to illustrate how short memories are, partly because of the way immigration is dealt with in the media – always focusing on 'newsworthy' events which are by their very nature short-lived. It is the lack of follow-up coverage of immigration which leaves this impression of always starting from scratch, as if people had no history. The media churn out the same old issues, out of touch with reality: a living, diverse and complex reality that is constantly evolving. IM'média, one of whose slogans is 'the agency that ensures follow-up', believes that immigration should be the subject of day-to-day coverage – just like the dollar exchange rate, the retail price index or the weather – by professional reporters and not by rising stars cutting their journalistic teeth on the compulsory issue of immigration before moving on to more 'serious' topics. A quick look at media round-ups of the 1980s speaks volumes in this respect: Gorbachev was widely acknowledged as the hero of the decade and Aids was the chief villain, but there was no mention of the young *beurs* who hit the headlines in 1983 – even though they probably helped to get François Mitterrand re-elected President in 1988 because he had managed to divide the Right over the issue of votes for migrant residents. Only IM'média rebroadcast film of the 'March For Equality' in *Les années quatre-vingt et l'immigration* (The 1980s and Immigration), an anthology of archive material provided for FR3's magazine *Rencontres*. The national media's way of handling news means that the latest story drives previous coverage out of collective memory. The row over whether schoolgirls should be allowed to wear Moslem scarves in class replaced the story of a bulldozed mosque, and was in turn ousted by the debate on illegal immigration and later by the official about-turn in favour of the integration of foreigners. This means that the media themselves have virtually no record of whole chunks of their own history, and television channels appear unable to make serious use of the programmes on immigration that have accumulated since television started in France. Similarly, a massive reserve of material at the Institut national de l'audiovisuel (INA - National Broadcasting Institute) remains untapped.

Faced with these policies leading to collective loss of memory, IM'média had the idea of setting up an independent archive to keep a record of immigration. As well as its own footage, which dates back to 1982, the agency began in 1987–1988 to establish an alternative network of independent journalists, programme makers and producers. Organizations like the Three Worlds Mediathèque, Inter Services Migrants (ISM) and the Agency for the Development of Intercultural Relations (ADRI) were struggling to renew their previously well-stocked information resources on immigration. Most serious of all, they were no longer producing any innovative material, despite recent administrative shake-ups and attempts at mergers. The television magazine *Mosaïques* proved incapable of managing its own stocks of film, which disappeared along with the programme itself in 1987. Buried in containers at the back of a cellar, items broadcast during the programme's 13 years of the existence are still unavailable, despite several attempts to set up an organization to manage them and put them to good use.

Consequently, the new-format programmes that replaced *Mosaïques* (*Ensembles aujourd'hui, Rencontres*) were on the lookout for new material. IM'média seized the opportunity to submit, in 1988, a series of co-produced features on subjects like a young cartoonist of immigrant origin, an Indian chef, the 'harkis' (Algerian soldiers who fought on the side of the French in the Algerian war of independence and are still housed in army camps) and a group of French Vietnamese repatriated after the French were thrown out of their former colony in 1954. In each case, IM'média asked to co-produce the programmes in order to remain in control of the material and be able to use it elsewhere, commercially or otherwise.

During 1988, when the subject of immigration had been put on the back burner, the FAS announced that it wanted to involve media professionals from an immigration background in devising and producing the new magazines, under the control of a well-established production company. After the idea was put out to tender, IM'média and Les Films du Sabre (acting as executive producer) were chosen to co-produce a series of 20 programmes, with an option for 20 more. Thus IM'média and Le Sabre co-produced 40 editions of *Rencontres* throughout 1989. A three-way agreement with the Association des rencontres audiovisuelles (ARA - Audiovisual Contacts Association) defined the role and contribution of each partner. Out of an average of 800,000 francs per programme, the FAS paid 500,000 francs through the ARA, with Le Sabre and IM'média paying two-thirds and one-third respectively of the remainder. The co-production was put together hastily and worked out in the end, despite long waits for payment.

The ARA, headed by former radio journalist Edouard Pellet, became increasingly touchy about editorial responsibility for the programme as the months went by, wanting to make all the major decisions itself. However IM'média, which had made sure from the beginning to have a cast-iron contract defining the conditions of its participation, continued to steer a straight course, making features and documentaries on major social themes according to its original mission: calling for repeal of the Pasqua law on foreigners, criticizing ideological and physical attacks on Islam, supporting rehousing of people in poor accommodation in Paris and Marseille, denouncing racist crimes in the run-up to the local elections of March 1989, backing the rights of foreigners in Europe, and so on. As an ex-journalist, Edouard Pellet was sympathetic to IM'média's point of view and they began to work together more closely. New regular spots were created to meet the needs of voluntary organizations, which were considered over-reluctant to contribute to the programme, and to provide room for comment by politicians and other prominent figures. One of the most successful regular features was 'foreigners' rights', devised by IM'média in cooperation with an immigrant workers' organization and presented by Senegalese legal adviser Assane Ba, former representative of a rent strike committee for immigrant workers living in government hostels. The large amount of mail sent to *Rencontres* was proof of the slot's popularity: 90 per cent of the letters asked for legal advice. Thus the programme moved closer to the ideal of dynamic interactivity on public television – too rare an occurrence in French broadcasting.

IM'média provided more than 13 hours of ready-to-broadcast programmes for *Rencontres*. This required the involvement of over 100 people working as researchers, journalists and technicians or assisting in other ways. Some were permanent staff members of the agency, others had temporary contracts and others were working as volunteers. They included many young people from an immigrant background for whom the project provided a unique opportunity to receive training and to get involved in television for the first time.

There is a saying in the French media that 'television drives you mad', and alongside its apparent success IM'média was going through an internal crisis. The root of the problem was a conflict between the collective development of the agency and individual opportunism, with some members demanding the same levels of pay as those practised in the mass media. This prompted a breakdown in staff relations and killed off some long-standing friendships. On the face of it the pay claims were justified, and it might have been possible to negotiate increases had they not been accompanied by a rejection of the agency's original mission in favour of the short-term personal convenience of a few people. While all this was going on, IM'média was snowed under with work and was in danger of becoming a mere sub-contractor for *Rencontres*. As weekly deadlines drew near, the agency toyed with the temptation to produce 'tissue-paper' images which could be thrown away after use, in clear contradiction with its commitment to provide follow-up in current affairs. To make matters worse, the dissident staff members were listened to and then wooed by the FAS and the ARA, and were even offered temporary contracts with the new-look *Rencontres* in 1990. Tissue-paper images paved the way for tissue-paper staff.

The years that followed saw a hardening of government immigration policy, with tighter police and employment controls. The 'integration' aspect concentrated on making it easier for long-standing immigrants to acquire French nationality and on making immigration part of common law. The FAS was charged with implementing this policy and openly stated its intention to use *Rencontres* to further the cause of integration as dictated by successive teams at the ministries of social affairs and budget planning. After being shuffled around various time-slots, the programme, renamed *Premier Service*, was broadcast daily at 7 am on France 3 in 1993–1994. In the process, it had shrunk from 26 to 13 minutes!

The magazine was a profitable outlet for the production companies responsible for it, and no-one seemed to worry about professional ethics any more. Apparently, everyone gradually lost interest in *Premier Service*. A few attempts were made to get back to a weekly two-hour format, but these were rejected by both the public and commercial channels. The ultimate irony was that the programme was continued in 1994 for fear that it might disappear altogether . . . in fact it is scheduled to go off the air in 1995.

Does this mean that the FAS, the government and the channels have given up the idea of any specific programmes for immigrants? This is a hard question to answer, because French officials are constantly shilly-shallying over matters of policy. They claim they want to integrate the subject of immigration into mainstream programmes and are sprinkling money around right, left and centre – but this policy is distressingly difficult to pin down. So far it has not been put in writing anywhere and does not form part of the channels' charters or guidelines. What can be perceived is that coverage of immigration is tending to get mixed in with coverage of social exclusion in general, even if this means strengthening the unwarranted comparison between immigration and poverty. As if occasionally seized with regret, the authorities schedule the odd 'specific' programme now and again. For instance the then boss of France 2 and France 3, Hervé Bourges, was anxious to reward the Arabs for their good behaviour during the Gulf War - in his fashion - by screening *Les Nuits du Ramadan* (Ramadan Nights), made by Tewfik Farès from 1991 to 1993. The next year it was Frédéric Mitterrand who took over the reins of this programme made specially for the Moslem community in France. Some local experiments have been carried out with Arabic-language cable channels, but these were somewhat confused and nothing came of them. As a preventive measure, the Higher Broadcasting Council (Conseil Supérieur de l'Audiovisuel, CSA) refuses to officially recognize Arabic-language channels on French cable. At the same time, French television, especially France 2 (formerly Antenne 2) and Canal Plus, is taking off in Africa. As always, the exchanges between France and its former colonies are on an unequal footing . . .

Television viewers from the immigrant communities have been kept on the sidelines of these political shenanigans even though they are the people mainly concerned, but they have not been idle in the debate. After providing plenty of business for video hire clubs, they have been flocking to buy satellite dishes which enable them to pick up channels from North Africa, Turkey and Pakistan. More than 100,000 migrant homes are now thought to be equipped to receive these channels via the Eutelsat satellite. The media and the political élite are now fussing about the supposed danger of Islamic fundamentalist propaganda being broadcast on these channels, pretending to be unaware that some of them actually provide efficient anti-fundamentalist material (especially Egyptian serials like *La Famille*, some religious chat shows and Adel Imam's films *Le Terroriste* and *Kebab et terrorisme*).

Paradoxically, the threat of fundamentalist proselytizing is at the moment coming mainly from channels broadcasting from Europe, and especially London, such as Muslim TV and MBC, which have Pakistani, Saudi or Kuwaiti funding. Moreover the Grey Wolves, a far-right Turkish nationalist group, and other fundamentalist Turkish groups are using various European independent or open channels, such as the Offener Kanal in Berlin, while European right-wing extremists are pirating programmes broadcast by the Ku Klux Klan, the Moonies or television evangelists for their video news networks.

In France the ministry of foreign affairs, with the backing of the communications and budget planning ministries, threw itself into new projects to fight fire with fire. Latest initiatives include the establishment in 1995 of a cable pay-channel called FAC (Franco-Arabe Câble) and run by Fouad Benhalla, former boss of Canal France International (CFI). Once again, the emphasis has shifted towards specific measures to 'encourage integration'. And in accordance with French tradition, the government is once again at the helm . . .

National and European networks

IM'média took advantage of its work for *Rencontres* to equip itself with Beta-SP filming and editing equipment. The agency set up a production arm, establishing IM'média Productions as a limited company, while the non-profit side reached out towards other parts of France and Europe. The developing world was not neglected, and special interest was taken in Algeria.

Since 1989 IM'média has been co-producing the series *Algérie en démocratie* with film director Merzak Allouache, who swapped his movie camera for a V8 to cover the upheavals in Algeria after the riots of October 1988. Although the technical quality leaves something to be desired, IM'média was won over by Merzak's determination to film history as it happened, like a one-man agency. Three programmes, *L'Après-octobre* (Post-october), *Femmes en mouvements* (Women on the move) and *Coincés à Alger* (Stuck in Algiers), co-produced and distributed by IM'média, have been sold to television companies all over the world.

After working with *Rencontres*, IM'média took advantage of a widespread renewed interest in documentaries to turn its attention to other new types of programme, such as *Reporters* on the now-defunct La Cinq, and to strengthen its ties with broadcasters. The trouble was that the agency was soon given to understand that, in order to survive, it had to stop bugging producers by harping on about immigration. What was wanted was more personal and imaginative work, unusual subjects and video-art. This drift away from IM'média's original mission got through to some of the team, who followed the new line on the pretext of covering protests by students, nurses and railway workers. Even the documentary *Voyage au pays de la Peuge* (A trip to Peugeotland), made by the agency in 1990, played down the role of immigrant labour in the history of the Peugeot car factories. That was probably why it received the National Heritage Prize at the Pompidou Centre's 'Cinéma du Réel' Festival!

However, IM'média took a stand against this process of denial and decided, on the contrary, to step up its role as media adviser to groups representing the unemployed, workers in insecure jobs, people in poor housing, and victims of the 'double punishment' (migrant residents who were born or grew up in France being deported after serving a prison sentence).

Where the trade union movement was concerned, IM'média was involved in the hopes raised by the Peugeot strike in autumn 1989. For once the workers' demands touched the hearts of ordinary French people. The media gave the movement ample coverage, showing pathetic pictures of workers' families at home. They included immigrant families talking about workers' complaints, without being branded as different. We had come a long way from Moslem fundamentalists fomenting dissent and violence in French factories. But all good things come to an end, and the Peugeot workers returned to the anonymity whence they had emerged. Later the strikers kicked themselves for handing over reponsibility for media coverage of their movement, with no attempt to create or control their own image. Some tried to write about their experiences; others began to collect scattered accounts of the strike in the form of photos, audio cassettes and V8 film. In an attempt to focus all this dissipated energy, IM'média scoured the Béthoncourt area (eastern France) where the workers lived and put together a local audiovisual network that brought into contact permanent and temporary workers, trade unions and militant immigrant groups. IM'média cameraman Samir Abdallah even used his experiences in the workers' housing estates to produce a new film about the survivors of this post-industrial cataclysm called *Laisses pas Béthon*.

IM'média has always sought to become a national network with regional branches where immigrants most need living media to make their voices heard, with major centres in Paris, Lyon, Marseille and Lille. To be honest, this has not been a great success. The agency started in Lyon but had to move the centre of its activities to Paris in 1984–1985. Nevertheless, the agency still served as a model for others. Small local broadcasting groups sprang up, specializing in production or distribution, often as part of regional organizations. They included Escale-Images in Lyon, Texture and Vidéorême in Lille, Requita in Villeneuve d'Asq, Vitécri in Toulouse, Trame-à-trame in Belfort and L'Yeux Ouverts in Nanterre. Sometimes these groups are in competition with IM'média but they try to stay in tune with its philosophy and fulfil more or less the same role of go-between with the local authorities and media. The chief obstacle to more open cooperation is their clique mentality. These new groups tend to be inward-looking, congratulating themselves on their ideas and jealously guarding their narrow notion of independence, but after this necessary stage of self-assertion, many move on to new forms of cooperation and coproductions. In addition, with the airtime available for immigration and social documentaries shrinking continually, new ideas for linking the two themes and getting them noticed start to appear. IM'média organizes monthly meetings known as Vidéo-réalités in Paris with the organization Avenir Vivable and Relais Ménilmontant, and a touring film festival (FISSA) focusing on the plight of the homeless has been started, aiming to cover the whole of France.

At European level, IM'média established a good working relationship with radical black British groups that had managed to penetrate the press, radio and television after the inner-city uprisings in the 1970s and 1980s, and to put black perspectives on the political and cultural agenda, with the Black Bookfair, Notting Hill Carnival, and so on. The agency also noted with interest the emergence of a new generation of performers and media workers forming part of the workshop movement. The British experience of multicultural programming and openings for independent producers seemed like the stuff dreams are made of compared to the way French broadcasting ostracizes immigration and social experiment, but we should beware of turning it into a myth. The dyed-in-the-wool British have lost nothing of their arrogance when it comes to showing who is really in charge. The BBC cannot get rid of a highly institutionalized, slightly paternalistic and complex-ridden style of race relations. Although the BBC's quota system ensures that some communities are represented on the staff, it also results in others being excluded and distorts the widely accepted general and political concept of 'black' as a term embracing all communities apart from the dominant whites. The old saying 'divide and rule' takes on its full significance here. One bone of contention: the now-defunct Afro-

Caribbean programme unit, in its series *Black on Europe*, dealt with the Afro-Caribbean diaspora in six European countries, leaving aside all other communities. From this sectarian viewpoint, Africa starts south of the Sahara, and Arab and Berber Africa disappear into the mists of Babylon!

Meanwhile, the sweeping public sector budget cuts carried out by the Thatcher government and the disbanding of financial backers accused of being too close to the Labour Party, revealed the limitations of the workshops. Although they retained their editorial and official independence, they were still dependent on outside finance. In order to defend themselves, they set up the Association of Black Workshops (ABW). The deregulation of the broadcasting industry sharpened the threat that the workshops' traditional sources of income might soon dry up and made them look at sponsorship and other ways of raising money. The ABW did the lobbying, tried to establish links with black people working in mainstream television and took part in alternative distribution networks such as Vokani Black and Third World Film Circuit. But the ABW, despite its smart new title of Black Media UK, did not seem able to cope with the scale of the economic challenge and, like other independent production companies, it was to undergo other untoward effects of this euphoric period. Collective political statement was giving way to the viewpoints of individual authors, a shift encouraged by white 'yuppies' (young urban professionals) and 'buppies' (black urban professionals). Groups like *Race Today* imploded.

The programme makers who emerged from the workshops have drifted from black politics towards a cultural élitism and trendy societal norms. In addition, commercial pressure means that what has been achieved is gradually being whittled away, and deregulation has been pushing things in the same direction. It was against this background that IM'média started working with newcomers like Migrant Media Collective in London and Hall Place Studios in Leeds.

Migrant Media, started by Ken Fero in 1989, concerns itself with the small communities concentrated in the London borough of Hackney, such as Turks, Kurds and Iraqi Arabs, Yemenis and North Africans. Fero, from Malta, is struggling against the tide of generosity extended mainly to Indians, Pakistanis and people of Caribbean origin. The task is particularly difficult because his own audience often consists of refugees and immigrants who have only recently arrived in Britain and enjoy little or no support in the country. It is no coincidence that Migrant Media made contact with IM'média at one of the many lectures organized by the British Film Institute about blacks in post-Maastricht Europe.

Migrant Media did get something resembling a quota from the local authorities, but Ken Fero also took advantage of his work with IM'média to convince himself that the worst was over. The coproduction of *Raus! Germany, The Other Story* and

Britain's Black Legacy in 1991 had a domino effect, and led to his making *After the Storm*, a 35-minute programme about the reaction of the Arab community in Britain to the Gulf War, for the BBC2 series *Birthrights*. In 1992 Migrant Media Limited – metamorphosed into a production company for the requirements of television – coproduced *Douce France* with IM'média for the *Critical Eye* series on Channel 4. The programme was ordered by Alan Fountain, who was then handling the commissioning of independent films and videos for the channel. In 1994 Migrant Media made another documentary for the *Critical Eye* series: *Tasting Freedom* was about the deportation of Algerian and black African refugees and their revolt in detention centres. Migrant Media and IM'media subsequently worked together on the story of Joy Gardner, a Jamaican woman killed by police who had come to deport her.

In addition to handling co-productions and one-off commissions from local and national channels, IM'média went all out to help voluntary, social and political groups in Britain, Germany, Scandinavia, Italy and the Benelux countries in order to use their communication capacities to best effect. With all of Europe in turmoil, priority was given to Germany, where racism had reared its head even before reunification. Young blacks from Germany had alerted IM'média to the situation in 1988. Some, arriving in London or Paris to study, set up camp on the banks of the Thames. Others, members of black German or Turkish organizations, followed training courses of six months or more at the agency, laying the groundwork for several programmes about German blacks, gangs of Turkish youngsters in Berlin, and so on. The Political Forum for Immigrants (IPF) in Germany, in connection with IM'média, increased audiovisual coverage of its work in aid of victims of racist attacks in 1991 and 1992, filming its investigations at hostels for refugees. At first the filming was done with S-VHS or high-band equipment – whatever happened to be available. The IPF gradually built up a video library and began cooperating with groups that had undertaken similar initiatives. Eventually the IPF acquired equipment compatible with IM'média's, and on this basis *Raus! Germany, The Other Story* (1991) and *Le Syndrome de Hoyerswerda* (co-produced with the IPF in November 1992) were made.

So the continuing story of racism in Europe, handled from the viewpoint of the people concerned, keeps chugging along, although it has its ups and downs. The topic crops up at festivals and hundreds of videocassettes are produced. Some television channels agree to broadcast them, in full or in part, and IM'média is perfectly willing to accept this piecemeal utilization to fit in with the channels' schedules. There are limits, however. For instance, *Viva cités* on FR3 wanted to re-edit a film about Germany, cutting out certain scenes in which immigrants were provoked into defending themselves. Instead, the channel wanted to show sinister-looking skinheads armed to the teeth with military equipment salvaged from the former Soviet Red Army, with an attractive young Turkish trainee acting as link woman. The aim was clearly to tug at the heartstrings of honest folk using images of immigrants as the innocent victims of ignorant yobs – but that's not IM'média's idea of television. If immigrants want to play at vigilantes, Rambo or Exterminator, why not? At least it shows that integration is working. There had also been complaints because *Raus! Germany, The Other Story* opened with the murder of a German who was killed in the metro by Ayhan Oztürk, a young Turk acting in self-defence, as if the idea was not acceptable to right-thinking people. A German court eventually acquitted Ayhan Oztürk.

These examples show the extent to which a clear or uneasy conscience can determine how people perceived as different are portrayed on television. Against this background, ideological or symbolic anti-racism can quickly become a poison that stifles the communities born of immigration. The French Jacobin model has a historical tendency to disown such communities, dissolving them by individual integration in the melting pot of the indivisible Republic. But times change, and with the arrival of the European Union and the global village so dear to Marshall McLuhan, the focus now is on negotiating collective self-determination in the broadest sense for these communities, which also provides a space for people to find their identities. The current fuss about Islam is proof of this. The factor of over-riding importance is not to get bogged down either in picturesque portrayals of immigrants or in lamenting their fate. Self-confidence and self-respect might be the driving force behind these forthcoming negotiations to ensure better representation of migrant communities and issues, both in public and commercial television and on the new cable and satellite channels.

From Monochrome to Technicolour

The history of PBME (Public Broadcasting for a Multicultural Europe)

Europe Singh

Education Officer, BBC, and Secretary of PBME

PBME (Public Broadcasting for a Multicultural Europe) has had a significant impact on European Broadcasting in the two or more years of its existence. Beginning with a Europe-wide conference in 1992, by the summer of 1994, it had published two issues of a hard hitting magazine *Spectrum*, had begun to influence the programme committees of the European Broadcasting Union and raised the debate around the employment and programme policies of broadcasters in The Netherlands, Germany, Belgium, Denmark and Sweden.

The transnational project began with the desire of two individuals involved in the *MOSAIC* project in BBC Education, Rakesh Bhanot and Europe Singh, to spread the lessons learnt in establishing that anti-racist broadcasting initiative (*MOSAIC*) to the other member states of the European Community. At first it was a desire to aid those attempting to hold back the racism and xenophobia that were beginning to develop in Europe, but after discussion with other media activists in Europe the emphasis began to change to encompass a much broader agenda. This development was not always easy and the relationship with the Dutch group STOA was not always a happy one. Although we had planned and completed the publicity for a conference as early as June 1991 that event did not take place until October 1992.

As part of the preparations for the conference, research was carried out by two researchers from STOA, funded by EC money, into the relationships between minorities and the broadcast media in seven different countries: The Netherlands, UK, Belgium, France, Denmark, Germany and Sweden.

The research revealed an uneven picture where some countries were striving to address the issues of employment and portrayal and others had not even though about them. The only consistent element was the very sensationalist and negative way in which news journalists treated stories involving these 'visible outsiders'. Even in the UK, which boasted of its liberal progress in media portrayal, a BBC Education producer, John Twitchin, exposed the problem-centred image of the black communities painted by news and current affairs programmes, light enter-tainment and drama. His series of documentaries – *The Black And White Media Show* – looked at the hidden and overt messages in British television that served to reinforce the racism and xenophobia of the viewing public. There was, in the UK however, a self-consciousness about the problem prompted by black communities and anti-racists that were forcing changes – both through the remit of Channel 4 to represent minority views and cultures and the BBC's Equal Opportunities initia-tives which looked at employment and portrayal. In the rest of Europe initiatives such as these were in their infancy in only two countries – The Netherlands and Belgium. The added difficulty faced by those wanting to change employment policies was that in some countries broadcasting was part of the civil service, which disqualified 'foreigners' from consideration – this was the case in Belgium. How-ever there was no guarantee that a lack of restrictions would produce a more diverse workforce. In France, with a large indigenous Arab community, resident communities from Francophone Africa and the Caribbean, there were no such restrictions on employment yet very few of these minorities were employed in broadcasting. They were present only as performers, foreign language broadcas-ters or, in the chic way of European TV, occasionally as presenters. There was a similar picture of employment in Germany, Sweden and Denmark.

On portrayal, the research was augmented by a survey conducted by Chris Lent of BBC Education for an EBU (European Broadcasting Union) Education sub-commit-tee meeting. Chris had asked European broadcasters to send examples of any programming that challenged racism and xenophobia or otherwise promoted a multicultural society. The most common form of broadcasting which included 'black and migrant' people was targeted, in all the countries surveyed (except UK) mainly in radio broadcasts – often local or at the margins of national broadcasting – to teach the minorities the national language or to give them information in their own language.

This casting of the settled ethnic minority communities as 'other' seemed to dominate their portrayal in every aspect of the media revealed by the Dutch research (this was also a phase in the development of the UK's output and, as already described, still has an impact). In mainstream news they were visible as performers or as problems. In drama as much as in news – they were the criminal, the illegal immigrant, the destitute or the victims of third world poverty. They, or 'their people', were the objects of pity and charity on a global scale.

These Third World images were the most insidious. They did not explain the complex web of the world economy enveloping the 'homelands as well as the migrant. Instead they reiterated notions of fecklessness, inability to make progress, primitiveness and violence. They served to reinforce the fears that were creating an embattled fortress Europe fending off the ladders of those desiring to clamber into the citadel. Of course, visible minorities already present in European nations were further marginalized by these images.

Despite this gloomy picture the rise of racism and xenophobia were forcing the issue of the role and responsibility of broadcasters on to the agenda of programme makers in all the states of the EC. The need for a response that promoted tolerance and valued diversity was slowly beginning to come under discussion and, in a few places, was bringing about small but significant changes.

The Dutch research also set out to find individuals in the seven countries who were active on the issues and could be invited to plan the European conference. The planning meeting took place in April 1992. Discussion focused on four major areas: employment, portrayal challenging racism, xenophobia and networking. During the discussion it was clear to the UK participants that there were wide gulfs between the understanding and perceptions of individuals from different countries on issues of race, migration and identity. Coming from a tradition in which self assertion of black communities had been won through struggle – it was difficult to cope with those who still saw these communities as 'foreigners' who needed things 'doing for them' rather than being active participants in a process. It was not only a question of patronizing attitudes but a lack of understanding of the role of migration in the post-war European economies – the 'guestworkers' were not extending the begging bowl but had put their hard labour into creating the wealth and the infrastructure of Europe. There was also amongst some, a lack of recognition of the role of the ex-colonies in laying the basis for the industrial development of Europe in the 17th, 18th and 19th centuries. The aims of the conference had to be broadened to accommodate these great deficits in understanding. Those participants who had been working on changes hoped that discussion and the exchange of experiences would sharpen the final positions in the conference.

The input of the BBC Television Equal Opportunities Department in the persons of Surinder Sharma and Jo Ann Surpliss, gave a cutting edge to the discussions on employment in broadcasting. By the time of the conference they had become part of the core of the project. Together with Louis Heinsman of the Dutch broadcasting company NOS, and Flip Voets of BRTN, the Flemish channel in Belgium they were also to become founder members of the PBME committee.

The European Broadcasting Union (EBU)

Parallel to these developments a conference on European Television and Immigration was being organized in Paris by Claire Frachon and Marion Vargaftig (the origin of this book) and the EBU education working party had put the issue of 'the challenge of a multicultural society and the campaign against racism and xenophobia' on to its agenda in a meeting in Valencia also in June 1992. This was the result of lobbying by Lea Martel of BRTN in Belgium and some of the BBC delegates. The EBU, a body that existed to run the Eurovision song contest and exchange news and sport items, was not as successful at establishing collective policy for its members. A code of conduct on violence had taken many years to agree. Guidelines on the portrayal of women had taken much effort but produced little in the way of concrete change. It had however, led to ongoing initiatives such as the Prix Nikki and the EBU women's conference that continue to raise the key issues around equality for men and women in broadcasting.

In Valencia, Chris Lent, the executive producer for *MOSAIC*, and Europe Singh, the project's education officer, attempted to map out the necessary elements of an anti-racist strategy:

- a multicultural programming policy that permeated all programme areas and ensured fair portrayal;

- an equal opportunities employment policy that ensured a diverse workforce to produce programmes that included a range of perspectives/cultures;

- niche programming to serve minority language communities;

- programming that challenged racism and xenophobia directly.

A lively debate was followed by recommendations to go to the EBU's main programme committee and the establishment of a 'committee of experts' chaired by Jos Tuerlinckx of BRTN. This latter body started with great promise with the hope of producing guidelines and co-ordinated strategies to energize educational broadcasting and other areas of programme making but it drifted into becoming an exchange opportunity for those producing multicultural magazine programmes around Europe e.g. *Couleur Locale* in Belgium. The exchange did allow for discussions on the different perspectives in the participating countries but despite the efforts of the chair, it was difficult to move ahead on any other area of policy.

The 1992 Conference

It was, by any measure, a great success. Robin Guthrie of the Council of Europe opened the event and Jonathan Powell, Controller of BBC1 gave the keynote address. A number of workshops provided the core output of the conference in the areas of: *Ethnic Minorities and Employment, Portrayal, Multicultural Broadcasting, Educational and Social Action Broadcasting to Challenge Racism and Xenophobia*, and *Networking*.

Participants from ten European countries included executives, policy makers, programme makers and personnel workers. Their feedback indicated that a whole range of agendas had been fulfilled by the event. In addition, the aims of the conference will be further progressed:

- through the European Broadcasting Union who are setting up a 'committee of experts';
- through the European Parliament: MEP Mary Bonotti gave a commitment to have a resolution in the European Parliament for the setting up of a European Foundation to further the aims of the conference; and
- a European Media Prize for best contribution to a multicultural society is being established with the CRE, ADO in The Netherlands and a German media organization.

The conference was concluded by the Dutch Minister of Health, Welfare and Culture, Mrs Hedy D'Ancona who gave her full support to the resolution for the European Parliament.

As always, the hidden agenda of the conference bore as much fruit as the 'official' programme. Many deals were struck, co-operation and co-production ideas generated and most significantly European networks were initiated.

The conference identified clear aims and objectives for PBME.

Aim

To discuss the role of public service broadcasting in a multicultural Europe and to develop a programme for action.

Objectives

- To formulate guidelines which enable public broadcasters to avoid negative portrayals of black and ethnic minorities and to strive towards high quality multicultural mainstream programming which promotes harmonious relations between different ethnic, religious and linguistic groups;

– To develop joint strategies for using educational and social action broadcasting as a means of countering racism and xenophobia;

– To set up networks to facilitate the aims of the conference, including a network of black and ethnic minority workers and organizations involved in broadcasting;

– To share good practice in establishing equal employment opportunities for black and ethnic minority broadcasters with European media organizations.

The multicultural debate

One of the key issues for the PBME has been in trying to define the term 'multicultural'. In Britain, amongst campaigners, this had become a glib term that often deflected serious analysis. It could be a way of softening the more difficult debates around racism and glossing over the difficulties of establishing pluralism. PBME members rapidly discovered that the French broadcasters would not accept the concept since in France there was only one culture. Top German executives flinched from the idea of an acceptance of the equal validity of different cultural expressions as much as they did from the notion of German Turks. Compared with these differences the debates in the UK were esoteric. The PBME struggled to define terms and offered the following formulation as a starting point for debate.

Multicultural programming

In this context 'multicultural' does not just refer to the national cultures of the European States, but includes the cultural diversity represented by people from other continents now settled in Europe. It is precisely the reaction of European people to this new diversity that has forced the issue of broadcasting and representation on to the agenda. The media, and television and radio in particular, help to affect attitudes and reinforce prejudices amongst the population. The way in which they represent these new communities is critical to the future health of the societies in which they exist. In most European states 'multicultural' programming has meant a half-hour slot on national television at some unpopular time, for black and migrant workers to make programmes for their own communities – possibly in their own languages. On radio, local radio has tended to devote some small amount of time to programming in the black/migrant languages present in the locality. Once again it has tended to be at unpopular times and restricted to certain sorts of output – e.g. music, cultural events. This could be better described as 'ghetto' programming since it cuts off the target communities from the society as whole.

Multicultural programming seeks to do the opposite. By making cultural diversity part of the reality of television and radio it aims to shift the focus of the listener and viewer away from the conflict model of us and them. For example, drama series set in the country should show its diversity. Quiz shows should represent in the mix of contestants, the diverse make-up of society. News and Current Affairs should not merely focus on the problems represented by black/migrant communities but see them as part of ongoing reality. The positive contributions made by the new Europeans should also be a subject of interest for news and current affairs. Documentaries should consult experts who also happen to be from ethnic minorities and not always choose commentators who are white, indigenous Europeans (and usually male).

The shifting of the reality reflected by television and radio towards a multicultural perspective would have a profound effect on the perceptions and attitudes of the viewing and listening public. It is within this 'multicultural context' that racist ideas can then be challenged by educational broadcasting, documentaries and studio discussions. One strategy without the other is difficult to sustain.

In the past broadcasters have adopted the position of 'present the facts and let the viewer decide'. The problem with this approach, is that it assumes the goodwill of the viewing audience. In a situation of unequal power relationships neutrality can merely support the existing inequality. Facts about racism and discrimination have to be presented in a way which makes clear our opposition to these anti-social behaviours. We would not, for instance, allow the audience to make up its mind about drug abuse.

Code of conduct

The pressure for change within European broadcasting grew irresistible in 1993, stimulated by events like the massacre of migrant workers in Solingen, Germany, racist murders in Britain and the rise of the *Front National* in France. The EBU programme committee, pressured by Lea Martel finally put the issue on the agenda of its 1994 conference. The PBME were invited to work on a code of conduct for European broadcasters and present it to the committee planning the session on 'addressing the needs of a multicultural society'.

At the conference held in Cardiff in June, delegates from Germany vigorously resisted the adoption of a code and the consensus settled for circulation of the code as guidelines. But the code meanwhile began to gain acceptance in wider circles. Journalists organizations, broadcasters who had been campaigning for change, community organizations and the Council of Europe's committees all began to argue support for the draft of the code of conduct produced by the PBME.

The code took each programming genre in television and radio and brought together the best practice from all over Europe – from casting in soap operas to choosing contestants for game shows – the code suggested ways that television and radio could include black and ethnic minority communities and act directly or indirectly to counter racism and xenophobia.

The future of European broadcasting

Undoubtedly the changes in technology, the new delivery systems of cable and satellite, the digital revolution, the establishment of global computer networks and the computerization of the production processes themselves, will have profound effects on all aspects of radio and television. Already cable companies are producing programming for linguistic and cultural minorities on a subscription basis. The danger of giving each community what they want on their own cable is the fragmentation of any multicultural community and the impossibility of addressing issues of mutual tolerance and co-existence. It could provide a temptation for some public broadcasters on the terrestrial channels to shirk their responsibilities to serve all their public and return to narrower schedules that addressed only the majority group – euro-centric, monocultural and certainly monolingual.

Perhaps an even greater danger witnessed in the success of cable in countries like Belgium is the threat to public broadcasting on the terrestrial channels funded by public tax (such as the BBC licence fee). A completely unfettered broadcasting market based solely on commercial principles could have little concern for issues of portrayal or fair employment or challenging the ideas that breed racial violence.

On the positive side, increasing numbers of black and ethnic minority people are involved in TV and radio production. The growth in employment of minority groups in the industry is slow but in some countries, for example Britain and The Netherlands, it is already having some impact on the variety of programming.

The most difficult issue remains the political power of extreme right-wing parties. Journalists all over Europe have struggled with the question of how to report them and their activities without making them look like respectable politicians or worse glamourizing their street thuggery. Many of these 'politicians' now serve in European governments e.g. Belgium and Italy, and their influence in the public TV and radio companies in these countries has increased. This poses a grave threat to the drive to create a more tolerant European community.

A mirror crack'd from side to side: Black independent producers and the television industry

Salim Salam

Independent Producer and Director

> 'Television is a mirror of society.'
> (Senior Dutch TV executive at Public Broadcasting for a Multicultural
> Europe conference, Noordwijkerhout, 1992)

I t's almost impossible to know where to start. I want to examine the situation of black independent production companies and black freelance personnel in the television industry here in Britain. There are issues concerning portrayal, employment and power involved; there's also a lot of confusion around, which has not helped constructive debate. And although I'm concentrating here on television, I could easily extend my analysis to the media as a whole.

First, some figures. There are approximately 3 million people of African, Caribbean and Asian origin in the UK, roughly 6 per cent of the population. That represents around 750,000 black households. That suggests black people pay to the BBC about £70 million every year through the licence fee. The ITV companies and Channel 4 (C4) make most of their money through advertising, but the cost of advertising products on television is of course allowed for in the price of those products. Consumers pay for it to the tune of some £144 per household per year, according to one recent survey. On these figures, black people pay something like £170 million annually to the BBC and ITV/C4. We have a powerful demographic case for better representation in the television industry.

I start from the principle that in the field of television, black people should be treated fairly. That doesn't only mean in the way we are represented in programmes; it also concerns, for example the editorial decisions that determine what programmes are made. In employment terms, it means taking actions that will alleviate the chronic under-employment of black production and post-production staff, actors, writers ... I could go on and on.

The Race Relations Act, 1976, made discrimination in employment illegal. Almost 20 years on, we know that in pure employment terms, black people are under-represented in the broadcasting institutions, and in the independent production sector. Most of us have had, at times, to suffer a shortage of opportunities to develop our craft, because employment and experience are disproportionately denied us. If television had eliminated discrimination in employment, you would expect to see black people forming about 6 per cent of the industry's technicians, producers and senior executives, administrative staff, and so on. We are nowhere near this.

A few years ago the BBC, to its credit, set itself a target of employing at least 8 per cent of its staff from the ethnic minorities. This initiative, monitored by the influential internal Directorate Implementation Group (DIG), has exceeded that target, but most of those staff are security personnel, cleaners, or other manual grade workers, not involved in production at all; there are hardly any black people at Producer and Senior Producer levels; and even fewer heads of department or other senior executives. Figures for the other broadcasters are harder to obtain, but are likely to be much worse. Deregulation and financial cutbacks probably mean employment opportunities for black people in television will be even more restricted in future, unless we can put these sorts of issues on the broadcasters' agenda as a real priority.

Under the terms of the 1990 Broadcasting Act, at least 25 per cent of all programmes of the four terrestrial channels now have to be made by independent production companies, but when it comes to commissioning, black companies and producers are marginalized by the big broadcasting institutions, both in the quantity and the type of work that tends to be offered. As an independent producer I'm grateful for the 25 per cent quota, as that means more money in the pot for independent commissions, and in theory there's more chance I'll get work. But while I don't mind competing for a share of the pot, I don't want always to be the last in line to be served.

There's no need to waste time justifying the need for a black independent sector. Just as in any other area of television, we need to be represented there. We need commercially successful black companies, and we need to be able to exert pressure on a system or production process that has so far largely *excluded* us, not *included* us. We also need enough of those black companies around to guarantee that there will be some who will want to work in a way which acknowledges a wider responsibility to the sector and the community, not just their individual financial or professional interests, otherwise we'll end up making sure some of us are alright, Jack, and forget the rest.

I've been talking as if there definitely is such a thing as a black independent sector. I wish I could be as sure of that as I would like to be. Certainly, there are more black people in television production than before, and for that we should be grateful. Yet we lack a sense of collective direction, our networking is informal and badly developed, and our influence on the industry at a strategic level is minimal. We lack a clear strategy for the future, and find it hard to work together. We cannot blame a white-dominated industry alone for this situation. In many ways, we are our own worst enemies.

The establishment of new black perspectives on television can only come from those black people involved in it; producers, technicians, media analysts, academics. At one level, that means we need to have black companies successfully operating in the independent sector. While we should continue to analyse, for example, the portrayal of black communities on television, we can't ignore the question of who made those images. If we do, we'll remain consumers, not producers, of the television we watch.

It's clear that black people do not get a fair deal from television, but what contribution can black independents make to improving the media's record on representation of black people on screen and off? Answer: It depends on many things, but *the most important factor is how black independents behave in the future, and how clearly we focus our efforts.*

It isn't simply a case of adopting a moralistic position; there are other considerations. In crude terms, we are businesses. Like the vast majority of independent production companies in Britain, we depend on the big broadcasters to survive. The four terrestrial channels between them spend hundreds of millions of pounds on programmes annually. Black independents, in order to survive financially, have to have access to a fair slice of this cake. If there is institutional discrimination in the broadcasting system, which there is, then it's probable that black independents don't get a fair share of commissions, which we don't. Without adequate financing, the quality and range of programmes black producers are able to make are restricted. Which brings me to the area of programming.

There are two multicultural programme departments in the 'mainstream' broadcasting organizations. The BBC's Multicultural Programmes Unit, headed by Narendra Morar, produces most of its programmes in-house; as C4's Commissioning Editor for Multicultural Programmes, Farrukh Dhondy commissions independents. Along with Samir Shah, Head of BBC News and Current Affairs, and Trevor Phillips, who heads the Current Affairs department at London Weekend Television, they are the most senior black executives in British television. The roles of Messrs. Dhondy and Morar are particularly interesting, because they lead departments set up specifically to respond to a perceived audience demand for 'black' programmes. Both have argued publicly that they are under no obligation to provide production work for black-owned companies, and that they have no responsibility to develop a black independent production sector. In the sense that they have no legal obligation to employ or commission *anyone* in particular, regardless of race or colour, they're right. Even so, it's disappointing to see that quite a few of the black programmes on TV are not made by black companies or technicians.

Entire series, like Carlton TV's *The Chrystal Rose Show* and C4's *Desmond's*, are made by white independent companies who may employ black researchers, actors, directors or producers, but who usually use mainly white crew and post-production staff, who are thus guaranteed the bulk of employment opportunities and economic benefit. A significant proportion of programmes in C4's *Black Bag* series and the BBC's *All Black* and *East* series, are made in a similar way. This underlines the fact that whatever happens in future to these two departments, they could only ever keep in work a very small number of production companies, and we will need to look elsewhere if we are to unlick the finance necessary to sustain a financially viable black independent production sector.

Unfortunately, the reluctance of these senior executives to form a positive working relationship with more than a few companies in the sector has contributed to the slow progress we've made. The financial issue is but one aspect; there are other, developmental questions. As well as being symbolic of a commitment to a distinct ethnic minority audience, they and their departments are also partly a product of the many formal and informal movements which have campaigned for black people to be better represented in the media, especially in senior positions. They were also in an ideal position to facilitate communication between black independents and the wider BBC/C4 organizations, and to encourage debate and business.

The fact that black producers, technicians and companies did not become a more established feature of the industry, has disadvantaged black producers in the competition for commissions (which is tightly-controlled and difficult to penetrate), and enabled other executives to justify their own lack of action.

Anyway, why should black programme makers be confined to making black programmes? We can make all kinds of programme from game shows to drama, from sitcoms and documentaries to pop promos and adverts. We should target the mainstream departments as our main potential source of work. It's obvious, but I don't see many black companies producing game shows etc., for the mainstream broadcaster. We know they can be very resistant, and it's a hard job to sell ideas even when there's no discrimination at work, but the pressure has to be increased nonetheless. And, to give credit where it's due, there are several white executives who have demonstrated that they are prepared to commission black programmes, or programmes from black producers. Their good example should be used to encourage the rest.

The spending power of the multicultural programme departments is minute in comparison to total spending on *all* independently-produced programmes. Personally, I don't want to fight over crumbs from the rich man's table. We need to establish commercial and artistic relationships with every programme department possible – in the BBC, Channel 4 and the regional ITV companies – and to win commissions. That's the bottom line, and we can accelerate the process by appreciating some of the lessons of the past.

How did we get here? To understand this we need to step back and see the response of television to black communities in a broader historical perspective. Many of the experiences of black people in television are mirrored by the experiences of black people in local government, in voluntary organizations, in society at large. Nor can we deny that any improvement there has been in the last thirty years is due much more to social dynamics than to enlightened or radical television executives. It's a common experience that institutions don't move until they're pushed. Television is no different; in the early days, programmes for black audiences were designed to ease our 'integration' into the 'host' community. Now that concept seems quaint.

We saw the political after-effects of the uprisings in Britain in the 1980s: a massive increase in public spending in the inner cities and on employment and training initiatives. They put social issues concerning black communities on the agenda of every relevant agency, and gave a fresh, urgent focus to equal opportunities thinking and practice. They drew attention to the representation of black people on television, and informed the debate taking place at that time about the workshop movement and its funding (this was in the years leading up to the birth of C4, who were looking to identify new sources of programming, and who had a remit to extend choice by catering more for various minority audiences). They were in part responsible for the realization that new approaches had to be tried to serving the black communities of Britain, hence new sorts of programmes – sitcoms, soaps – and new multicultural programme departments.

The earliest black film-makers in Britain – Horace Ové (*A Hole in Babylon*, *Pressure*, *Playing Away*) being perhaps the most significant, certainly the most prolific – started off in the 1960s in true isolation, struggling for finance in an era when racism was much more overt, equal opportunities in the distant future, and the idea there should be dedicated public funding for black film-makers virtually unimaginable. The video revolution had not yet happened, transforming the public face and working practices of television as it was later to do, and they were unable to rely on stable periods of employment. Yet they got their films made. They inspired the next generation of black British film-makers like Menelik Shabazz (*Burning an Illusion*) and Imruh Caesar, now Imruh Bakari (*Riots and Rumours of Riots*) who went on to form with others – Isaac Julien, Lena Gopal, John Akomfrah, Nadine Marsh-Edwards, Mahmood Jamal *et al.* – the black workshops: Sankokfa, Black Audio Collective, Ceddo and Retake. For too many reasons than there is space to discuss, the efforts of these individuals, and others from the same period who made an equal if not greater contribution, have failed to establish a strong black independent production, distribution and training infrastructure.

Some people argue that the workshop movement, and the few black people in positions of influence, have acted as a block to the development of black people in film and television, leading to the creation of an élite within the black television and film community. This history demands a book in its own right, but the lesson it should teach us is that we need to plan *now* for the future. The danger of viewing ourselves solely as individuals or individual companies, with no responsibility for the long-term development of a black production sector, is that we'll never be taken seriously as a distinct part of either the independent sector or the industry generally. All we'll do is help to perpetuate the confusion and inequalities of the present situation. We'll remain divided, atomised, competing with each other for resources which become ever more scarce. Instead, we need to work to achieve a critical mass, a point in our economic development which will enable more of us to aim as high as we want in this business, and for that aim to be a realistic one.

The satellite/cable revolution has added a new dimension to the debate, but it's still a relatively small factor. It has begun the process of making subscription and pay-per-view acceptable to a British audience. It has provided an opportunity for culturally-specific stations such as TV Asia, to provide films and magazine programmes for subscribers who want programmes from a cultural tradition they recognize, and in mother-tongue languages. However, TV Asia does not have the financial resources to commission a significant number of independently-made productions, buying in most of its programmes cheaply from India and Pakistan, or sticking to equally cheap, live studio-based formats. Similarly, most of the black stations on satellite and cable are music video-dominated services made in the USA.

I'm conscious of having skimmed over these important subjects in obscene haste, and of completely ignoring others. I could have, for example, explored the potential for a terrestrial multicultural channel funded by a mix of advertising and subscription (public subsidy of such a channel, as happens with SBS in Australia, being out of the question in the current climate). This could be one response to the problem of inadequate airtime for the mix and quantity of programmes needed to satisfy black audience demand. Equally, I could have discussed the whole process of commissioning, which is crucial to our future, and the quality and types of programmes that are being made on black people's behalf. Those discussions will have to wait.

The debate about black people and television has to be able to discuss these issues clear-sightedly and honestly. They affect not just black people, but the whole of the broadcasting establishment. Actually, I am and will remain a supporter of the BBC in its current form as a body funded by licence fee, with a public service requirement. I am not torn between my belief in that and my anger at the BBC's failure to serve black people properly. I appreciate the uncertainty that has hit BBC staff in the light of the recent 'Producer Choice' reforms, which have cut production costs and jobs, are naturally seen as a threat to the livelihoods of BBC staff, and have been resisted by the unions. But sometimes your emotions are pulled in different directions.

As a believer in the right of people to form unions, and as someone who is opposed to political interference in the media, I didn't like the political pressure put on the BBC in the period before this year's renewal of the BBC Charter and funding. It's the same political arrogance which imposed on the ITV network a ridiculous bidding system that made a sick joke of the serious matter of allocating franchises. But I have to say that my sympathy is qualified, because I know there's waste in the broadcasting institutions, and I know black people have been badly served over decades by television people and institutions, including the broadcast unions and producers' trade associations.

My point is that the creation of what we might term identifiable black perspectives on television, depends on our recognizing a common interest in establishing a dialogue between ourselves; and between us and the wider industry. With the exception of some small-circulation journals, the *Black to the Future* debates at the Edinburgh TV Festival, or the occasional forum at other festivals, there's virtually no public discussion about our future in television and television's attitude to us.

It's something that should be going on all the time.

Thirty years after the first black British film makers started up, we remain a fragmented sector, unable or unwilling to speak or act as though we have a shared interest. Yet the rewards for us all as individuals and as communities, not to mention the benefits to British television, could be huge. At the risk of appearing idealistic and naïve, I want to repeat firmly that we do have common interests which we can hope to achieve, but only if enough of us work together for them. And that process has to start now, because it is already too late.

The Council of Europe's guidelines 1972–1992

Antonio Perotti

Director of the Centre d'Information et d'Etudes sur les Migrations Internationales (CIEMI)

The studies of the links between television and immigration described in this book highlight the shortcomings of European broadcasters in this respect. Despite a wide variety of contexts, whether or not the country in question includes national groups speaking different languages (such as Belgium, Switzerland and Luxembourg) or has specific policies towards ethnic minorities and immigrants (like France and the UK), television news and other programmes seem to have trouble getting to grips with the multicultural nature of society and the rights and requirements of minorities.

Television's difficulty in taking account of the diversity of society (or maybe its inability to do so), especially when this diversity is based on the inequality of immigrant groups, can be discerned in all official policies, even though different terms are used (*immigrants* in France, *ethnic minorities* in the UK and the Netherlands, *guest workers* and *foreigners* in Germany).

Although such terminology is not simply a neutral way of describing the same groups – it implies different policies on the integration and assimilation of immi-

76

grants – it does not seem to have implications for answering the basic questions concerning the relationship between television as a means of communication and the cultural and social diversity of society. So rather than labour the point, I will concentrate on examining the overall direction of official national policies on broadcasting and immigrants (whether or not they are described as *minority* groups in the sociological sense) and comparing it with the guidelines put forward by the Council of Europe.

Taking a historical approach to the aims of official policy on TV programmes for immigrant groups, I have encountered time and time again the five guidelines put forward at the end of the 1970s in a comparative study-report on the media and immigration in some European host countries and some countries of origin. The report was commissioned from two Belgian researchers by the Council of Cultural Cooperation in 1979 as part of a project on culture and the media.[1] These guidelines were as follows:

- To help immigrants understand and adapt to the host society.
- To provide immigrants with information resources in their own language about their country of origin and to enable them to find out more about their own culture.
- To give immigrants and minorities access to the media.
- To give society as a whole a better understanding of immigrant communities by familiarizing people with immigration as part of their own history.
- To encourage understanding in what is now a multicultural and multi-ethnic society.

These objectives, barely outlined in the late 1970s, have undergone significant development since then. Although some major host countries have tried to link them, greater stress has usually been placed on one or another. The different emphasis may depend on which generation is concerned (first-generation adults are more liable to be targets of the first and second guidelines; young people of the second generation are more likely to be concerned by the third). It may also depend on an immigrant community's linguistic and cultural needs, or the information and education required to develop intercommunity relations.

This development has been the result of several factors, some linked to the demographic and social evolution of the various immigrant communities, others touching on legal and technological changes in the media themselves. Perhaps the most important of these are firstly, privatization and secondly, cable and satellite broad-

---

1   B. Ducoli, A. Martinow-Remiche, *Les grands médias au service de l'identité culturelle ds travailleurs migrants*, Council of Europe, Strasbourg, 1979. Two breochures: DECS/DC (79).

casting, which has tended to stress linguistic rather than political boundaries.

The Council of Europe's initial approach, 1972–1979

Robert Wangermée and Holde Lhoest's book, *L'après-télévision. Une antimythologie de l'audiovisuel*,[1] was published in 1973 under the patronage of the Council of Europe. The first overview of its kind to appear in Europe, it raised questions about the future of new communications technology such as video, cable and satellite broadcasts – all largely unfamiliar to Europeans at the time. The new means of communication were not widely applied, although they were already the subject of widespread enthusiastic comment. Video and local television in particular were put forward as remedies for all the ills of modern civilization: the lack of communication resulting from urbanization, the destruction of family-based cultures and, of course, the nature of mass media, perceived as an impersonal, one-way means of communication to which the public had no right of reply. *L'après-télévision* went against the tide of thinking at the time, attempting to put these budding utopias back into perspective and to look at their political, economic and social implications.

Between 1972 and 1979, the Council of Europe's Council of Cultural Cooperation commissioned from European communication experts and those working in or responsible for local and professional media, at least 50 case studies dealing with the various aspects of how the new media were being used, especially in the field of education. From 1975 onwards, these surveys focused in particular on local, regional and community television, looking at subjects such as communication and the community, the role of television in the sociocultural development of new towns, the growth of cable television in towns, community television services, and viewer participation through local television centres. All these surveys were used as background for a wide-ranging conference, *Médias communautaires*, organized in Liège, Belgium, in December 1978 by the Council of Europe with the support of the Belgian Ministry for French Culture. In 1980, the Council of Europe published an important book by Paul Beaud on local television and experiments with broadcasting in Europe[2] which set out both to assess the discussions and conclusions of the Liège conference and to provide an overview of the 50 case studies.

It was against this background of research that in 1979 the Council of Cultural Cooperation financed the report on the media and immigrant workers referred to in footnote 1. It was based on surveys carried out in 10 host countries (Belgium, Denmark, France, Germany, Luxembourg, The Netherlands, Norway, Sweden,

---

1 Hachette Littérature, Paris.

2 Paul Beaud, *Médias communautaires? Radios et télévisions locales et expériences d'animation audiovisuelle en Europe*, Council of Europe, Strasbourg, 1980. The bibliography gives a complete list of references to surveys published by the Council of Europe.

Switzerland and the UK) and five countries of origin (Greece, Italy, Portugal, Spain and Turkey), and reached the following conclusion: most European TV stations at the time were producing programmes specifically for immigrants, in their own languages and in cooperation with national television in their countries of origin, with the aim of informing immigrants about the situation in their homelands and their new countries of residence. People from the countries in question were called on to help produce these programmes.

Generally speaking, the report noted numerous criticisms of these programmes, pointing to:

- Their brevity, inadequate form and content, apparent lack of connection with the everyday conditions in which immigrants lived, lack of debate about why they had left their homelands, the situation in their countries of origin and their contribution to the economy;

- Shortage of information about the history of immigration in the host country and on the main cultures involved, their origins and the most significant figures to have emerged from them;

- Lack of investigation into the way these different cultures develop, both in host countries and in the countries of origin.

At the end of the report, three working recommendations were made:

- Better coordination between production units in different countries and the organization of meetings between programme heads and exchanges of programmes in order to achieve this;

- Programming of general broadcasts to take account of substantial immigrant communities, especially in the choice of films and sports news;

- Greater efforts to make use of immigrants as a source of news on matters affecting them.

The surveys mentioned above did not lead to specific guidelines from any Council of Europe body. This is a matter for regret given the relevance of the conclusions reached by the surveys, which were the first of their kind. Moreover, since there was no real effort to make the results of the research known, only a restricted group of people are aware of them.

From the Tampere conference (1983) to the Cologne symposium (1986)

After the initial, provisional survey commissioned by the Council of Europe in

1979, another analysis was carried out at an international conference organized under the auspices of UNESCO at Tampere, Finland, in 1983. This second overview, clearly structured from a scientific viewpoint, examined the role of the media concerning immigrants in several European countries.[1]

The final report noted the serious handicaps and conditions of inequality in which relations between the media and immigrants had been conducted thus far, and made the following suggestions as a basis for a new relationship:

- Because of their legal status and socioeconomic position, migrant workers often have only restricted access to the usual channels of communication. Consequently they cannot fully exercise their rights of freedom of speech and opinion;

- The media and other means of communication can help to foster fundamental human rights. It is therefore important to ensure that migrant workers have equal access to and participation in the media;

- Migrant workers have an inalienable right to regularly receive news in their own language concerning both their country of origin and the host country;

- Migrant workers should not be regarded solely as consumers of information or be expected to *undergo* cultural adaptation; they should also be active in the processes of communication and cultural creation.

The Tampere conference emphasized the legal angle of the issue, as its title and conclusions make clear, but many national reports submitted to the conference underlined the sociological and cultural aspects. Participants were unanimous in pointing to the negative image of immigrants and minorities as portrayed by television, leading the Council of Europe to look again at the educational aspects of TV broadcasts following another project entitled *Education and the cultural development of immigrants* (1981–1985).

From 2 to 4 December 1986 the Council of Europe helped to organize an international symposium on *Migrants and the media: from guest workers to linguistic minorities*, backed by various broadcasters in the Federal Republic of Germany and by the government delegate responsible for foreign community affairs.

The aims of the symposium were to evaluate how foreigners living in West Germany were portrayed, to examine various aspects of their relations with the media

---

1 T. Hujanen, *The role of information in the realization of the human rights of migrant workers*, Report of the International Conference, Tampere, June 1983, University of Tampere, Finland, 1984.

and to make proposals for the future work of the media that would foster better understanding between the various foreign and cultural groups. Although the gathering focused on West German television, it was attended by programme heads, journalists and editors from ten or so European countries, including Turkey, which has a large migrant community in Germany, and from Canada.

An analysis by experts of the content of TV programmes during the first nine months of 1986 reached the following conclusions:

- Minorities of foreign origin have very limited access to the media, either as participants in various types of programme, as media professionals involved in producing programmes or as sources of news. Issues involving foreign minorities are usually channelled through third parties which generally enjoy privileged access to the media, such as political parties, trade unions, performing artistes and cultural organizations.

- Portrayal of the life and culture of foreign minorities is limited to a very restricted range of subjects (cooking, sport, tourism), and some nationalities are over-represented compared to others (Italian, Greek and Spanish immigrants are better represented than Turks).

- In news coverage of immigration, what often comes across most strongly is the suggestion that immigrants are a *burden* on and a *threat* to the host country.

A second negative point to emerge from the Cologne symposium concerned the involvement of foreign communities in pilot projects for cable broadcasting in West Germany. It had been expected that the development of this new technology would open up fresh prospects for expanding and diversifying what the media had to offer minorities of foreign origin, but a review of cable broadcasting experiments in Dortmund, Ludwigshafen and Berlin proved generally disappointing in this respect.

A number of structural problems were raised:

- Producing programmes aimed at target groups, and especially those broadcast in foreign languages, calls for exceptional investment in terms of finance, editing and design.

- If the programmes are to be favourably received by communities of foreign origin, correct conditions for reception are essential (cable networks, proper equipment, publicity for the programmes). One problem is that cable television is not yet widespread in districts with a high proportion of foreign minorities.

- Because few foreign households have cable services, it is difficult to obtain advertising income.

- The different foreign communities in West Germany do not share the same aspirations and interests. These vary and develop according to the length of stay in the country and many other factors.

The shortage of funds and of professionals with the journalistic and management ability necessary to produce programmes of quality for foreign communities largely explains the current situation in this new field of broadcasting. Minorities are either ignored in cable programmes (as happened with the Ludwigshafen pilot project), or given programmes taken almost entirely from the national broadcasting company of the target group's country of origin (for instance, Türkisch Deutsch-TD 1, the cable channel aimed at Turks living in Berlin). Only the cable television experiment in the Dortmund region seemed to be giving encouraging results.

The Cologne symposium recorded a similar lack of satisfaction with the situation in the UK, despite the fact that official bodies such as the Independent Broadcasting Authority (IBA) theoretically had wide-ranging powers to take account of the specific interests of ethnic and linguistic minorities. Although the IBA had made significant progress in providing broadcasting services to educational establishments with a view to fostering communication between different cultural communities, no satisfactory answer had been found to the question of how minorities should be represented in general mass-audience programmes.

Generally speaking, the mass media pay little attention to immigrants' practical difficulties and especially the complex relations between their culture of origin and their new environment in the host country. In its conclusions, the Cologne symposium called on the media in West Germany to make a more active contribution to contacts and understanding between Germans and minorities of foreign origin. German broadcasting law explicitly states that the relevant media should foster understanding between peoples.

The conclusions of the symposium confirmed first of all the general need to expand and diversify media production concerning foreign communities and to improve its quality. This would obviously require sufficient financial and technical resources, as well as painstaking work by well-informed professionals having close links with the subjects they would be dealing with.

Journalists were advised to modify their usual vocabulary; to avoid terms with connotations that were liable to provoke or strengthen resentment and rejection of foreign minorities on the part of the host country's population; to increase the number of reports and features dealing in depth with the lives and cultural contributions of foreign communities in West Germany, in order both to spread awareness of their cultural traditions and to highlight new aspects and forms of expression arising from their experiences in German society (historical or cultural series of interest to both Germans and foreigners, such as programmes about Arab culture in Europe, the history of Turco-German relations, and so on).

Throughout the media, action to achieve these aims should be taken at three levels:

- In the training of media professionals. Steps should be taken to encourage people from foreign communities to train as journalists, programme makers, presenters, and so on. The *multicultural* nature of society should be taken into account during initial and continuing training for media professionals.

- In encouraging people from foreign communities to play an active part in the production and broadcasting of news by the mass media. Accurate portrayal of the daily lives and experiences of foreign minorities is not possible without first-hand accounts and contributions from the people concerned. With this in mind, the following measures were suggested: increased use of members of foreign communities as news sources, programme advisers and local newspaper correspondents; representation of foreign minorities on supervisory bodies responsible for overseeing public broadcasting in West Germany.

- In the field of cooperation. As far as possible, cooperation should be increased and broadened between all media professionals dealing with subjects concerning foreign minorities and multicultural issues.

Finally, the Cologne symposium underlined the importance of cooperation between the mass media at European level (in the form of coproductions, programme exchanges and possibly meetings between professionals, production of European programmes, etc.) in order to jointly promote the cultural development of immigrants and ethnic and linguistic minorities, as well as to encourage contacts and understanding between the different cultures which have formed an integral part of European history and which will be part of our common future.

The Cologne symposium did not lead to any specific recommendations from Council of Europe bodies. The Council merely sponsored, published and distributed a summary of the main reports.[1]

---

1   Council of Europe, symposium on *Migrants and the media: from guest workers to linguistic minorities*, DEC/EGT (87) 2, Strasbourg, 1987.

From the Noordwijkerhout conference (1988) to the reports on intercommunity relations (1991)

In recent years two themes have recurred frequently in the Council of Europe's debates: concern with respect for diversity in broadcasting (opposing multimedia concentrations and monopolies), respect for the role of broadcasting as a service to the public on the part of both public and private channels, and therefore respect for cultural diversity in society as a whole, a role that television, as a public service, should play in developing intercommunity relations, a vital condition for fostering a form of democracy based on freedom of speech and information and on social unity.

The first of these concerns is particularly apparent in the work of the Steering Committee on Mass Communication Methods; the second has been dealt with chiefly by the Steering Committee on Migration and the Cultural Cooperation Council. In other words, it is an attempt to put into practice Article 10 of the European Convention on Human Rights, to work on the assumption that *freedom of expression and information is necessary for the social, economic, cultural and political development of all human beings, and is a condition of the harmonious advancement of social and cultural groups, nations and the international community.*[1]

In November 1988, at a ministerial conference on the politics of mass communication, the ministers agreed in the first resolution on political objectives to employ political, legal or other means to achieve common aims in the field of broadcasting, *to develop the cultural and educational aspect of television and encourage programming that reflects and optimizes the cultural richness and diversity of Europe and its different identities.*[2]

As several surveys by the Council of Europe have shown, relations between the media and immigration are conducted on an unequal footing. Immigration, associated with the idea of difference, seems to go against one of the functions of the media – integrating people into the fabric of society – because social unity is often regarded as the unity of a single group, the majority. As Len Masterman points out:

> We can easily imagine that in Europe, media are less and less the bastions of the freedom of expression than weapons used to serve powerful groups of interests. Even developed democracies have given birth to new forms of poverty and inequality: opposition between those who have easily

---

1 Declaration on Freedom of Expression and Information, adopted by the Committee of Ministers on 29 April 1982. See: Council of Europe, recommendations adopted by the Committee of Ministers of the Council of Europe in the area of the media (DH.MM (91) 1), Strasbourg, 1991.

2 Council of Europe, Activities of the Council of Europe in the field of the media, Human Rights Department, Strasbourg, 1991.

access to media and those who remain outsiders; inequality between those who have the power to define and those who are defined; inequality between those who talk of the world they know and understand, and those whose experiences are automatically situated and interpreted by others; inequality, in other words, between those who profit from the media and those who do not have access to them.[1]

This bleak picture was confirmed by participants at the Noordwijkerhout symposium on *Immigrants, the Media and Cultural Diversity*, organized by the Council of Europe with the Dutch Ministry of Well-Being, Health and Cultural Affairs from 29 November to 1 December 1988.

More than 120 journalists and civil servants took part in the debates. They were unanimous on one observation: television – like radio and the press – does not adequately reflect the diversity of multicultural society today, partly because broadcasting companies and professional training bodies are not easily accessible to minority groups.

At the end of the symposium, the participants proposed that the Council of Europe's Ministerial Committee and the governments of its member states should acknowledge the right of minority groups and immigrants to express themselves in the media and that this right should be included in the documents setting out the public channels' obligations. To encourage the state sector media to fulfil their obligations in this respect, the participants suggested that governments, when allocating funds to the media, should be obliged to award subsidies to channels with a policy of recruiting and providing initial and continuing training for journalists and programme makers of immigrant origin.

Colleges of journalism should include in their initial and continuing training programmes the knowledge needed to understand the social and cultural circumstances in which immigrant communities live, as well as the sociocultural, economic and political background of their countries of origin.

The participants even suggested that representatives of democratic immigrant associations and ethnic groups should be included on the boards of management of the state media, in the same way as other interest groups are represented. This recommendation was taken up by the European Parliament in 1988, in Recommendation 1089, para. 21.IX.b).[2]

The symposium participants recommended introducing a European media prize,

---

1 Len Masterman, *The Development of Education in the Europe of the 1980s*, Council of Europe, Education and Culture, Strasbourg, 1968.

2 Recommendation 1089 (1988), adopted by the European Parliament on 7 October 1988.

under the auspices of the Council of Europe or the European Broadcasting Union, to be awarded annually for the best TV programme about immigrants, ethnic minorities and intercommunity relations. They also suggested setting up a European production fund to encourage the making and broadcasting of multicultural programmes. The fund would grant subsidies, particularly to independent producers of immigrant origin, independent production companies run by immigrants and international coproductions. It would be an independent body with a board of management made up of media experts, including immigrants. The Council of Europe, the European Community and interested member states could help to finance the fund and get it under way.

These recommendations were adopted by the European Parliament in Recommendation 1089[1] and by the group of experts on intercommunity relations in their final report presented in late 1991. The European Parliament also recommended carrying out a comparative study of the member states' media policies on foreign communities and ethnic minorities. To date this recommendation has not been implemented.

Experts in intercommunity relations emphasize two points: training of journalists and drawing up a code of conduct for the profession.

> In order to combat stereotyped opinions about immigrants and their countries of origin and to ensure that the media do not give false information about them, journalists and radio and television broadcasters must be made more aware of the culture and lifestyles of those countries. It is also important that they should understand what the lives of immigrants and members of ethnic groups are like in the host country. It must be emphasized that these issues should be dealt with in a totally professional manner. Mass communications training establishments and journalists' organizations should be perfectly aware of these problems and should make sure that room is made for them in training programmes at all levels. Training establishments should also ensure that immigrants and members of ethnic groups do not encounter difficulties in enrolling for their courses. Governments can provide an incentive in this respect by increasing the funds available for grants and subsidies for students from these groups.

> Journalists' organizations may also find it helpful to draw up codes of conduct for their members, laying down the major principles of correct professional practice in a multiethnic society by drawing journalists'

---

1   Ibid. para 21, VI.

attention to the sensitive issues raised by coverage of subjects connected with intercommunity and interethnic relations.

I consider that the proposal for a code of conduct (whether it is drawn up by professional organizations as suggested above or by individual TV channels) should be put into practice as a matter of urgency, given the present and potential social and political mood.

Conclusion

Over the past 15 years, several reports have referred to the deliberations of the Council of Europe's group of experts. On the other hand, very few of the directives or clear, practical guidelines given, have been embodied in documents liable to have a political impact. This is disappointing, especially concerning the policies of public channels, where it would be relatively easy to take action. Does this mean we should give up the fight?

The current situation in broadcasting illustrated in this book, with its limitations and tentative experiments, suggests (as Robert Wangermée and Holde Lhoest did in *L'après-télévision. Une antimythologie de l'audiovisuel*) that we should not get too excited about the prospects of television taking account of the diversity introduced into our society by immigration. This is still a long way off.

But this book should encourage us to increase the opportunities for European-level meetings – as the Council of Europe was trying to do – between those who play a part in deciding communication and cultural policy, those who produce general or specific programmes for national or local television, and ordinary people who would like to become involved in producing and broadcasting news, in the social communication process as a whole. Such people do exist, as the experiments described in this book show.

The way the Council of Europe's thinking on this subject has changed over the past 15 years shows that relations between television and immigrants has undergone a degree of development, even if this has not been regular.

From broadcasts produced exclusively in immigrants' language of origin, programme makers have moved on to attempting to work the social and cultural aspects of their lives and intercommunity relations into general-interest programmes: from taking account of a social problem to taking account of a social phenomenon.

It is in that direction that this book opens up important prospects for future work. Although the contribution of international organizations such as the Council of Europe has had no significant direct impact on improving official policy, it may have influenced debate on this subject, which is no mean achievement.

Part II
Countries

AUSTRIA

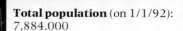

Total population (on 1/1/92):
7,884,000

Foreign population (on 1/1/92):
512,200
6.6 per cent of the total population

Distribution by country of origin:[*]
Former Yugoslavia	144,000
Turkey	63,320
Germany	14,400
Poland	14,400
Romania	8,640
Hungary	8,640
Former Czechoslovakia	7,200

[*]On 1/1/91

Sources: Louis Rallu & Alain Blum,
*European Population / Démographie
européenne*, Vol. 1: country by country
analysis, John Libbey Eurotext, Paris,
1991; SOPEMI, *Trends in International
Migration*, Paris, OECD, 1993 (based
on the Austrian Central Statistics
Bureau).

Heimat, fremde Heimat. Photo: ORF

AUSTRIA

1

IMMIGRATION HISTORY

Austria is something of an exception in its immigration patterns. Whereas most of Western Europe has accepted large numbers of foreigners, mostly from Mediterranean countries, Austria has for a long time been an open door to Eastern Europe.

About 2.6 million people have come to Austria since 1945, either as refugees or asylum-seekers, or as transmigrants. Some 550,000 were just passing through. Another 1.4 million stayed in the country for a few months or years before either continuing westwards or returning to their homelands.

Three main phases have marked the history of immigration in Austria: an increase in the number of foreigners entering the country in the late 1950s and early 1970s, a period of stagnation from 1973 to the mid-1980s, and a further increase from then onwards.

Between 1945 and 1981, waves of new immigrants often followed political crises to the east. Hundreds of thousands of Hungarians arrived in 1956 and 1957, and 162,000 Czechs and Slovaks came in 1968 and 1969. In 1981-1982, some 130,000 Poles spent some time in Austria.

After 1987 the number of asylum-seekers from Eastern Europe and the Middle East was back up to over 20,000 a year. Initially they came mainly from Hungary, Poland and Czechoslovakia, prior to the collapse of communism in those countries. From 1990 onwards they were replaced by refugees from Romania, Turkey, Iran and Bulgaria. As more East European nations opened their borders, Austria stopped being the only way to get from the Balkans and Eastern Europe to the north and west.

Many of these political refugees only regarded Austria as a staging post and did not bother to request asylum. In 1989 the country became the focal point for migration between the two Germanies: more than 45,000 former East German citizens crossed the Austro-Hungarian border between July and October 1989. Some 250,000 Jews from the Soviet Union arrived in Austria between 1976 and 1989 but most left shortly afterwards.

Since the early 1960s Austria has also taken in foreign workers, but the number allowed in has been reduced significantly since the recession of the mid-1970s.

A law governing the employment of foreigners was passed in 1975, following a consensus between the chambers of commerce, trade unions, the Church and the Ministry of Social Affairs. Broadly speaking, it lays down that the number of foreign workers allowed to enter Austria depends on the country's labour needs. The major principles of this law have changed little over the years. Austria still refuses to become a country of immigration, and the concept of integration concerns very few immigrants.

By 1984 there were officially only 139,000 foreign workers in Austria, 40 per cent fewer than ten years previously, yet by the end of the decade extra labour was being sought in Yugoslavia and Turkey. It is worth pointing out that Austria is also a country of *emigrant* workers: latest figures show 413,400 foreigners living in Austria and 430,000 Austrians living abroad.

An important change in the law came in 1990, when foreigners legally resident in the country before 1 April of that year were given until 1 October to apply for a work permit, thus allowing many unrecognized asylum-seekers to put their papers in order. The issue of clandestine workers (of whom there are estimated to be some 200,000) is the centre of heated political debate. On 24 November 1992 the French daily *Le Monde* reported that Austria's right-wing Freedom Party was calling for a referendum to back its call for a total halt to immigration.

The integration of foreigners has been made somewhat easier; they can now apply for Austrian nationality after living in Vienna for four years – or ten years in the rest of the country.

A new law, the *Fremdengesetz*, was adopted in January 1993, making it easier to expel the growing number of illegal immigrants from the country – something that is happening almost every day. People entering Austria must now have a work permit before they are allowed to live there. Foreigners already in residence are required to have a valid work permit and to have ten square metres of living space available. Anyone who is out of work for more than six months can have their residence permit withdrawn and be expelled from the country. This harsh law has been strongly criticized by the Green party, human rights organizations (the largest is SOS Mitmensch) and the Church.

On 1 July 1993 another law was adopted, the *Aufenthalstsgesetz*, concerning residence permits for people from outside the European Union. It lays down quotas for each of the nine Austrian federal states, averaging about 9 per cent. The law also includes a paragraph on helping to integrate foreigners living in Austria, but nothing concrete has yet been done in this respect.

Earlier, in October 1992, the Viennese Integration Fund was launched with a government contribution of $3 million. The aims of the fund include helping Bosnian refugees to learn German and find work, starting special lessons for Bosnian children, advising foreigners in their own languages, helping them find accommodation, and so on. Austria also has about 50 state- financed information centres for foreigners spread throughout the country. These centres have just set up an advisory committee to devise better ways to assist integration.

Major cities have government information and reception centres for foreigners. In Vienna alone there are about 100. Primary schools with large numbers of foreign children employ teachers who speak the children's own languages as well as German-speaking staff.

2

THE BROADCASTING SCENE

Austria is one of the few European countries whose public television still has a monopoly (until 1995 at least). But in addition to the two channels of the ORF (Österreichischer Rundfunk), Austrian viewers can receive most of the German channels and these attract more than 15 per cent of the total audience.

The state channels, ORF1 and ORF2, are financed by the licence fee plus 20 minutes of advertising per day. ORF1 was launched in 1955 and ORF2 in 1970. Between them they broadcast 14 hours a day from 9 am, a total of 11,000 hours a year. Their schedules are complementary and are designed for a wide audience: in 1990 they offered 39 per cent fiction and 13 per cent news plus a variety of other topics such as economics (8 per cent), entertainment (9 per cent), religion, culture and music (7 per cent each) and children's programmes (5 per cent).

During the first half of 1991, ORF1 and ORF2 won 79 per cent of the total audience. The other 21 per cent watched foreign channels: ARD (5 per cent), ZDF (2.6 per cent), Sat 1 (3.1 per cent) and RTL Plus (4.4 per cent).

3

CHANNEL POLICIES

Austria's broadcasting law obliges ORF to take an interest in all sectors of the Austrian population and their democratic coexistence. This a particularly important factor because of the large number of immigrants and ethnic groups speaking foreign languages who have lived in the country for a long time.

Magazine programmes for immigrants

The idea of making television programmes especially for ethnic minorities arose in 1987 after a change in policy at ORF2. The appearance of local programmes increased demands by Slovenians and Croats for their own broadcasts. A model was devised for three 30-minute programmes to go out simultaneously: one for the Slovenians in Carinthia, *Dober dan Koroska* (Hello Carinthia), one for the Croats in Burgenland, *Dober dan Gradisce* (Hello Burgenland), and one for the minorities in other states, *Heimat, fremde Heimat* (Homeland, Foreign Homeland). The transmission was split up in this way because there are hardly any immigrant workers in Carinthia and Burgenland. The three programmes, which include 10 per cent of entertainment such as music and dance, are broadcast from 1 pm to 1.30 pm on Sundays by ORF2, the only channel that can broadcast to all nine states.

➤*DOBER DAN KOROSKA* (Hello Carinthia) is aimed at the 50,000 Slovenians living in Carinthia. The language used is Carinthian Slovenian, with a detailed summary in German at the start of the programme.

➤*DOBAR DAN HRVATI* (Hello Croats) is intended for the Croat minority of 30,000 living in Burgenland. The language used is old Croat, but most of the features are subtitled in German.

➤*HEIMAT, FREMDE HEIMAT* (Homeland, Foreign Homeland) is aimed at the 300,000 immigrants living in the rest of Austria, including Vienna. The programme includes interviews, comment and entertainment and is subtitled in German.

The Croat and Slovenian scripts are written by native speakers from the radio stations in Klagenfurt and Eisenstadt. For the third programme, ORF set up a central editorial office in Vienna. The programme was launched in two stages for financial and practical reasons; starting with a 20-minute weekly magazine on 2 April 1989, it went up to 30 minutes in 1990.

The audience for these programmes is hard to estimate. The target groups reckon that about half those belonging to the minority concerned watch the broadcasts regularly. Polls carried out by Teletest put the number of viewers per programme between 20,000 and 200,000, varying according to the season, the weather and what is on the other channels. A minimum of 150,000 viewers per year for the three programmes (20,000 of them in Carinthia and 15,000 in Burgenland) may be considered a realistic average. It should also be borne in mind that some families record the programmes and pass on their videocassettes to friends and family.

From the beginning, it has been editorial policy for all the magazines not just to provide factual information but to help Austrians and minorities live together. *Dober dan Koroska* and *Dober dan Gradisce* introduced subjects such as sketches of Croat villages in Burgenland, detailed features on cultural activities and videoclips produced in Carinthia. The cultural mix was strengthened by the addition of extracts from German programmes in the two magazines.

The central editorial office devised a programme for all the minorities living in Austria, whether they were part of well-established foreign communities or had just arrived, and including Slovenians and Croats living outside Carinthia and Burgenland. *Heimat, Fremde Heimat* has also produced special programmes for Albanians, Anatolians, Armenians, Arameans, Slovenians in Carniola, Croats in Burgenland and Croatia, Kurds, Macedonians, Iranians, Poles, Romanians, Serbs, Slovaks, Italians from the Trentino region of northern Italy, Czechs, Turks, Hungarians, Ukrainians, Romanies and Assyrians. The general theme of the broadcasts is ethnic identity, either seen from the immigrants' viewpoint so as to show the particular culture of the various groups, or from an outsider's viewpoint so as to strengthen understanding among Austrians and other minorities.

The magazines have also given rise to a regular help and advice service for immigrants set up by the central editorial office. Staffed by 15 people able to answer questions about practical problems such as housing and red tape, it is backed up by a special children's hotline run by people speaking minority languages. Both services operate seven days a week in eight languages (the Slav languages plus Armenian, Kurdish and Turkish) and work in cooperation with the ORF's family programmes department.

In 1994 the German satellite channel 3 SAT began broadcasting a half-hour international summary of *Heimat, Fremde Heimat* twice a month. Dubbed in German, it can be picked up by German- speakers from North Africa to Russia. Recent subjects have included the fact that foreigners cannot stand for election in Austria, the history of Hungarian costume among Hungarians in Austria and the role of religion for the country's officially recognized ethnic groups.

The central editorial office has achieved recognition as an authority on ethnic issues, with ORF and its news department often seeking its assistance and advice. But above all, it has managed to make Austrians generally more aware of the problems of ethnic minorities.

Mainstream programmes

ORF has broadcast many programmes about ethnic minorities, foreigners, refugees and the struggle against racism since 1993.

ORF 2's weekly magazine *Inlandsreport*, which goes out from 8.15 pm to 9.05 pm on Thursdays, has broadcast several documentaries produced by the channel on topics such as the Austrian political landscape and the extreme-right Freiheiliche Partei Österreichs (FPOe), and the new laws regarding foreigners. In June 1993, for instance, 'Ausländer – Nein Danke' (Foreigners – No Thanks) dealt with the content and consequences of the new law on residence permits due to be introduced the following month, strongly criticizing the effects the law was likely to have. *Inlandsreport* also includes various five- or ten-minute reports on latest developments regarding foreigners and immigrants. The magazine is repeated by 3 SAT on Fridays from 12.15 pm to 1 pm.

Other mainstream programmes include the sitcom *Kaisermühlenblues* (Kaisermühlen is a neighbourhood of Vienna) which has proved popular with both the public and the critics. First shown on ORF 1 in 1993, the original six 50-minute episodes were repeated in 1994 and followed by six new episodes. The programme is broadcast at 8.15 pm on Sundays and repeated on 3 SAT at 8 pm on Wednesdays. *Kaisermühlenblues* takes a humorous look at relations between Austrians and foreigners or refugees and shows how racism and prejudice arise in everyday life. The main roles are taken by well-known actors. Six further episodes were planned for autumn 1994. The magazine for young people, *X-Large*, shown on Sundays from 5.10 pm to 6 pm, often deals with the problems of racism and fascism in Austria.

BELGIUM

Total population (on 1/1/92):
10,045,000

Foreign population (on 1/1/92):
922,500
9.18 per cent of the total population

Distribution by country of origin:

Italy	240,000
Morocco	145,600
France	94,900
Turkey	88,400
Netherlands	67,700
Spain	51,100
Germany	28,500
United Kingdom	24,200
Greece	20,600
Portugal	17,800
Zaire	12,800
United States of America	11,700
Algeria	11,000
Former Yugoslavia	6,500
Tunisia	6,400

Source: SOPEMI, *Trends in International Migration*, Paris, OECD, 1993.

Sindbad, la calligraphie. Photo: RTBF

BELGIUM

1

IMMIGRATION HISTORY

The history of immigration in Belgium can be divided into four main periods:

- 1946-1956: the Italian decade.
- 1956-1964: the start of diversification, with the arrival of immigrants from Spain, Greece, Morocco and Turkey.
- the late 1960s and early 1970s: from immigrant workers to ethnic minorities.
- 1980-1992: the integration of ethnic minorities began.

On 20 June 1946 an agreement was signed in Rome between Italy and Belgium covering the arrival of 50,000 Italian workers for Belgian coal mines. The accord marked the start of a wave of Italian immigration that lasted until August 1956, when many Italians were among the victims of a mining accident at Marcinelle. Belgium then turned to other nations liable to send cheap labour: first Spain, then Greece, then Morocco and Turkey. The economic boom of the 1960s led to the hiring of large numbers of workers from North Africa.

Like other west European countries, Belgium cut back on and eventually stopped immigration because of the recession in the early 1970s. In 1982 there were actually more foreigners leaving than entering the country. With immigration at a standstill, immigrant workers gradually came to be regarded as ethnic minorities. This process was hastened by the 1984 Nationality Act, which granted Belgian nationality to 54,000 children born to Belgian women married to foreigners.

In 1981 Belgium adopted a law aimed at 'curbing certain acts resulting from racism and xenophobia' (Law of 30 July 1981, known as the Moureaux Law).

During the 1980s the Belgians attempted to define a national immigration policy.

This resulted, among other things, in the creation in March 1989 of a Royal Commission for Immigration Policy, headed by Flemish Christian Socialist Paula d'Hondt. Meanwhile the government set up an interministerial committee for immigration policy, including the relevant ministers and community and regional leaders. The Royal Commission's four-year mandate gave it two main missions: to make public recommendations in reports issued every six months, and 'to coordinate, supervise and support the policies followed in this area by the various ministerial departments, communities, regions and local authorities' (Royal Decree of 7 March 1989). It was this second set of tasks that concerned the fight against racism.

The provisions of the Moureaux Law proved insufficient, as shown by the Brussels riots of 1990-1991 and the alarming results of the November 1991 elections in which the extreme-right Vlaams Blok party did well. The future of the Royal Commission, whose mandate ended in March 1993, is still uncertain.

The law of 15 February 1993 set up a Centre for Equal Opportunity and the Struggle against Racism. Article 2 states that the Centre's purpose is to promote equal opportunity and combat all forms of discrimination, exclusion, restriction or preference based on race, colour, family background, origin or nationality. Its most important tasks include:

- Making recommendations to government authorities and private bodies based on the results of the Centre's own surveys and research;

- Helping people in search of advice about their rights and obligations, within the limits of the Centre's mandate as defined by Article 2. Information and advice are given about how to make sure these rights are enforced;

- Testing in the courts the provisions of the law of 30 July 1981, which aims to suppress racism and xenophobia.

Belgium has three main language communities: 5.9 million Flemish-speakers, 4.2 million French-speakers and 65,000 German-speakers. All are recognized by the constitution and have their own institutions. Foreign minorities, who make up 9.18 per cent of the population (nearly a million people), are not mentioned in the constitution. The distribution by nationality varies according to the region. Wallonia, where the first immigrants arrived in the 1950s, has strong Italian and French minorities; Flanders, where immigration only took off in the 1970s, has mainly Turkish and Moroccan minorities.

2

THE BROADCASTING SCENE

Public channels

French-speaking Belgium

The two public channels of the French-speaking community, RTBF 1 and Télé 21, are run by the RTBF (Radio télévision belge de la communauté française de Belgique). Both have been receiving income from advertising since 1989.

❶ **RTBF 1**, started in 1953, broadcasts nine hours of programmes a day, from 12.30 pm on weekdays and all day at weekends – a total of 4,115 hours in 1991. A mainstream channel, it gives priority to fiction (40.5 per cent of airtime in 1991) and news (29.1 per cent). Entertainment is given 8.1 per cent. RTBF 1 faces strong competition from a private channel and from the three main French channels TF1, France 2 and France 3. In 1991 it obtained 20.7 per cent of the audience – putting it in second place behind the privately owned Radio-Télé Luxembourg-Télévision Indépendante (RTL-TVI) – and average viewing time was 265 minutes a day.

❷ **TELE 21** has been so called since 1988, when it took over from Télé 2, launched in 1977. It describes itself as 'the extra channel offered by the public broadcasting service' and its schedules are complementary to those of RTBF 1. Télé 21 offers more cultural programmes for a more targeted audience. Broadcasting begins at 2 pm on Mondays, Fridays and Sundays, 12.30 pm on Saturdays and 3.15 pm on Tuesdays, Wednesdays and Thursdays – a total of 3,024 hours in 1991. Fiction and news take up roughly the same number of hours (21.9 per cent and 20.8 per cent respectively), sport comes third with 14.3 per cent, followed by art and science (10.1 per cent) and music programmes (10 per cent). Télé 21 attracted 2.7 per cent of viewers in 1991. From 1993 to March 1994, Télé 21 became Arte 21 because of the RTBF's participation in the Franco-German channel Arte, and Arte's schedule was broadcast in the evenings from 7 pm.

Flemish-speaking Belgium

Like its French-language counterpart, BRTN (Belgische Radio Televisie) has two public channels, BRT 1 (or TV 1), started in 1953, and BRT 2 (or TV 2), started in 1977. An important difference between the two authorities is that BRTN's only income is from licence fees.

❶ **TV 1** broadcasts for longer than its sister channel. It offers about ten hours of mainstream programmes a day, starting at 2 pm, weekends included.

❷ **TV 2** only starts its programmes at about 7 pm and does not broadcast on Sundays.

BRT 1 and BRT 2 broadcast a total of 4,650 hours in 1991. Fiction programmes had most airtime (33.3 per cent), followed by newscasts (14.8 per cent), entertainment (11.5 per cent), sport (9.4 per cent), news magazines (8.7 per cent) and educational programmes (7 per cent).

With 26.5 per cent of the market in December 1991 and 26.6 per cent in September 1992, BRT came second in the audience ratings after the privately owned VTM. BRT 2's market share was 9.7 per cent in December 1991, ahead of the Dutch channels, but the following year it faced stronger competition from VTM and its market share had slipped to 7.9 per cent by September 1992.

Private channels

French-speaking Belgium

❶ **RTL-TVI**, a cable channel, began broadcasting from Luxembourg in 1985 as RTL-Télévision. In 1987 it was legalized under the new name. Financed entirely by advertising, it broadcasts 14 hours a day – more than 5,900 hours in 1991. The emphasis is on entertainment, with 65 per cent fiction and 9 per cent variety, game and quiz shows, but news is not neglected (9 per cent). RTL-TVI attracts the biggest audience in French-speaking Belgium, with 27.2 per cent of the market in 1991. This share goes up to 39 per cent between 7 pm and 8 pm, except on Saturdays.

❷ **CANAL PLUS TVCF**, an encoded cable channel, is the result of an agreement between RTBF, which owns only 14 per cent of the capital, and Canal Plus France. TVCF stands for Télévision de la Communauté Française de Belgique. Launched in 1989, it had 96,000 subscribers in October 1992. Like its French counterpart, it offers mainly films (60 per cent in 1992), sport (15 per cent) and documentaries (10 per cent), and broadcasts 24 hours a day.

Flemish-speaking Belgium

❸ **Vlaamse Televisie Maatschappij (VTM)** The Flemish government authorized this private channel in 1989, thereby giving it a monopoly of television advertising in the region. Most of VTM's shareholders are from the press, which must by law own at least 51 per cent of the company.

VTM broadcasts nine hours a day, a total of 3,255 hours in 1991, and aims to provide a schedule with a regional flavour (some 53 per cent of the programmes, not counting advertising, were locally produced in 1991) and to give a dominant place to news (14 per cent). Entertainment is still the major category, with foreign and Flemish soaps and series, films (26 in 1991) and a dozen different game and quiz shows.

On the air from 5 pm to 11 pm, VTM picked up 43.6 per cent of market share in December 1991, far ahead of the three Dutch channels (which attract about 10 per cent of the total audience) and the two public channels. By September 1992 VTM's market share had edged up to 45.5 per cent.

3

CHANNEL POLICIES

❶ **RTBF**. At the moment there is no legislation governing the production of programmes specifically for immigrant groups. The government has issued no guidelines and no obligations are mentioned in the RTBF statutes.

However, Belgium's French-speaking community did take a stand concerning the Arabic-language radio stations in Brussels after a series of violent clashes between the police and young people from some poorer parts of the capital in May 1991. The unrest was due to unemployment and low standards of living generally. Most of the troublemakers seemed to be young Moroccans, although people of 11 different nationalities were arrested, including Belgians.

The Consultative Council for population groups of foreign origin in the French-speaking Community (part of the Ministry of French Culture) said the media should allocate airtime to foreign communities 'if we believe that they are made up of individuals and groups with their own symbols and messages that should be more widely known. This could be done in three ways:

– *Hiring journalists and presenters of foreign origin*. The proposal of the Royal Commission for Immigration Policy to increase the number of journalists and presenters of foreign origin should be supported in order to focus on the communities these people come from and to provide different views of the role they are liable to occupy in society. More generally, it would be desirable to include people of foreign origin on programmes in which members of the public take part. At the moment people of foreign origin are relegated to debates on topics that specifically concern them.

– *People of foreign origin should also appear in the RTBF's usual programmes*. It should become the rule for foreigners to be included in broadcasts that mention important events and for cultural groups of foreign origin to produce their own programmes. The council also hopes that the existing programmes made for immigrants should be turned into multicultural magazines, focusing both on the diversity of Belgian culture and on the cultural contributions of immigrants' countries of origin, and with the aim of giving everyone access to culture as it arises and spreads due to the presence of foreign population groups in Belgium. These types of programme should also play an informative role, while observing the usual journalistic code of conduct in force in a public service.

-Community television. The Council would like longer time slots reserved for cultural minorities in the regions and more importance accorded to their views.'

❷ **BRTN**. Since 1988 the BRT has had a 'positive action policy'. Initially the aim was to have more women in programmes and on the channel's staff, and to upgrade their image. In 1992 the board of directors decided to extend the policy to all those of foreign origin, much as the BBC had done in Britain. In practical terms, this meant that people of foreign origin should be better represented on the staff; special attention should be paid to the content of programmes dealing with ethnic minorities so as to avoid negative impressions that might reinforce existing prejudices; specific programmes should be produced for the ethnic minorities in Flanders and Brussels; and the channel should take part in the initiatives launched by other European channels, the European Union and other organizations working on relations between the media and immigrants.

Magazine programmes for immigrants

❶ **RTBF**. Until January 1994, three programmes for immigrant groups were produced and broadcast regularly: *Sindbad* for North Africans, *Hasret* for Turks and *Spotkania* for Poles. *Hasret* and *Spotkania* were taken off the air in January 1994 for 'budgetary reasons'.

These three programmes were inspired by a television magazine called *Inter-Wallonie*, which was launched by the Liège production centre in 1965 on the same lines as the radio programme *La Wallonie accueille des étrangers* (Wallonia welcomes foreigners). Intended for Italians working in the coal mines of French-speaking Wallonia, the radio programme spawned a series of similar magazines for Belgium's other immigrant communities: Greek, Spanish, Polish, Yugoslav, Portuguese and finally Arab. The programmes dealt with social, political and economic themes, discussing issues such as immigrants' problems at work, whether foreigners should have the right to vote, integration of illegal immigrants, the setting up of advice groups and recognition of Islam.

The *Inter-Wallonie* model remained practically unchanged until 1985 but underwent a major transformation in 1987 following changes in broadcasting, new immigration patterns and budget restrictions. Once the Spanish channel TVE and the Italian RAI became available in Belgium on cable, magazines like *Ciao amici*, the first television programme for immigrants started in December 1971, and *Para vosotros*, started in 1972, became superfluous and were dropped. *Zdravo* (for the Yugoslav community) and *Noticias* (for the Portuguese) were also taken off the air. *Zdravo* and *Noticias* were made up mainly of features provided by the home countries and put together in the Liège studios. One programme that survived the cuts was *Ileikoum* (For You), a 15-minute magazine for North African community launched by Khiti-Amina Benhachem in 1973 on the model of an earlier radio programme. Broadcast one Saturday a month at 9.50 am, *Ileikoum* was composed of social and cultural reports and entertainment.

After the violent clashes at Forest in the Brussels suburbs in May 1991, the *Ileikoum* crew filmed a sequence with the main groups involved: young people, their parents, the police and city officials. When shown in May, it proved to be a landmark in the history of the magazine. The violence had caused a political and psychological shake-up in Belgium, and the North African community started calling for 'personal fulfilment in accordance with the structures of the host country and integration, respecting their own culture'.[1] The RTBF's response was to replace *Ileikoum* by *Sindbad*, the first broadcast going out at 9 pm on Monday, 9 September 1991.

➤*SINDBAD* is aimed chiefly at the North African community but is also of interest to other immigrant groups and to Belgians. It is broadcast in Arabic and/or French, with French subtitles for the Arabic sequences, and lasts 30 minutes. Produced by Khiti-Amina Benhachem and Mehrdad Taghian, and presented by Khiti-Amina Benhachem, *Sindbad* aims to provide a space for meetings and discussion between Belgians and young immigrants on the one hand, and the youngsters and their parents on the other.

The magazine may include two or three topics or have a single theme. It covers news, culture, music and information about services and deals with social, political and cultural subjects affecting the North African community. *Sindbad* is broadcast by Télé 21 on alternate Saturdays at 6.30 pm and repeated the next day. It is also shown on RTBF at 10 am on alternate Saturdays, and on TV5 Europe one Thursday per month at 10.30 am, with a repeat at 4 am on Friday.

The question of whether the form and content of the programmes were adapted to the target group was raised at the highest level of the broadcasting authorities following the unrest of May 1991. It was decided that from September the length of *Sindbad* would be cut from 40 to 30 minutes, but the programme would be produced twice instead of once a month. Whereas it had formerly been conceived as a cultural magazine for a specific group, it was agreed that the new format would

1 *Le Ligueur*, 34, 6 September 1991.

take account of changes in the immigrant communities. For instance, there were no longer many immigrants who spoke only their own languages; most of the new generation only knew their parents' language as a second language. As a result, *Sindbad* became more Belgian- oriented; French was used more often by the presenter and in interviews, and the same standards of objectivity were required as for any other news programme or magazine.

The first broadcast of the revamped *Sindbad* looked at Forest, a few months after the uprising, from the viewpoint of young Belgians and Moroccans, mayor Magda de Galan, police officers, Moroccan social workers and police auxiliaries hired afterwards. The second programme, broadcast on 23 September 1991, was entitled 'What will become of them?' and asked questions about the future of second-generation immigrants as they left school. In December 1991 *Sindbad* produced a special Christmas edition, talking to a Moroccan family about the festivals of Mouloud, which celebrates the birth of the Prophet Mohammed, and Adha, commemorating Abraham's sacrifice. Children were interviewed about the distribution of toys for the feast of Saint Nicholas and a Moroccan national troupe performed traditional dances. Other noteworthy editions included one on aspects of Arab culture shown on 13 January 1992, with sequences on calligraphy and classical musician Hamza Eddine; one on the month of Ramadan broadcast on 20 April 1992; and one devoted to the tense atmosphere in some parts of Brussels which the media claimed was caused by gangs of young North Africans.

In 1993/1994 the producers of *Sindbad* tried to maintain a balance between social and cultural subjects, while keeping the programme accessible to both Belgians and ethnic minorities.

In this period of financial problems for the RTBF, *Sindbad* is the only remaining programme dealing with immigration, integration, minorities and multicultural issues. The format alternates between full-length case studies and series of shorter items. Subjects tackled recently have included: Ramadan in Brussels (a chance for non-Moslems and Belgians to meet and get to know Moslems living in Belgium); the Gnawas brotherhood of Morocco, who practice music and trance-dancing and carry out healing ceremonies; teenage second-generation people making a video and giving their views on integration and the rift between their two cultures; Moslem mosaics, a programme introducing geometric art, which is one of the main aspects of Moslem culture; and 100 years of Belgian immigration.

➤*HASRET* (Nostalgia), a monthly 30-minute programme aimed at the Turkish community, was produced by the RTBF's Liège studios and broadcast at 10 am on Saturdays by RTBF 1. Subtitled in French and filmed entirely in Belgium, it focused on the previous month's major news stories.

➤*SPOTKANIA* (Encounters), aimed at the Polish community, was produced by the Liège studios in conjunction with Polish television in Warsaw, which contributed regular news features and entertainment spots. RTBF added studio discussions with guests and packaged the programme. *Spotkania* was shown at 10 am on Saturdays by RTBF 1.

Both *Hasret* and *Spotkania* were taken off the air in January 1994.

RTBF-Liège also shows the old magazines *Ciao amici*, *Para vosotros* and *Zdravo* (replaced by *Musiques d'Europe* from 1 January 1992), as well as *Inter-regards* (an Arab programme), *Nychtologa* (for Greeks) and *Entre dois cais* (for the Portuguese).

❷ **BRTN** used to produce a two-part magazine, *Babel*, for the Turkish and Moroccan communities. In dialect with Flemish subtitles, the 40-minute programme was split evenly between *Babel-Turquie* and *Babel-Maroc*. Broadcast weekly on TV 1 from September 1991, it was composed of features supplied by the Turkish and Moroccan broadcasting authorities. The production crew included some Flemish-speaking Turks and Moroccans.

➤*BABEL*, started early in 1985, was originally made for seven immigrant communities in Flanders (Moroccan, Turkish, Greek, Italian, Spanish, Yugoslav and Portuguese). Features on the different groups made up a single programme broadcast once a month by TV 1 at midday on Sundays, and repeated at 3 pm on Saturdays. The format was soon judged too costly and the following year it was made for Turks and Moroccans only. In 1988 *Babel* went weekly, then it was cut from 40 to 30 minutes and the repeats were dropped.

For Flemish television officials, *Babel* was more the work of one man, producer Bert Goovaert, than a real BRT production. The programme was therefore tolerated, but not really recognized. Questions were raised about *Babel*'s usefulness following the Brussels disturbances in May 1991 but nothing was actually done, although the events led to changes in the statutes governing BRT's radio programmes. The two main issues raised were how to bring the format up to date and whether such programmes should still be made at all, given the financial problems of Flemish public television and the need to make cuts.

Babel was finally taken off the air in 1992. Interest in broadcasts in Turkish had waned since Turkish radio and television programmes became available on cable in the cities of Antwerp, Ghent, Saint-Nicolas and Limburg in late 1990. Moreover, the second and third generations were using Flemish as their first language. It was largely for these reasons that the Italian, Spanish, Serbo-Croat, Portuguese and Greek sections of *Babel* had been dropped in 1986.

➤*COULEUR LOCALE*, a 30-minute magazine launched in January 1993, aims to provide a link between 'old and new' Belgians. It is usually made up of two or three reports and covers all aspects of Belgium's multicultural society. Part of the programme is reserved for features on writers and artists from migrant families and for world music. Subjects dealt with in 1994 have included living conditions in a Romany camp, the reactions of survivors of the Holocaust to the film *Schindler's List*, illegal immigrants in Belgium, racism in discotheques and asylum-seekers' employment problems.

Originally broadcast by TV 2 at 8 pm on Thursdays and repeated at midday on Saturdays, *Couleur locale* attracted an estimated 100,000 to 200,000 viewers – between 3 per cent and 5 per cent of the total audience in Flanders. The person in charge of the programme felt this was encouraging for a programme on the second channel. From September 1994 the magazine was switched to 8 pm on Fridays, with a repeat broadcast at 10 pm on Sundays, with the aim of boosting the audience. The production team of *Couleur locale* is made up of 13 people, including three journalists with an ethnic background, and the programme is presented by a Belgian-Senegalese woman.

❸ **RTL-TV1**. The Belgian subsidiary of RTL schedules a programme that has been made in Italian by the parent company in Luxembourg since 1980.

➤*BUONA DOMENICA*, which lasts an hour, is produced in cooperation with the RAI. Broadcast weekly with no subtitles, it is largely cultural in content.

Mainstream programmes

Some of RTBF's mainstream programmes take account of the multicultural society in Belgium, such as the monthly news magazine *Au nom de la loi* (In the Name of the Law). Produced since 1979 by the RTBF studio in Charleroi, the programme devoted three editions to the subject of immigration between October 1991 and May 1992. The first, broadcast in October 1991, looked at the way political refugees were dealt with and how long they had to wait before being recognized as asylum-seekers. The second, broadcast at 8.10 pm on Wednesday 15 January 1992, was about illegal immigration from Poland and the third, broadcast in May 1992, showed how a family of Hungarian origin was protected by villagers after being ordered to leave Belgium.

The cultural programmes *Carré noir* and *Cargo de nuit* have also shown features on issues and personalities from other communities. One example was *Mizike Mama*, a 52-minute musical documentary about the Belgian polyphonic group Zap Mama, a symbol of cultural fusion. Broadcast on 25 January 1992 by Télé 21, *Mizike Mama* was made by Violaine de Villiers and coproduced by *Cargo de nuit* and Morgane Films. Through interviews with singer Marie Daulne, the film reveals the relationship between African and European cultures, the emotional force unleashed when they are blended and the creative urge sparked by mixed origins, all illustrated by the singer's original rendering of music from Zaire. The documentary won prizes at the Strasbourg International Festival of Human Rights and the Créteil International Women's Film Festival in 1992 and was bought by the Danish channel TV 2.

RTBF also buys and broadcasts documentaries such as Anne Deligne's *Sango Nini, What's new?*, which was produced by the Brussels Broadcasting Centre and Cobra Films. *Sango Nini* takes the viewer to Matongué du Nord, a quiet Brussels neighbourhood home to most of the Zaireans who live in Belgium. Gradually, faces and figures are introduced that bring the neighbourhood to life. In 1991 the documentary won awards at a documentary festival in Marseilles and at the Filmer à Tout Prix festival in Brussels.

A theme evening entitled *Etranges Étrangers* was produced by Arte 21 and broadcast simultaneously by Arte and Télé 21 from 8.40 pm on Sunday 14 November 1993. Studio discussions were interwoven with documentaries and extracts from films. The programmes shown aimed to look at issues raised by immigration through a multicultural lens, showing the contribution made by immigrants to 'national culture'. On the agenda were:

➤*JE PARLE FRANÇAIS COMME TARZAN*, a documentary by Miel van Hoggenbernt tracing the life of a Turkish immigrant in Belgium for 18 years and married to a Spanish woman.

➤*RUE DE LA PERLE*, a cartoon made by North African children from Brussels at the Graphoui workshop.

➤*LA TÊTE À L'ENVERS*, made by Violaine de Villiers and produced by CBA, the RTBF and Paradise Films, shows two young North African women living in Europe since childhood who meet in Belgium. Although they come from very different backgrounds, they have in common their two, apparently irreconcilable, cultures. Yet their inventiveness and thirst for knowledge enable them to cope with the tension and contradictions between these cultures.

➤*NOUS SOMMES TOUS DES ÉTRANGERS*, by Alexandre Wajnberg and Annie Thonon. Using research into our genetic heritage, they demonstrate that the differences and similarities between all human beings are so great that the concept of race is meaningless.

The RTBF is currently making a documentary called *Les Nouveaux Belges* (The New Belgians) focusing in particular on the Turkish community in Brussels. It was due to be broadcast in autumn 1994.

At 2 pm on Sundays, Télé 21 takes a look at other cultures in *Reflets* (Reflections), which incorporates features made by French-language television companies in Africa, the Indian Ocean and South-East Asia. It is produced by the RTBF and the CIRTEF (International Council of French-language Radio and Television).

Cable and satellite programmes

Because of Belgium's geographical position, its small size and linguistic and cultural divisions, it was receiving television programmes from abroad well before foreign channels became available by cable and satellite. The wide variety of channels that can be picked up nowadays is one of the characteristics of Belgian television. Cable, introduced in 1961 and now reaching 97 per cent of households, is the most widespread method of broadcasting. About 40 different cable companies offer an average of 25 channels each, and some networks have as many as 35 channels.

French-language community television operates in most major cities, such as Brussels, Liège, Namur, Charleroi, Tournai and Verviers. There are no programmes made specifically for immigrants but related issues are often raised in news and current affairs reports.

4

INITIATIVES

❶ **REGARDS CROISES NORD-SUD.** The sixth Namur International French-Language Film Festival, held from 26 September to 5 October 1991, took a special interest in films from developing countries, especially Africa. Télé 21 contributed by giving an African emphasis to its programme *Regards croisés*, shown on Saturdays at 10 pm. Over four weeks the broadcast featured films such as *Yeelen* and *Tabataba*, plus three documentaries: *Colporteur de son état*, about the making of the film *Tilaï*, by Idrissa Ouedraogo; *Sango Nini* by Anne Deligne, about Zaireans in Brussels; and *Djembefola*, by Laurent Chevalier, about Guinean percussionist Mamady Keita, who lives in Brussels.

❷ **THE MEDIA PRIZE FOR A HARMONIOUS SOCIETY** was introduced in 1992 by the Royal Commission for Immigration Policy (now the Centre for Equal Opportunity) and the King Baudouin Foundation. The award is for journalists working in the press and broadcasting who give particularly impartial, balanced and sensitive coverage to the subjects of immigration and foreigners in Belgium, thus helping to foster the development of a harmonious society. The prize is given annually to the person directly responsible for the report or programme concerned, and alternates between the press and broadcasting on the one hand and the French-speaking and Flemish-speaking communities on the other (German-speaking journalists are eligible for either award). Juries put forward suggestions and the final decision lies with a management committee.

In 1992 the prize was awarded to two newspaper journalists, Martine Vande-meulebroucke of *Le Soir* and Guido Fonteyn of *Standard*. In 1993 the winners were Jacques Malpas and all those who worked with him on *36 heures pour la démocratie*, produced and broadcast by RTBF. The company decided in March 1992 to devote a large chunk of its schedule and resources to a discussion of the issues raised by democracy, intolerance and social exclusion. Several programmes and sequences focused on immigration. The prize will enable Jacques Malpas and his colleagues to launch a new series of programmes dealing specifically with the problems of immigration and exclusion. In addition, a special prize went to RTBF sports journalist Michel Lecomte for his original film on the Atlas football club of Brussels.

❸ EUROPEAN REGIONAL TELEVISION AND IMMIGRATION. Discussions on this theme were organized by the RTBF in Liège on 22 and 23 October 1992 to mark the tenth anniversary of CIRCOM (International Cooperative for Research and Action in Communication).

The participants, mostly television programme producers, were invited to take part in four workshops: immigration from the third world, immigration from Eastern Europe, racism in a multicultural society, and 'we are all immigrants'.

❹ FILMER A TOUT PRIX. The sixth film festival with this title, held in Brussels from 19 to 24 October 1993, included a section on the theme 'Ethnic communities and cross- cultural fertilization: an urban culture for the 1990s?'

❺ GUIDELINES FOR REPORTERS. In June 1994 the 'media and immigrants' group of the Belgian Professional Journalists' Association published a series of recommendations for news reports regarding people of foreign origin. They included:

- Do not mention a person's nationality, country of origin, ethnic group, colour, religion or culture unless such information is relevant to the story.

- Avoid generalization and over-simplification.

- Avoid exaggeration and creating problems where none exist.

- Take a critical view of racism and the political far right.

CZECH REPUBLIC
& SLOVAKIA

Total population (on 1/1/93):
Czech Republic: 10,500,000
Slovakia: 5,300,000

Foreign population:
No figures are currently available.

Romale. Photo: Gilles Stassart

CZECH REPUBLIC & SLOVAKIA

1

IMMIGRATION HISTORY

The outstanding feature of population movements in the former Czechoslovakia is large-scale emigration to western Europe. From the mid-1950s until 1989, more people left the country than entered it. The number of emigrants was particularly high between 1965 and 1970. Many people left after the Prague Spring of 1968, before the borders were completely closed; most went to Austria, West Germany, Switzerland, the United States and Canada. More than 20,000 people emigrated legally between 1968 and 1969, and another 70,000 left clandestinely. After the 1970s visas became harder to obtain and border checks were stepped up, making it more difficult to emigrate, either legally or illegally.

Between 1981 and 1989, official statistics show 3,000 people emigrating per year, but this does not include those who left on tourist visas or on the pretext of visiting their families abroad to get round the official emigration process. The number of illegal emigrants during this period is thought to have been more than twice the number who left legally. By way of comparison, only about 1,000 people a year immigrated to Czechoslovakia during the 1980s, not counting foreign workers. Most came from the former Eastern Bloc and from countries which had signed labour agreements with Czechoslovakia (Germany and Hungary, followed by Poland in June 1992).

Since the start of the 1990s, large numbers of workers have continued to leave the Czech Republic and Slovakia (as they have become since January 1993) – usually short-term emigration for seasonal work to west European countries, especially

Germany and Austria. There has also been a significant increase in immigration: from around 1,000 people a year in the 1980s to 3,282 in 1990 and 7,382 in 1991, with more than 70 per cent going to the Czech Republic. During the 1980s, most immigrants came from the former Soviet Union and from central and Eastern Europe. In 1990 and 1991 they were mainly from Poland, the former Soviet Union, Germany, the United States, Canada and Australia, including Czechs and Slovaks returning from areas affected by the Chernobyl nuclear disaster and those returning from exile in the traditional host countries. Nonetheless, immigration is still low compared to most of western Europe, even if refugees from Romania, Bulgaria and the former Soviet Union are included in the figures.

Within a few years the Czech Republic and Slovakia have become a focal point for illegal immigration to the rest of Europe. People from North Africa, the Middle East and especially Asia go through Prague on their way to neighbouring countries, usually Germany. On account of this trend, one of the main features of Czech and Slovak immigration policy is now tighter border controls. On 4 March 1992, the parliament of the Czech and Slovak Federative Republic (which oversaw the transitional period) passed a law laying down the conditions under which foreigners could enter, stay in and leave the country. It came into force on 1 October 1992.

In fact, since the Czechoslovak State came into existence in 1918, it has had a significant proportion of ethnic minorities. According to the 1991 census, the 600,000 Hungarians make up the largest group – 4 per cent of the total population. The vast majority – 96 per cent – are concentrated in Slovakia, where they represent 11 per cent of the population and are often in violent conflict with Slovaks. The second largest group are Romanies, about 70 per cent of whom live in Slovakia. Romany nationality has been officially recognized since 1991 but many Romanies prefer to declare a different nationality, making it hard to compile accurate statistics. Demographers estimate that there will be between 450,000 and 500,000 Romanies in the two republics by 2005, whereas Romany organizations put the figure at 800,000. Despite their official recognition as a minority, Romanies were often victims of discrimination under the former communist regime and they are still far from being accepted by Czech and Slovak society. Since the 1980s, and especially after the 'velvet divorce' of January 1993, large numbers of Romanies have emigrated from Slovakia to Bohemia and Moravia – the former 'Czech lands' that make up most of what is now the Czech Republic. In these countries already subject to strong social tensions, this significant trend worries both the authorities and Romanies who have lived in the region for many years.

Other minorities are, in decreasing order of size, Poles, Germans, Ukrainians and Ruthenians, who are relatively well integrated into society. In the March 1991 census, Moravians and Silesians were also registered as separate nationalities.

CZECH REPUBLIC

2

THE BROADCASTING SCENE

The disappearance of the Czech and Slovak Federative Republic in January 1993 led to radical changes in Czech and Slovak broadcasting. The federal channel F1, which had covered all of Czech and Slovak territory, was dissolved.

A law passed in October 1991 had already abolished the state monopoly on broadcasting and allowed licences to be granted to private television companies. Another law, dating from 7 November 1991, established the principle of the autonomy of radio and television and their independence from the political authorities.

Prior to the partition of Czechslovakia, viewers had the choice between three channels:

- F1, a mainstream federal channel covering the whole of the country which broadcast two-thirds of its programmes in Czech and the other third in Slovak.

- CTV, a Czech regional channel covering all of Bohemia and Moravia.

- OK 3, launched in May 1990, which covered 40 per cent of Czech territory.

Public channels

In 1994 Czech public television, CT, had two complementary channels run by a joint governing body:

❶ **CT 1**, which replaced CTV, is a mainstream, mass-audience channel, offering 55 per cent Czech programmes and 45 per cent foreign programmes. It covers 98 per cent of the country and broadcasts 126 hours a week.

❷ **CT 2**, which replaced OK 3, offers more cultural programmes and aims to appeal to minorities. It is not allowed to broadcast advertising. Like its sister channel, it covers 98 per cent of the country and broadcasts 112 hours a week.

The two channels combined provide 38 per cent entertainment, 24 per cent features and documentaries, 21 per cent news, 9 per cent sport and 8 per cent educational programmes.

The public channels' revenue comes mainly from the licence fee – a pittance because the fee is set very low and many people are exempt from payment. The government also provides subsidies and CT 1 is allowed to broadcast some advertising (3 per cent of airtime, compared to 10 per cent for private channels).

Private channels

Czechs are among the world's most enthusiastic television fans, watching an average of three hours a day. The recent arrival on the scene of two privately owned channels has given them a wider choice of programmes.

❶ **NOVA**, the first national private channel, was launched in February 1994. Financed entirely by advertising, it is 70 per cent owned by CEDC, an American-Canadian company, and 30 per cent by the Czech savings bank. Nova sets out to compete directly with the state channels, putting out its news broadcasts at the same times, for instance. Most of its schedule is made up of foreign programmes – it has signed agreements with Disney, Columbia, MTV, CNN and the National Geographic Society – but its licence stipulates that it must broadcast a quarter of Czech programmes.

❷ **PREMIERA**, a privately owned regional channel, went on the air in June 1993. Broadcasting 110 hours a week to Prague and central Bohemia, it was initially financed exclusively by Italian capital. In December 1993 Czech interests took over 55 per cent of the company (the Investment Bank bought 35 per cent, while the Marcucci family reduced its stake to 45 per cent). About 95 per cent of Primiera's programmes are purchased. In March 1994 the company asked for authorization to be relayed by cable and satellite in order to cover the whole of Czech territory.

Cable television is booming in Czech Republic cities, with some 400,000 subscribers registered in 1994. The leading cable companies are Kabel Plus and Codis.

Czechs can also pick up some land-based broadcasts from neighbouring countries. Austria's ORF is the most popular in Bohemia and Moravia, ahead of the Polish and German channels.

3
CHANNEL POLICIES

Magazine programmes for immigrants

❷ **CT**. No legislation specifies that television companies should show special programmes for immigrants but CT, as a public service, undertakes to respect minorities and allow them to express their opinions on the air.

The need to broadcast programmes for Romanies has been discussed at meetings between government representatives and the Romany Civil Initiative, the organization which became the leading mouthpiece of this group after November 1989.

➤*ROMALE – THE ROMANIES' MAGAZINE* is a fortnightly programme lasting 20 minutes and broadcast at 11.30 pm on alternate Wednesdays. In 1994 it was broadcast on the first channel one week and repeated on the second channel the next. It aims to show what the lives of Romanies in the Czech Republic are like and is produced in turn by television studios in the cities of Prague, Brno and Ostrava, each dealing with both general and specifically regional problems. The features and interviews cover topics such as children's education, housing, unemployment, security and Romany culture. *Romale* is the only regular magazine on Czech television targeted at a minority, and though it can still sometimes be didactic and clumsy in its approach, it represents an interesting attempt to reduce social tension. In Ostrava and northern Moravia about 15 per cent of the population are Romany and in 1992 it was in this region that the most crimes were committed against this population group.

Romale was started by the federal channel F1 in October 1991, when the studios in Bratislava and Kosice, now part of Slovakia, also contributed programmes and the magazine included three languages, Czech, Slovak and Romany.

Mainstream programmes

The Czech channels are becoming aware of the important role mainstream programmes can play in tackling the subject of minorities, combating racism and communicating with refugees.

➤*OKO*, a 20-minute fortnightly news magazine, goes out on alternate Mondays. Produced by the independent company Febio and broadcast since 1992, *OKO* was originally scheduled at 10.30 pm but its popularity (30 per cent of the total audience) allowed it to be brought forward to 9.10 pm in January 1994. It is shown first on CT 1 and repeated on CT 2 at midday on Wednesdays. There is a possibility that the magazine may go weekly from January 1995.

OKO always deals with a single, topical theme. The programmes are made by leading Czech film directors such as Vera Chytilova, Ivan Passer and Ian Nemec, or by promising newcomers. On 17 January 1994, for instance, *OKO* tackled the subject of racism, with Petr Vaclav looking at discrimination against Vietnamese, Africans and Romanies living in the Czech Republic. Other recent broadcasts have featured the integration of Romanies, the problems faced by young people, the Jewish community, and minorities in general.

Fero Fenic, head of Febio, is currently working with a Romany professor on a magazine about minorities and refugees. The 20- minute programmes have been provisionally scheduled by the second channel from January 1995.

A series of documentaries produced by the Film and Sociology Foundation and broadcast on the CTV second channel from September 1991 until 1993 frequently raised the issues of minorities and refugees. For instance, *Cuoc Song o Dormitory*, a 36-minute programme made by Petr Vaclav, was an account of the federative republic's 'isolated and angry Vietnamese minority'. The series went out on Thursdays at 9.30 pm. Other productions included:

➤*CEKARNA ANEB TAKOVÉ PROBLÉMY JSME NEMELI* (The Waiting Room, or We didn't have problems like that) is a 32- minute film about political refugee camps made by Vladislav Kvasnicka and broadcast in October 1991.

In autumn 1990 Kvasnicka, a producer with the company Kratky Film, helped a deserter from the Soviet army to obtain the right to stay in the federative republic. Later Kvasnicka took an interest in the problems of refugees and became one of the promoters of the law on refugees negotiated by the federal assembly in December 1990. It was his interest in the subject that led the interior ministry to suggest he made The Waiting Room.

➤*STRACH NECHALI DOMA* (They left their Fear at Home), a 32-minute documentary, is also the work of Vladislav Kvasnicka. Broadcast on 26 January 1992, it highlights the problems faced by Czechs in Volhynia, a region of Ukraine contaminated by the Chernobyl nuclear disaster, before they returned to the federative republic.

➤*Z DEMOVA DOMU* (From the House in our Home Country), also on the subject of Czechs returning from Ukraine, was made by Olga Sommerova. This 42-minute documentary shows them settling into their new homes and the reactions of neighbours to their arrival. It was broadcast on 8 March 1992.

➤*HO-CI-MINOVI VNUCI* (The Children of Ho Chi Minh) is a 30-minute documentary about Vietnamese people living and working in the town of Zlin. Made by R.

Lauterkrane and the Brno television studios, it was broadcast on 21 January 1991.

In 1991 and 1992 the federal channel F1 devoted some magazine programmes to the issue of racial discrimination against minorities.

➤*S.U.S. – Soky, ulety, srandy* (Shocks, Getaways and Giggles) was a magazine for teenagers broadcast fortnightly by F1 – at 9 am on Saturdays with a repeat at 2 pm on Tuesdays. Produced by the Prague studios, the 45-minute programme deals with issues such as social exclusion, racism against Romanies and immigrants, drugs, prostitution and unemployment.

SLOVAKIA

2

THE BROADCASTING SCENE

The broadcasting law of October 1991 abolished the state monopoly in the federative republic, and in July 1993 the Slovak parliament adopted a new broadcasting bill paving the way for a dual public/private television system.

Before partition, viewers in Slovakia could choose between three channels:

- F1, the federal channel.
- STV, a Slovak regional channel.
- TA 3, established in the spring of 1990, which covered 32 per cent of Slovak territory. It was based on the same model as OK 3, offering mainly foreign programmes purchased from companies such as Arte, CFI, CNN, 3 Sat, TV5 and MTV.

Public channels

The reorganization in broadcasting that followed partition gave Slovakia two public channels run by Slovenska Televizia (ST):

❶ **STV 1** is a mainstream channel designed for a mass audience. It broadcasts 94 hours a week and covers 95 per cent of the country.

❷ **STV 2** broadcasts 50 hours a week and offers more cultural and educational programmes, complementing STV 1's schedules. Covering 88.8 per cent of the country, it is targeted more at special-interest groups and minorities. In 1995, STV

2 will have to share its frequency with the private sector, with STV 2 on the air from 5 am to 5 pm and the future private company from 5 pm to 5 am. In July 1994, no licence had yet been granted to a private television company wanting to run a national channel.

The Czech and Slovak public channels exchange some programmes, particularly daily newscasts, news magazines and entertainment.

STV 1 and STV 2 combined broadcast 40 per cent newscasts and current affairs programmes. Slovak programmes account for 66 per cent of airtime.

Private channels

❶ **TELEVIZIA SEVER**, Slovakia's first privately owned regional channel, broadcasts two to three hours a day from Zilina, in the northwest of the country. It was launched on 3 January 1994.

Growing numbers of Slovaks are able to receive programmes by satellite; in 1993, 28.2 per cent of households were equipped with dish aerials. Cable is also expanding rapidly, although it is less widespread than in the Czech Republic. Bratislava is expected to be totally cabled sometime in 1995.

3
CHANNEL POLICIES

Magazine programmes for immigrants

❶ **STV** Like Czech public television, STV undertakes to respect minorities and allow them to air their views. As far back as 1983, Slovak television started producing a 15-minute weekly magazine for the Hungarian minority. The programme has had various titles, including *Udolasti v Madarskom Jazyku*. In 1994 it was being broadcast by STV 2 and was called *Hirmagazin*.

▶*HIRMAGAZIN*, produced by the Bratislava studios, is also known in Slovak as *Madarsky Magazin*. It now lasts 30 minutes and is made up of three-to-five-minute features in Hungarian with Slovak subtitles. Broadcast three Saturdays a month at 4.20 pm, it deals mainly with social, cultural and economic issues affecting the Hungarian minority in Slovakia. Slovak television researcher Ivan Kralik said of the programme: 'On the whole, its tone is critical but not controversial, because Slovaks and Hungarians living in the same towns or villages try to solve nationality and language problems in a practical way within the community.'

➤*NARODNOSTNY MAGAZIN* is a 30-minute programme aimed at the German, Ukrainian and Russine minorities in Slovakia. It is broadcast by STV 2 at 4.20 pm on the Saturdays when *Hirmagazin* is not shown, and deals mostly with the lives of these minorities in Slovakia. Six programmes are in Russine and six in Ukrainian (both sets produced by the Kosice regional studio) and four in German (produced by the Banaka Bystrica regional studio).

➤*ROMALE*, the Romanies' magazine, is broadcast by STV 2 one Saturday a month at 1.30 pm. The half-hour programme is produced in turn by the regional studios in Bratislava, Kosice and Banska Bystrica, alternating documentaries and groups of shorter features. *Romale* sets out to reflect the cultural life and social problems of Romanies and is broadcast in Slovak with interviews in the Romany language. (See the description of *Romale* in the Czech section.)

Mainstream programmes

From time to time Slovak television tackles the subject of minorities, race relations and tolerance in its documentaries, news magazines and educational programmes, and, more recently, in fiction. Four 30-minute documentaries about Jews in Slovakia were produced in 1994, with the aim of highlighting past and present Jewish cultural contributions to the life of the country. The Hungarian department of the Bratislava studio, which produces *Hirmagazin*, prepares between four and six short features a month for the evening news broadcast, and the number is expected to increase in 1995.

Slovak television also shows programmes with the languages, symbols and values of minorities for a wider audience. One example is the yearly broadcasts of the Hungarian Folk Festival in Gombasek and the Russine and Ukrainian Folk Festival in Svidnik.

Documentaries made before partition included:

➤*DETI VETRA* (Children of the Wind), a series of 13×30-minute documentaries on the history and present lives of Romanies in Europe. It was produced by H. Slivka with the Bratislava studio and the German company Schwarzwald Film. Shown on the federal channel F1 from 17 October 1991 to 29 January 1992 and by the German regional channel SWF, *Deti Vetra* received the annual Czechoslovak Television Award. The series was later repeated by TA 3.

DENMARK

Total population (on 1/1/92):
5,171,000

Foreign population:
169,500
3.3 per cent of the total population

Distribution by country of origin:

Turkey	32,000
Former Yugoslavia	10,700
United Kingdom	10,500
Norway	10,300
Iran	8,800
Germany	8,600
Sweden	8,300
Pakistan	6,100
Sri Lanka	5,300
Poland	4,900
United States of America	4,400
Vietnam	3,800
Lebanon	3,700
Iraq	3,200
Morocco	3,200

Source: SOPEMI, *Trends in International Migration*, Paris, OECD, 1993.

Kolonihaven. Photo: Statens Filmcentral

DENMARK

1

IMMIGRATION HISTORY

Taking in immigrants is part of Danish history, as Bille August's film *Pelle the Conqueror* shows. (The film won the Golden Palm award at the Cannes Film Festival in 1988.) Swedish immigrants arrived in Denmark in the 19th century, when Denmark was more prosperous than Sweden. Most of the economic refugees, including many Turks and Yugoslavs, came in the late 1960s, during the industrial boom era. Like the rest of Europe, Denmark closed its borders in 1970, except for people joining members of their families.

Non-naturalized foreigners (in official Danish statistics, an immigrant is defined as 'a foreign national living in Denmark') made up 3.3 per cent of the population on 1 January 1992. Of the 169,500 people of 156 different nationalities, a third are from Scandinavia, and a third from the European Union and North America. Less than a quarter are refugees. The others (more than 70,000 people) are third-world immigrants.

The government's clearly stated immigration policy, based on the concept of respect and mutual understanding, is to integrate immigrants into Danish society. In 1983 former interior minister Britta Schall Holberg described the principles of this policy as follows: 'An integration policy presupposes tolerance of, and respect for, differences and the right of everyone – whether Turkish, Pakistani, Jewish or an inhabitant of Copenhagen – to be on Danish soil. It implies respect for the culture and distinctive nature of immigrants on the grounds that their culture may exert a positive influence in Danish society.'

People from ethnic minorities are therefore regarded as citizens with the same rights and obligations as Danes. Nonetheless, the 1983 law on foreigners, amended in 1986 and again in June 1992, places certain limitations on family reunification and on the issuing of residence permits to the foreign wives of both immigrants and Danes.

With the economy in recession, foreigners have once more become scapegoats. The spirit of tolerance and support for the oppressed (which had been an example to other nations since October 1943, when the Danes helped more than 7,000 Danish Jews fleeing Nazi Germany to escape to Sweden) seems to be evaporating as the years go by.

There has been an increase in racist attacks, especially against refugees from the former Yugoslavia who represent the majority of the asylum seekers to arrive in Denmark since 1992. The issue of immigrants and refugees is one of the Danish people's major concerns: a recent opinion poll revealed general anxiety about rising unemployment and disapproval of what are regarded as excessive welfare benefits for foreigners. Unemployment in Denmark is running at over 12 per cent, and immigrants are four times more likely to be affected than Danes.

Tension also exists between Danes and the 6,000 Inuit from the province of Greenland – a closed Danish colony for more than 200 years – as well as people from the Faroe Islands.

2
THE BROADCASTING SCENE

Public channels

❶ **TV 1/DR** Governed by the state broadcasting authority, Danmarks Radio, TV1, also known as DR, is the oldest national channel, with the first test broadcasts carried out in 1951. It is financed entirely from the licence fee. Programmes start in the early afternoon, and the total weekly volume is 59 hours. TV 1, a mainstream channel, is trying to cope with two demands: offering a large proportion of cultural and news programmes, as its charter requires, and facing up to competition from TV 2. Of the 3,254 hours of programmes broadcast in 1991, fiction represented 31 per cent, documentaries 22 per cent, sport 15 per cent and entertainment 13 per cent, with news and other programmes making up the rest of the schedule. TV 1 attracts just over a third of the total audience (37 per cent during the first quarter of 1992, with a particularly low average viewing time of 166 minutes a day).

❷ **TV 2** Denmark's second channel, launched in 1988, gets most of its income from advertising, and licence fee revenue makes up only 30 per cent of its budget.

Both its statutes and working methods give it a sort of autonomy – not exactly public but not really private either. TV 2 offers a national schedule of eight hours a day, plus an hour of local programmes broadcast by eight regional stations. Out of more than 2,000 hours a year, TV 2 broadcasts mainly fiction (55 per cent in 1991) and magazines (28 per cent). Its audience – 41 per cent of the market in 1991 – is larger than that of TV 1.

Private channels

Denmark does not have any land-based private channels. The Danish and foreign cable channels compete fiercely with the two state channels. As a result of an ambitious national policy, more than half of households have been cabled, making 24 national or foreign channels available. These include Kanal 2, an encoded pay-channel broadcasting to Copenhagen and the surrounding area, which started in 1984. It puts out 22 hours of programmes a day, made up mostly of fiction (50 per cent, including 10 per cent cartoons) and sport (15 per cent).

3

CHANNEL POLICIES

❶ **TV 1/DR**. In 1977 the director of Danmarks Radio ruled that programmes – and not just those radio programmes intended for immigrants – should aim to encourage 'the adaptation of immigrant groups to Danish society by taking account, as far as possible, of the cultures of the various minorities'. Danish broadcasting is legally obliged to serve the entire population and as immigrants, in all their diversity, form part of that population, mainstream progammes are also supposed to be intended for them.

One of the recommendations made to the Danish broadcasting authorities by the Council of Europe at the symposium on *Immigrants, the Media and Cultural Diversity*, organized with the Dutch Ministry of Well-Being, Health and Cultural Affairs in Noordwijkerhout from 29 November to 1 December 1988, was:

> Danish broadcasting should, through its programme production, enable Danish society to embrace many cultures with mutual respect for basic democratic standards, by encouraging the integration of immigrants and by helping them to take part in the life of Danish society on an equal footing, while at the same time preserving their language, culture and religion as far as they wish; Danish broadcasting should also contribute to giving the rest of the population a balanced and truthful picture of immigrants and their culture.

However, unlike Danish radio, which puts out cultural and news programmes in Arabic, Urdu, Turkish, Serbo- Croat and Inuktitut five days a week, TV 1/DR still offers no specific programmes for immigrants. The heads of Danish television said at the October 1992 conference in Noordwijkerhout that they did not wish to produce a specific magazine programme and were reticent about multicultural broadcasting (which goes against the directives given by the DR in the late 1970s). The channel does occasionally produce documentaries about immigration and racism. These are usually made by the news magazine department, which works closely with the television news section.

Mainstream programmes

In autumn 1991, the refugee question was a major concern in Denmark and it was against this background that TV 1 produced and broadcast two programmes about immigration that caused quite a stir: *Flugten til Europa* (Besieged Europe) and a special issue of the magazine *45 minutter* (45 Minutes).

➤*FLUGTEN TIL EUROPA*, an hour-long programme, was broadcast at 9.15 pm on 4 November 1991 and repeated on 14 November. Directors Hans Bülow and Paul-Erik Heilbuth spent several months travelling in Europe and North Africa, following in the footsteps of people wishing to enter *rich* Europe illegally. Filming took place in Algeria, Greece, Italy, France, Germany, Spain and Poland. It shows the various routes used by illegal immigrants to reach Europe: squashed into the hold of a boat, facing army helicopters and patrols at the Austro-Hungarian border, crossing the Alps into France. Some sequences were filmed using a hidden camera, especially those about the conditions in which immigrants live and work (building sites in Poland, tomato-picking in Italy, clothing workshops in France). In the words of the directors: 'The programme thus became a description of the future of Europe: cornered by the wish to close its borders, to put an end to cheap labour and to get rid of immigrants.'

At the 32nd television festival in Monte Carlo in February 1992, *Flugten til Europa* was awarded the prize for best news magazine.

➤*45 MINUTTER* is broadcast weekly on TV 1. On 5 November 1991, the day after *Flugten til Europa* was first shown, it dealt with the issue of economic refugees in Denmark. The programme makers felt that: 'As will happen in other countries when the European Community opens its borders, the Danes will be faced with the following choice: increase aid to developing countries or turn Denmark into a closed state, with its frontiers controlled by the army'. In the studio, Danes with widely differing opinions gave their points of view on the subject. The programme was repeated on 11 November.

➤*ET LIGEGYLDIGT MORD* (An Accidental Murder) After the resurgence of xenophobia among young people in Denmark, TV 1 broadcast this weekly serial as part of the young people's magazine *Transit* from 25 May to 29 June 1992. It was directed by Johnny Andersen and Mediehuses Svendborg and financed by the trade union Lands Organization, the Danish Ministry of Social Affairs and the channel.

The story showed how complex the truth can sometimes be: four young Danes kill Reza, a young Iranian refugee, at a discotheque in a small village. The murderers say they had no motive to commit the crime. The directors commented: 'The idea of the serial was not so much to describe the trial, the problems of refugees or why they had fled their country, but to focus on young people unleashing their anger, frustration and feelings of emptiness on foreigners'.

➤*KOLONIHAVEN* was a 53-minute documentary about the Inuit in Denmark, coproduced by the Statens Filmcentral (Danish National Film Institute), Film and Lyd, and Danmarks Radio/TV in 1990.

Greenland, the world's biggest island, was a Danish colony for more than 200 years. Some 6,000 of its inhabitants now live in Denmark. Director Lise Roos wanted to meet some of these Inuit and listen to their stories in order to highlight the prejudices many people hold against this minority.

The documentary received first prize at the Anthropological Film Festival held in Pärnu, Estonia, in October 1991. It was broadcast in December 1990 and repeated on 26 June 1991.

➤*DEN SAGTMODIGE MORDER* (The Silent Killer), a 68-minute documentary made by Paul Martinsen, was first broadcast on 16 June 1988 and subsequently won the 1988 Prix Europa and the 1989 Prix Italia. It traces the story of a 31-year-old Turkish woman who is stabbed to death in the street in Denmark by an 18-year-old cousin. The investigation of the motives for the murder – incomprehensible to westerners – took the television crew to the woman's home village in Turkey to seek an explanation in the Turkish vendetta system. The documentary asks whether western justice can be applied to Turkish immigrants in Copenhagen. The documentary was bought and broadcast by several European channels, including the Franco-German channel Arte.

All the above programmes were repeated during a special four-week schedule about racism, xenophobia and the integration of foreigners, organized in September and October 1993. The schedule went out both on TV 1 and on the three DR radio stations. (Further details are given in the 'Initiatives' section at the end of this chapter.)

➤*SUGARLAND*, a family saga of three 90- minute episodes, was in preparation in July 1994. Written and directed by Annette Olsen and coproduced with Polish television, it covers the period from the late 19th century to the end of the First World War when Danish farmers were bringing in Polish workers to grow sugar beet, which they called 'white gold'.

Programmes for children and young people

➤*CLOSE UP – A TRAGEDY WITH A HAPPY ENDING*, which won the Youth Prize at the Munich film festival in June 1994, was one of the 15-minute documentaries about racism produced by 14 state television channels in Europe in 1993. Intended for children aged 10 to 12, they were the idea of the European Broadcasting Union.

Cecille Olrik, who made the Danish film, set out to demonstrate the absurdity of racism through the story of a threatened friendship between two boys – one Danish, the other Turkish. In January 1994 she told *Spectrum*, 'the Magazine of Public Broadcasting for a Multicultural Europe (PBME)': 'We need to recognize that there is a difference between the reticence of communities that feel unwelcome and rejection by the "host community"'.

❷ **TV 2**, the semi-public channel, has no specific magazine programme for immigrants. Lally Hoffmann, head of news and documentaries until late 1993, explained: 'I did not start a magazine about and for immigrants for two reasons: there are not many foreigners in Denmark and, more importantly, I am not convinced that Danes would want to watch such a programme. The Danes are the guardians of the well-being of foreigners in our society.' She added: 'We do deal with the problems of immigrants, but not in ghetto-magazines. We talk about immigrants whenever we can in the hope that viewers will integrate them into their daily lives. The world is shrinking and we are all the richer for having a multicultural outlook.'

Nonetheless, *Fakta*, the news and documentaries programme responsible for some 400 hours of programmes a year, has recently broadcast some documentaries and magazines on the theme of immigration. In-house productions include:

➤*MAN SKAL VAERE RUND FOR AT BO I EN GLOBUS* (You have to be Round to fit in a Globe) is a documentary series of three 30-minute programmes made by Annette Olsen: *Kunsten at overleve* (The Art of Survival), *Kampen om vindmøller* (Tilting at Windmills), and *Ukendt jord* (Unknown Land). They went out at 9 pm on 4, 9 and 16 December 1991 and attracted from 12 to 18 per cent of the total audience. The series focuses on how foreigners adapt to life in Denmark and how Danes react to them: Polish Jews in the 1970s, a little boy who fled the Iran-Iraq war on his own, and Turkish Moslems who wanted to be buried in their own country. The programmes won a special Prix Europa in 1992.

The series was continued in 1993, this time looking at the lives of three European women. *Iboja, born in Slovakia*, has lived in Denmark since 1946, after surviving

Auschwitz. *Julia, born in Ukraine*, arrived in Denmark in 1913 with the many Polish women seeking seasonal work in the sugar beet fields. Now aged 93, she still lives on the island where she worked all her life. *Paulina, born in Sarajevo*, came to Denmark as a tourist in the late 1960s and later decided to move there. She had never really been interested in politics before the Balkans conflict, but now helps to look after her compatriots living on the Flotel Europa, a ship providing accommodation for refugees and moored in central Copenhagen.

➤*FAKTEREN*, a monthly news magazine, goes out on TV 2 from 9 to 9.50 pm and attracts from 20 to 30 per cent of viewers. In the autumn of 1991 it showed *Maelk og honning* (Milk and Honey), about a Turkish village.

➤*MIT TYRKISKE LIV* (My Turkish Life), a serial broadcast in March 1991, tells the story of a Turkish boy living in Denmark and how he returns to a traditional village in Turkey.

➤*CLOSE UP*, a 25-minute documentary broadcast on 14 September 1993, is about three young people who arrived in Denmark with their parents in the late 1960s – one from Pakistan, one from Turkey, one from Yugoslavia – and how they fit into Danish society. A hidden camera that followed them as they sampled Copenhagen nightlife showed that they were victims of discrimination, especially in discotheques. *Close Up*, made by Ulla Pors Nielsen, aroused much comment in Denmark and police were forced to investigate discrimination charges because of the sequences filmed with a hidden camera.

Programmes bought from outside production companies include:

➤*MADSEN'S HOTEL*, a 40-minute documentary directed and produced by Annette Olsen and Sphinx Television, was broadcast on 14 April 1990. Madsen is a hotel owner who opens his establishment to Tamil and Sri Lankan refugees. The programme won a special Prix Europa in 1991.

➤*RAPPORT*, a monthly magazine of political and social news lasting 50 to 60 minutes, goes out at 10 pm and attracts about 20 per cent of viewers. It showed several foreign programmes in 1991 and 1992: *Enfance Interdite* (Forbidden Childhood), three programmes by Gilles de Maistre and Hervé Chabalier; *Banlieue*, about the French suburbs, produced by the Capa French news agency; *Kateb Yacine*, a French-Belgian-Algerian production about the life of the poet and his cultural cleavage; *First Tuesday, 24 hours in Tuzla*, a Serbo-Croat love story; *Ansigt til ansigt* (the French series *Vis-à-vis*) from the agency Point du jour; France 2's programme on National Front leader Jean-Marie Le Pen made for the magazine *Envoyé Spécial*.

TV 2's choice of a young black American woman to present *Rapport* excited much comment from immigrant community leaders. Filomenita Mongaya-Hogsholm, a journalist and film maker of Indonesian origin, said: 'While the steps taken by TV2 are welcome, it should not be forgotten that the real blacks in Europe are Turkish, Pakistani, Tamil or of Arab origin. Denmark still has a long way to go if it is to reflect the whole of society and not simply the majority'.

Cable, satellite and local channels

Half the Danish population is equipped for cable and can receive 24 national and foreign channels. This means that some immigrants in Denmark can watch the weekly magazine *Mosaik* produced by the first Swedish channel.

There are five local channels in Copenhagen which deal with issues affecting immigrants. Byens Lys (City Lights), which can be received by 1.5 million people, has been broadcasting on cable for an hour and a half a day (an hour of which is produced in-house) since 1990, from 6.30 pm to 8 pm. It is basically a videotext information service about organizations for immigrants and refugees and about the third world, in Turkish, Farsi, Spanish and Danish. Many volunteers and a few paid staff, of 13 different nationalities, work for the channel. Quality is expected to improve with the support of the association Kulturmode Film and Video, which also makes professional multicultural programmes.

Various other local channels have been set up elsewhere in Denmark, such as Indsame and TV Stop. Their quality also leaves something to be desired.

4

INITIATIVES

Denmark has various workshops where anyone can suggest a subject and may be offered film and video equipment and the means to edit a programme. These workshops are managed by the Danish Film Institute, DR television or local authorities. However, the distribution system is such that the programmes made there are usually only shown on local channels or in schools.

For many years the Ministry of Social Affairs and the Committee of Aid to Refugees subsidized programmes about the culture of immigrants and refugees. Unfortunately this assistance has now been suspended. However, the Danish National Film Institute (for documentaries) and the Danish Film Institute (for fiction) may still subsidize programmes by up to 50 per cent of the total budget. They have thus co-produced and distributed many films about immigrants and refugees, and have hired several immigrant directors.

The educational and cable networks also help to distribute films made, for instance, by Ester Heller's Heller Films, and by Kulturmode Film and Video run by Ali Alwon and Karen Hjort. These parallel distribution networks are important to professionals of foreign origin, who do not often have access to the mainstream programmes of the national channels.

In 1993, 'European year of old people and solidarity between generations', Ester Heller, a film maker of Indian origin who lives and works in Denmark, had the chance to show her documentary *Old in a Foreign Country* at international conferences in Denmark, the Netherlands, England and Scotland.

❶ **FESTIVAL DET ABNE VINDUE** (The Open Window Festival) showed 240 international films and videos about refugees and immigrants between 1988 and 1991, some made by refugees and immigrants themselves. Started by the Goethe Institute of Copenhagen and the National Film Institute, the festival was taken up by other Danish cities: Arhus, Odense and Alborg. The aim was to choose quality productions and make them known to a wide audience.

For four years the festival's schedule included films for children and young people, documentaries, experimental films, video productions and full-length films: an extremely varied selection, both in the different types of production and the way they presented foreigners in society.

Although the festival was a success for the first two years, in 1990 and 1991 it proved much less popular with the public at large. Only the teachers, social workers and film makers concerned turned up – all people who were already only too aware of the problems raised. More requests were made for special showings to schools and other groups.

The organizers decided to stop the festival but use the experience they had acquired to emphasize selecting quality films for targeted audiences. In 1993 they also showed more ethnographic productions in the new cinema at the Danish National Museum and put on an exhibition, with the aim of attracting a different type of filmgoer. The same schedule was later presented in Bonn, Germany. Sadly, there were no plans to stage any similar events in 1994.

Organizer Andreas Steinmann said the four years of the festival had shown that good films on the subject were being made. Many of those shown were later bought for broadcasting on television. Demand for films on refugees and immigrants had actually increased and they were being more widely distributed. 'Films alone cannot change public opinion', Andreas Steinmann said, 'but they can often provide new and unusual points of view. They make people think and encourage discussion. Small steps towards dialogue are steps in the right direction.'

❷ **DR – THEME: STRANGERS?** On the initiative of DR director-general Finn Slumstrup, TV 1 and the three DR radio stations broadcast a special four-week schedule about racism, xenophobia and the integration of foreigners from 13 September to 10 October 1993. The aim was 'to inform the public and stimulate national debate about refugees and immigration' as thousands of refugees from the former Yugoslavia were seeking asylum in Denmark. Various relevant programmes, like the BBC's *The March*, were rebroadcast. Others were made specially for the schedule, such as a documentary about a family from Chile, in Denmark for 15 years and unsure whether they wanted to go home, or one about old people and the difficulty of living out their final years in a society so different from their country of origin. Several programmes, both for adults and children, highlighted the cultural contribution made by immigrants, asked why people leave their homelands, or examined the problems that arise when two cultures meet or clash.

The special schedule was an important idea, but some of the programmes were considered clumsy or inappropriate by several broadcasting professionals with an immigrant background. A particular object of criticism was a made-for-television film about a Danish farmer who 'wins' a young Thai bride from a bet.

FRANCE

Total population (on 1/1/92):
57,372,000

Foreign population (on 1/3/90):
3,607,590
6.4 per cent of the total population

Distribution by country of origin:

Portugal	645,578
Algeria	619,923
Morocco	584,708
Italy	253,679
Spain	216,015
Tunisia	207,496
Turkey	201,480
Former Yugoslavia	51,697
Poland	46,283
Senegal	45,260
Cambodia	44,029
Mali	34,937
Laos	31,643
Vietnam	31,171
Cameroon	19,145
Côte d'Ivoire	16,987
Congo	12,235

Source: INSEE (French National
Statistics Office), latest population
census in March 1990. Also based on
SOPEMI, *Trends in International
Migration*, Paris, OECD, 1993.

Vis-à-vis: Rose et Nejma. Photo: Point du Jour

FRANCE

1

IMMIGRATION HISTORY

Long before immigration became a major political issue in France, it was a fact of life in history and population statistics. Eighteen million French people – about a third of the population – are descended from immigrants who arrived one, two or three generations ago.

Before the Second World War, immigration policy was closely linked to the hiring of immigrant workers and was left more or less entirely to industry. It was only after the war that the government took charge of the issue. On 2 November 1945 the National Immigration Office (ONI) was created by decree, but its new policies, designed to meet both economic and demographic needs, proved difficult to put into practice. Companies found ways of securing cheap foreign labour in the informal economy, and the ONI was forced to grant these immigrants working papers after the event. The task of helping immigrants and their families to settle in remained with the private sector, especially the Social Service for Aid to Emigrants, founded in 1921.

In 1952 the French Office for the Protection of Refugees and Stateless People (OFPRA) was set up specifically to help refugees. The government delegated some of its powers to this body, which was soon given the right to grant the status of refugee.

The 1960s saw the state gradually losing control over immigration flows. Large numbers of Spanish and Portuguese workers entered France illegally, and many subsequently managed to obtain work and residence permits: 79 out of every 100 in 1965. During the early 1960s about a million immigrants arrived on French soil and the number of foreigners living in France reached 2.3 million. The latter figure did not include Algerians, who were only counted as foreigners after Algeria won its independence from France in 1962. The number of Portuguese entering France rose from 20,000 in 1959 to 200,000 in 1965.

As immigration increased and the public became aware of the poor housing and living conditions endured by many immigrants, especially in shanty towns, the government decided to take action to help them. In 1959 the Social Action Fund (FAS) was created to assist Algerians, and in 1964 its work was extended to cover all foreigners. In 1957 the National Society of Construction for Algerian Workers (SONAOTRA) was founded; all immigrant workers were eligible for its help from 1962. The Population and Immigration Department, whose original aim was to keep a closer watch on arrivals, was set up in 1966. From 1971 it was also given the task of formulating population policy under the supervision of the National Institute for Population Studies and the Higher Council for Population and the Family. Today the Population and Immigration Department has three main roles:

– to study and formulate population policy;
– to conduct and coordinate immigration policy, in conjunction with the other relevant bodies;
– to follow and define naturalization policy.

The law of 1 July 1972 regarding the struggle against racism introduced sentences for provocation and libel, as well as for segregation in public places, in employment and in government and the civil service.

The government's concern about the immigration issue led to the creation on 7 June 1974 of the post of secretary of state responsible for immigrant workers. The job went first to André Postel-Vinay, then to Paul Dijoud (1974-1977), then to Lionel Stoléru (1977-1981). It was in July 1974, during Postel-Vinay's brief appointment, that the government decided to suspend immigration by foreign workers. The official decree banning them from entering France did not really stop immigration; what it did do was increase the number of foreign wives and children joining workers already in the country. Between 1975 and 1984, some 472,000 foreigners arrived in France.

After 1975 foreigners of different nationalities started coming to France. Between 1975 and 1982 the number of Turks rose from 50,000 a year to 123,000, and the number of Africans went up from 81,000 to 157,000. To these figures must be added the growing number of political refugees – 163,000 in 1983, 75,000 of them from South-East Asia.

The Bonnet Law of 10 January 1980 amended the decree of 2 November 1945, making the ONI responsible for matters connected with immigrant workers returning to their home countries and for social work to help immigrants. In 1988 the ONI's name was changed to Office of International Migration (OMI), but its role remained the same.

Since 1981 the various French governments, most of them socialist, have tried to stabilize the number of immigrants, encouraging measures to help them that also benefit the population as a whole and trying to decentralize the services concerned. Meanwhile, as immigration became a political hot potato with the rise of the extreme-right National Front, governments were forced to adopt more specific measures. In 1982 a plan to reform the Social Action Fund was launched, aimed in particular at decentralizing its work. Regional Committees for the Integration of Immigrants were set up in ten regions, and regional authorities were asked to draw up an annual programme for the integration of immigrants.

A law passed in 1981 gave immigrants the right to create non- profit associations, and allowed the Social Action Fund to finance four times as many organizations that help immigrants. The amount of loans doubled between 1980 and 1986.

In 1983 the government, anxious to avoid social tension, set up the National Council for the Prevention of Crime, the Commission for Neighbourhood Social Development, and urban-area contracts, which represented a new departure in integration policy. The contracts are agreements between the state and local authorities aimed at establishing an overall programme concerning the integration of immigrants. They focus mainly on housing but social and cultural activities are also covered. Local groups of the Commission for Neighbourhood Social Development seek ways in which the state and municipal authorities can work together in this domain, encouraging local people to join in and trying to improve management of urban areas. These groups were later swallowed up by the Interministerial Commission for Cities and Urban Social Development, started in October 1988. Education Priority Areas were created in 1981 with the aim of 'helping to correct social inequalities by selective strengthening of educational work in areas and social groups where the failure rate is highest'.[1]

In 1983, partly as a result of the *beur* movement started by second-generation North Africans, France introduced a single type of residence permit for all foreigners, the ten-year *carte de séjour*. The next year saw the emergence of SOS Racism, which was launched to look for ways of combating the National Front and which developed into a movement aimed at reforming French society from within. Along with groups such as the Movement against Racism and Anti-Semitism and for Peace (MRAP), and the Group to Inform and Support Immigrant Workers (GISTI), SOS Racism protested against certain parts of the Pasqua Law, which was based on a policy of encouraging immigrant workers to return to their home countries and

---

1   *Immigrés: réussir l'intégration*, report to the Prime Minister, General Secretary for Integration, Paris, June 1990.

stepping up of border controls. The Pasqua Law was finally judged too repressive and was amended by the Joxe Law of 1989.

The National Council for Immigrant Populations was established in 1984 as a consultative body to give advice on issues such as housing, living conditions, employment, education and training, as well as on social and cultural work. Its 57 members include representatives of immigrant communities, trade unions, employers' organizations and the various ministerial departments that deal with immigration issues.

In November 1989 the government rearranged the advice and decision-making bodies responsible for integration:

- The Interministerial Committee for Integration was given the job of defining, managing and coordinating government policy on integrating foreigners or people of foreign origin living in France. The Committee reports to the Prime Minister's office.

- The General Secretary for Integration, appointed for two years, prepares the work of the interministerial committee and supervises the implementation of its decisions with the help of a coordination committee made up of a member of each of the ministries represented. Hubert Prévot, chairman of the Social Action Fund, was appointed to the post of General Secretary for Integration in December 1989.

- The Council for Integration, set up in March 1990, is made up of nine experts elected for three years and chaired by Marceau Long. Its mandate was extended in February 1994 and Marceau Long was retained as chairman. The Council's role is to give opinions and make any relevant proposals at the request of the Prime Minister and the Interministerial Committee for Integration. It also prepares an annual report to the Prime Minister.

Major measures taken since 1990 include those initiated by the Ministers for Cities – a post created in December 1990 and held in turn by Michel Delebarre, François Loncle and Bernard Tapie. In 1990, 80 million francs was provided to improve the situation in what were considered the 60 most needy urban areas. Edith Cresson's government also contributed. In the Cabinet reshuffle of 17 May 1991 the post of secretary of state for integration was created and given to Kofi Yamgnane, who comes from Togo and is mayor of Saint-Coulitz in Brittany.

The Sapin Law of 31 December 1991 was aimed at curbing illicit labour by introducing heavy penalties for employers who hired workers without declaring them to the authorities. The law also set a time limit after which clandestine immigrants could not be expelled from France, significantly reducing the number of foreigners who suffered the 'double punishment' of being thrown out of the country as soon as they left prison. At the same time the government attempted to lengthen the time people caught trying to enter the country illegally could be held by the French police by introducing the highly controversial Marchand Amendment, which sought to legalize the 'transit centres' where they were detained. The law was finally adopted in June 1992 after being revised by Paul Quilès.

The law of 22 July 1993, which marked the return to power of the political right, introduced sweeping reforms to the regulations governing the acquisition of French nationality. One of the main changes was that children born in France to foreign parents no longer automatically become French once they reach the age of majority. Instead, they are required to 'express the wish' to acquire French nationality to a magistrates' court between the ages of 16 and 21. Another change is that a foreigner who marries a French person now has to wait two years instead of six months before he or she can apply for French nationality.

To sum up, French immigration policy is still dominated by action that covers the population as a whole: measures are introduced to help the poorer social groups and thus automatically help a substantial number of immigrants. Integration measures at local level depend to a large extent on the individual municipalities and are liable to be changed or abandoned if a different political group comes to power.

2

THE BROADCASTING SCENE

Since the ORTF, the French radio and television authority, was split into six separate bodies in 1974, French broadcasting has come under a succession of governing bodies. In 1982 the Higher Broadcasting Authority was established, to be replaced in 1986 by the National Commission of Communication and Freedoms, itself replaced in 1989 by the Higher Broadcasting Council. The series of laws that brought in these changes led to a new era in French broadcasting, with privately owned, mostly mass-audience, channels creating an imbalance in the market in favour of the newly privatized TF1 and a drop in resources for the public sector. The Higher Broadcasting Council is responsible for all aspects of broadcasting, such as monitoring freedom of communication, attributing frequencies and enforcing the various public and private channels' statutes.

Public channels

❶ **FRANCE 2**, a mainstream channel with a 'cultural, educational and social role', receives 53 per cent of its revenue from the licence fee. The ORTF's second channel, launched in 1964, became Antenne 2 in 1975 and France 2 in September 1992. It is broadcast in France by land and on some cable networks. Since 1992 France 2 has been broadcasting 24 hours a day and attracted 21.4 per cent of the audience in 1991. The channel tries to cater for a mass audience while fulfilling its public service role; in 1991 it broadcast 7,887 hours of programmes, including 31 per cent made-for-television fiction (18.8 per cent intended for children and young people), 21.4 per cent news, 15.5 per cent documentaries and magazines (6.38 per cent for children and young people), 15 per cent music and entertainment (4.5 per cent for children and young people), 6.2 per cent sport and 4.5 per cent cinema films.

❷ **FRANCE 3** combines national and regional programmes via a network of 13 regional stations and 25 news centres controlled by a national board of managers. France's third channel, launched in 1969, became FR3 in 1975 and France 3 in September 1992. It receives 63.8 per cent of its income from the licence fee and is broadcast by land and cable. Under French law, France 3 has the specific role of 'producing and scheduling programmes about life in the regions'. Although the number of broadcasts produced in regional languages has been falling for the past three years, more regional magazine programmes have been made since 1991 and seven local stations have been opened. Inter-regional and cross-border programmes have also been made possible by agreements with public and private partners. France 3 attracts 11.8 per cent of the total audience and broadcasts an average of 18 hours a day (5,941 hours a year). The national schedule includes 26.1 per cent documentaries (4.58 per cent for children and young people), 15.9 per cent news and news magazines, 16 per cent music and entertainment (5.9 per cent for children and young people), 9.2 per cent sport and 6 per cent cinema films. Regional programmes are broadcast every day before the 1 pm and 6.30 pm newscasts, on Saturday afternoons, late on Wednesday evenings, and at various times when regional events are in the news.

Joint management for Antenne 2 and FR3 was introduced in August 1989, one of its tasks being to make sure their schedules were complementary. The two channels became France Télévision from 7 September 1992.

❸ **ARTE** (Association relative aux télévisions européennes) is a Franco-German cultural channel with a European outlook. Launched on 28 September 1992 on the frequency formerly occupied by La Cinq (a private channel that went off the air because of financial problems in April of that year), Arte has a French arm in Paris, Société d'édition de programmes de télévision (La Sept), and a German arm in Baden-Baden (Arte Deutschland TV, a subsidiary of the public channels ARD and ZDF). La Sept, created in May 1989 as a French public cultural channel, was first broadcast in France by cable only, with a 'window' on France 3 on Saturdays, before merging with Arte. The German part of the operation includes both ZDF and ARD with its nine regional stations in Munich, Frankfurt, Hamburg, Bremen, Stuttgart, Berlin, Saarbrücken, Baden-Baden and Cologne. La Sept and Arte Deutschland TV both send programmes to the Arte head office in Strasbourg, a European Economic Interest Grouping responsible for scheduling, newscasts, and dubbing and subtitling of programmes.

Arte is the only channel financed entirely from public funds. Its budget in 1992 was 1.2 billion francs. The French government contributed a further 160 million francs to launch it on La Cinq's old frequency, which covers 85 per cent of the country and can reach 30 million French and German homes. Although Arte cannot accept advertising, it is encouraged to seek its own resources through sponsorship. At the moment Arte is a bilingual channel broadcasting programmes in French and German and films from all over the world. Its ultimate aim is to become multilingual.

With an audience of around 1.1 per cent, Arte is on the air from 7 pm to late night. One of the main features of its scheduling is an evening's programmes based on a single theme, with a mix of documentaries, fiction and archive film. Three such evenings go on the air each week. Documentaries are an important part of Arte's programming (30 per cent), especially the work of directors regarded as 'difficult'. It also aims to be the channel of quality films, of which it offers a wide international selection, and to provide original made-for-television fiction, with numerous co-productions. One evening a week is devoted to music of all kinds, including opera, ballet and jazz. Theatre-lovers have one evening a month when some of Europe's top names are featured, with successful plays sometimes produced especially for television. Arte's news programmes aim to take a European view of events and to offer a different angle from that of the other channels. They include a short daily newscast, a weekly current affairs magazine that provides both French and German viewpoints and a weekly programme on what is going on behind the scenes in politics.

❹ **LA CINQUIEME**, the new educational channel, was launched on 15 December 1994 on the frequency occupied in the evenings by Arte. It will broadcast from 7 am to 7 pm. The company's main shareholders are the state (51 per cent) and the French National Employment Agency (15 per cent), and it will be chaired by Jean-Marie Cavada, who produces and presents the popular discussion programme *La Marche du siècle* on France 3. La Cinquième plans to make knowledge accessible to all, offering both mainstream programmes and broadcasts responding to specific needs for information on employment, training, career guidance, health, the environment and family matters. Programmes for children and young people will form a major part of its schedules, with special fiction, cartoons, games and interactive educational broadcasts shown daily.

❺ **TV 5** is a mainstream channel that aims to make the best of French-language television more widely known to an international audience. Launched in January 1984 as TV 5 Europe, it is broadcast by satellite and relayed by cable to about 100 countries all over the world. Starting in western and Eastern Europe, it rapidly expanded to cover Africa from October 1992. The Russian satellite Stationar 12, which made TV 5 available to the Indian Ocean nations of Mauritius and Madagascar, also beams the channel to Asian countries such as Thailand. TV 5, which aims to offer a range of viewpoints, broadcasts from 18 to 20 hours a day. Its programmes are taken from a variety of French-language channels (half of them from France, with the rest divided between Swiss, Belgian, Canadian and African channels). African programmes received a boost with the launch of TV 5-Afrique and now account for four hours daily.

Private channels

❶ **TF1** was privatized in 1987 when a group of shareholders, led by the Bouygues company, took over 55 per cent of the company. It inherited the frequency of French television's first channel, which was launched full-time in 1948 after broadcasting four hours a day since 1937. The first public channel became TF1 in 1975. It is broadcast by land and by cable in some neighbouring countries, as well as by satellite.

Under the terms of its mandate, TF1 must ensure 'honesty and pluralism' in its newscasts and programmes, respecting the various currents of opinion in the country. TF1's viewing figures have continued to rise since privatization (reaching an average of 42 per cent in 1991) and the company has not altered its schedules significantly for several years. It aims to reach a mass audience with a range of entertainment, games and reality shows during prime time, and relies heavily on the popularity of its star presenters. TF1 has cut back on fiction since 1989. Documentaries and magazines are broadcast fairly frequently late in the evening, although the more personal style of documentary has practically disappeared from the schedules. Broadcasting 24 hours a day (8,736 hours in 1991), TF1 offers 40.9 per cent fiction (27.1 per cent for children and young people), 17.1 per cent music and entertainment (14.3 per cent for children and young people), 14.7 per cent news, 9.5 per cent documentaries and magazines, 3.4 per cent sport and 3.3 per cent cinema films. Children's programmes take up 13.5 per cent of the schedule (82 per cent fiction, 54 per cent of which is imported and mostly in the form of cartoons).

❷ **CANAL PLUS**, an encoded pay-channel launched in November 1984, had 3.5

million subscribers in 1992. Broadcast by land to 87 per cent of France, it has undertaken not to be partisan in its scheduling and to warn viewers when programmes are liable to upset or offend viewers, especially those judged unsuitable for children. The channel is also committed to broadcasting at least 45 minutes of unencoded programmes per day. These include newscasts, entertainment and a look at current films and concerts.

Canal Plus, with around 4.5 per cent of the total audience, has found its niche as the entertainment channel, offering an original mix of half mainstream programmes and half cinema films. It broadcasts round the clock and in 1991 its 7,786 hours of programmes were divided between cinema films (45.8 per cent), made-for-television fiction (20.5 per cent, about a third of it aimed at children and young people), documentaries (11.8 per cent, often unencoded), sport (7.1 per cent), music and entertainment (5.9 per cent) and news (5.7 per cent). With the experience gained in France, Canal Plus has exported its formula to Spain, Belgium, Germany and some African countries (it was launched in Senegal, where is is known as Canal Horizons, in December 1991 via the Intelsat VI satellite).

❸ **M6** was started in March 1987 and reaches 80 per cent of France with its land-based broadcasts. It can also be received by satellite in Europe and North Africa. Like the other channels, M6 has pledged to respect different viewpoints and beliefs, and not to offend its viewers. It broadcasts 24 hours a day (8,760 hours in 1991) and its audience is increasing (from 8 per cent in 1991 to 12 per cent in 1992). In 1991 the schedule included 34.1 per cent made-for-television fiction (85.7 per cent of which is American and broadcast on prime time), 31.2 per cent music and entertainment (mainly videoclips, but magazine programmes are gaining ground), 17.8 per cent documentaries, 4.5 per cent news (with the emphasis on regional news – seven major cities each have a six-minute daily slot – and working closely with the regional press), and 0.7 per cent sport.

Encouraged by its success, M6 has started producing more of its own programmes.

3

CHANNEL POLICIES

The statutes of France 2 and France 3 as public service channels stipulate that they should 'schedule and broadcast documentaries on economic, social, scientific and technical issues in the contemporary world, as well as magazines or series of programmes covering the various aspects of national cultural life, including the cultural activities of the various foreign communities living in France'.

Nonetheless France, unlike other European countries, has never considered that producing a magazine for immigrants was part of its role.

Magazine programmes for immigrants

French channels do not seem to have any regular policy regarding magazines specifically for immigrants, despite the country's long tradition of immigration. It is only recently that such programmes have been produced at all.

France 3 has since 1976 broadcast a succession of four magazines, financed mainly by the Social Action Fund (Fond d'Action Sociale, FAS). Scheduling is often haphazard and at times when few people are watching.

➤*MOSAIQUES*, started in 1976, went out on Sundays from 10 am to midday. It had several roles: helping to make foreign culture better known in France, enabling immigrants to maintain ties with their country of origin and bringing the various communities into contact. *Mosaïques* described itself as a 'public service and entertainment' programme open to both French viewers and immigrants.

Unlike magazines produced for immigrants by other European channels, which are usually financed by public television, *Mosaïques* was funded to a large extent by the Social Action Fund, part of the Ministry of Social Affairs. The fund both bought airtime for the programme and paid the production costs. The budget, voted anew each year, went to a nonprofit organization known initially as the Office for the Cultural Promotion of Immigrants, then as Information on Culture and Immigration, and most recently as the Agency for the Development of Intercultural Relations (ADRI), which subcontracted production of the programme (except for a short period when FR3 acted as executive producer).

The seven countries with which France once had labour agreements (Morocco, Tunisia, Algeria, Yugoslavia, Portugal, Turkey and Spain) contributed to the programme by providing regular features.

At first *Mosaïques* was made in immigrants' own languages, using presenters of different nationalities, and each section was subtitled, translated or repeated in the language of the next presenter. Topics covered included folk music, practical and cultural information, as well as features on the countries of origin, immigrants' lives in France, hostels, immigrants' organizations, literacy, women's issues and school problems. The atmosphere was friendly, with paternalistic overtones. Immigrants' organizations thought the programme was deliberately rather amateurish, but they agreed that such a magazine was needed and that it seemed to be popular.

The Gaspard Report, published in 1982, threw a spanner in the works, pointing out that *Mosaïques*' audience was falling, that it was costly to produce and was scheduled at an unsuitable time. Françoise Gaspard, a member of parliament and mayor of the town of Dreux, had been commissioned to write the report by François

Autain, secretary of state responsible for immigrants, as part of a plan to integrate immigrants into French society being worked out by the socialists in power at the time. The report also raised the question of whether such programmes might actually be helping to maintain immigrants outside the mainstream of society, and whether it might not be better to deal with these issues as part of the channels' regular schedules.

Françoise Gaspard did not think that *Mosaïques* should be taken off the air, but she did consider it old-fashioned. The programme should be updated and adapted to the needs of a new generation, the report said.

Although many people agreed that the report's criticism was justified, the proposals made were considered dangerous and premature; it was feared that the Social Action Fund might withdraw its support before making sure the channels were willing to take over. The programme was maintained – with a few minor alterations. In 1987 the magazine took on a different format incorporating news, features made in France and abroad, stories and cartoons for children, entertainment, sport and practical information. The new-look *Mosaïques* also aimed to show that immigrants could succeed and find a place in French society without losing touch with their original culture; interviews with such people were included alongside reports of the work of organizations and community groups. From 5 April 1987 the length of the programme was cut to an hour and a half. Several surveys carried out in 1986 and 1987 showed that it was less popular, that it was scheduled at an unsuitable time and that many people felt too much attention was paid to the North African community at the expense of other communities.

Programme advisers felt that young film makers with an immigrant background should be allowed to contribute to the magazine and that the format should be updated to take account of competition from other channels. By early summer, a proposal for a new programme to start in September had been submitted for consideration to the Social Action Fund, which had a new board of managers. On 4 October 1987 *Mosaïques* was taken off the air without warning – even the production crew was not told in advance – and replaced by *Ensemble aujourd'hui*. The programme was still produced by the Agency for the Development of Intercultural Relations, still subject to government control and still went out on Sundays – but its outlook and producers had changed.

►*ENSEMBLE AUJOURD'HUI* (Together Today) lasted a year, from November 1987 to December 1988. Some viewers complained when it was suddenly shifted from 10 am to 9 am; others disliked the move back to a paternalistic tone. Nonetheless, the programme was making an effort to be more receptive to its audience, with features presented in a more up-to-date style and covering a wider range of subjects.

Ensemble aujourd'hui disappeared as suddenly as its predecessor. Claude Evin, Minister of Solidarity, Health and Social Protection, met members of the Social Action Fund's board of managers on 22 November 1988 to tell them of the government's new immigration policies. He informed them that a new programme was to be launched in January 1989 and a new organization set up to handle production.

►*RENCONTRES* (Encounters[1]) was targeted at a young audience of ethnic background but welcomed other viewers. It aimed to keep in step with the new generation being integrated into French society. The Agency for the Development of Intercultural Relations moved out of the picture and a new organization, the Audiovisual Contacts Association (Association Rencontres Audiovisuelles, ARA), was set up to produce the programme. The association was given a three-year mandate by the Social Action Fund and the government's Population and Immigration Department.

In November 1988 public and private producers were invited to bid for the right to produce the new programme. The winners were Les Films du Sabre and the agency IM'média, run by Mogniss Abdallah.

The pilot programme, given the title of *Rencontres* with the first broadcast scheduled for 29 January 1989, featured a succession of rapid sequences showing news from immigrants' home countries, legal advice, a music and culture slot, daily life and history. The stated objective of the programme was 'to increase knowledge of the conditions in which immigrants or people of ethnic background are being integrated into French society by encouraging greater receptiveness and providing information about the contributions made by the communities concerned to the host country'. The programme was targeted at, but not restricted to, an audience of ethnic background, and it was hoped it would reach a mass audience. It was supposed to 'respect the differences between types of viewer and different generations, with the emphasis on a young audience, and with the aim of presenting immigrant communities in a better light'.

This fast-moving magazine with a young outlook, incorporating jingles and video-clips, was tailored to fit the current style of French television. Its content was geared to the second generation and to more recent immigrants who had previously been disregarded by broadcasters, such as South-East Asians, Chinese, Pakistanis and Lebanese. The format was the same each week: a guest who gave his or her opinion on the news and features shown, a comedy sketch, a special feature presented by

---

1   Details of the saga of these magazine programmes are taken from Catherine Humblot's article, 'Les émissions spécifiques: de *Mosaïques* à *Rencontres*', in *Migrations-Société*, 4, CIEMI, Paris, August 1989.

Karim Hacène, a description of a successful individual or group, reports on social problems and the difficulties of daily life, cultural features and a legal advice slot.

In April 1990 the programme was moved from Sunday to Saturday afternoons, and the duration was reduced to an hour. At the end of the year FR3 entered the partnership by paying the broadcasting rights.

Rencontres was taken off the air for good in late 1991 by the Minister for Social Affairs and Integration, Jean-Louis Bianco, following its rescheduling by FR3. No other programme was brought in to replace it in 1992 and the ARA was put on ice.

➤*PREMIER SERVICE* (First Service) is the most recent magazine of its type on France 3, which continues to contribute to the partnership. Various production companies were invited to put forward ideas for the programme and the format suggested by the Point du Jour agency was chosen by the Social Action Fund in December 1992. The magazine was broadcast from 7 am to 7.30 am from 1 February to 30 June 1993, and was back on the air at the same early hour in September – but lasting only 13 minutes. *Premier Service* is aimed at all those who live in France, whatever their origin. It aims to help people in their daily lives, bring them into contact with others and entertain them right from the start of the day.

Brigitte Vincent, well-known for her work as a journalist in the Caribbean and on Radio France, is the programme's friendly presenter. Her team includes Mouss, a young actor of Algerian origin who looks after the practical advice section, and Assan Ba, of Senegalese origin, who introduces the legal slot. A studio guest comments on the two daily features that may concern a look back at the story of immigration, minorities elsewhere as seen by television abroad, descriptions of individuals and organizations, news and a diary of cultural events.

The programme was scheduled for a further series from September to December 1994 – unfortunately still at 7 am, an anti-social time which is liable to ensure it has only a tiny audience. The latest series has a new format focusing on the studio guest and concentrating on one theme each week. The producers of *Premier Service* are trying to get it repeated as a single, hour-long programme on France 3 once a week and to have the whole series re-broadcast as part of a collection of pro-grammes packaged by the Social Action Fund for immigrants' organizations. This magazine was finally stopped at the end of 1994 by the Minister for Social Affairs.

Mainstream programmes

❶ **France 2** sees its role as mainly cultural, educational and social, with particular emphasis on current affairs. Its news and general-interest magazines (like those of its predecessor, Antenne 2) quite often feature immigration in France and elsewhere. Some examples are:

➤*GEOPOLIS*, Claude Serillon's weekly magazine devoted an issue to immigration in the Paris region on 20 November 1993. Maps and statistics were used to paint a detailed picture of the different types of immigrant who have arrived in the French capital over the past 150 years.

➤*ENVOYE SPECIAL*, a prime-time weekly magazine presented by Paul Nahon and Bernard Benyamin, has frequently dealt with the subject of immigration, whether legal or illegal, and the problems of integration and living in exile.

➤*PREMIERE LIGNE*, a weekly documentary slot that tackles important social issues. One excellent documentary by Jean-Claude Guidicelli, Patrick Weil and Alain Wieder, entitled 'From Father to Son, France and its Foreigners', was broadcast on 5 January 1994 and repeated on TV 5 on 11 April. Through a series of interviews, it traces the history of immigration in France as well as integration in schools and in the workplace.

The growing importance of immigration as a political issue in recent years has meant that it also comes up in political broadcasts such as *L'Heure de vérité*.

People with an immigrant background are under-represented in French made-for-television fiction compared to the rest of Europe, and the United Kingdom in particular. Crime series such as *David Lansky* and *Le Lyonnais* have occasionally used immigrant characters or set the action in immigrant districts such as the Chinese neighbourhood of Paris, but these instances are still few and far between. It was not really until 1990 that black actors began to appear in television drama, whereas in the UK the first multicultural sitcoms were shown in 1972.

France 2 is also expected to devote airtime to religious broadcasts. Catholics, Protestants, Jews and Moslems share the schedule on Sunday mornings from 8.45 am to midday, also providing the opportunity for a glance at other cultures.

In 1992 and 1993, France 2 broadcast special programmes during the month of Ramadan, when Moslems fast from sunrise to sunset. *Les Nuits du Ramadan* (Ramadan Nights) showed the traditional festivities of singing and dancing, along with film and features on the Arab and Moslem worlds.

Children and young people's programmes that have featured immigrants include:

➤*GOAL*, made by Alya Production in 13 ×26-minute episodes, was first shown in June 1992 at 4.40 pm as part of the *Giga* programme. *Goal* tells the story of a group of youngsters who share a passion for football and whose varied backgrounds provide an accurate reflection of French society: Richard's father is Spanish, Olivier's parents are French, Jorge is a brown-skinned Brazilian and Luis comes from a working-class suburb of Lyon.

➤*SECONDE B*, a sitcom shown at 5 pm daily early in 1994, is about life in a secondary school near Paris. The tone has been altered slightly since the first series, broadcast in the spring of 1993, which was regarded as too didactic, but the series still deals mainly with serious, topical subjects such as neo-Nazis and racism.

❷ **France 3** has both national and regional responsibilities regarding programme production and scheduling, and aims to present the opinions of the different cultural, social and professional groups in France as well as the various spiritual and philosophical points of view.

In an effort to fulfil this role, the channel has coproduced and broadcast documentaries such as:

➤*L'HORLOGE DU VILLAGE* (The Village Clock), made by Philippe Costantini, was coproduced with the Portuguese television company RTP. It describes a village in northern Portugal from which many people have emigrated, and the reunions and conflicts that occur when they return each summer. This 75-minute documentary, one of a trilogy on Portuguese emigration, was broadcast in April 1990 and in February 1992 as part of the programme *Océaniques*.

➤*RACINES* (Roots), a series of 40 × 26-minute documentaries, was broadcast in 1989 and 1990 as part of *Rencontres*, at 9 am on Saturdays, then at 2 pm on Sundays. The programmes looked at the history of France through the eyes of a variety of immigrant families, giving viewers food for thought about how they had been integrated into society. The man behind *Racines* was historian Gérard Noiriel, founder of AFHIS (the Association for Making History), and coproduced by the Social Action Fund, the Audiovisual Contacts Association, Anabase (a private company and subsidiary of the Expand group) and AFHIS. Executive producer Mohamed Charbagi said: 'This series is made with the aim of talking about the ethnic and cultural diversity of the French people by describing the historical melting pot which our country has become and because of which it is now a multicultural and multiracial nation'.

Racines deals with subjects affecting either a specific immigrant community or a broader topic such as xenophobia or authors living in exile. Each programme looks at four aspects of immigration: the various immigrant flows, what happens to young people, religion and roots.

Some titles speak for themselves: 'Armenians: Ploughing Up Memories', and 'Samsara: the Transmigration of Laos', both by Axel Clévenot, 'Sweet Gascony', by José Vieira, and 'The Mosque with Three Borders', by Derri Berkani.

At 2 pm on Saturdays during the summer of 1991, Michel Polac introduced *Spécial Racines*, a documentary followed by a debate on the subject of integration, as part of *Rencontres*. A selection of the *Racines* documentaries were also broadcast at 7 am from Monday to Friday during January 1993.

➤*PLANETE CHAUDE*, a Saturday evening documentary slot presented by journalist Bernard Rapp, looks at the harsher facts of life in the modern world.

➤*VIS-A-VIS* is a series of ten 52-minute documentaries produced by the Point du Jour agency. It is based on the original idea of filming (using the 'compressed video' technique) a conversation between two people who in normal circumstances would probably never have met. The first in the series, broadcast on 26 September 1992, was called 'Rose and Nejma'. Rose is a 35-year-old Haitian woman who lives in Brooklyn, New York; Nejma, 29, is of Algerian origin and lives in Gennevilliers, near Paris. Their discussion shed light on life in the poorer parts of big cities, and on strategies for survival.

France 3 also broadcasts some children's programmes made by the National Centre of Educational Documentation. For instance the 11 February 1992 edition of *Paroles d'école* looked at the issues of immigration and integration.

➤*GENERATION 3* has been broadcast every weekday morning since September 1993. Introduced by Marie-Laure Augry, it focuses on a major theme each week, with one guest bringing together a variety of points of view. Moroccan author Tahar Ben Jelloun was the guest during the week that featured immigration and integration.

France 3's regional and national magazines regularly show reports and debates on problems connected with immigration and on other cultures.

➤*LA MARCHE DU SIECLE*, Jean-Marie Cavada's popular current affairs programme broadcast nationally on Wednesday evenings, has often dealt with immigration, either directly or as part of broader social issues such as unemployment, exclusion, Islam in France and problems in the suburbs.

➤*SAGA-CITES*, a weekly magazine broadcast at midday on Sundays, is about life in the poorer Paris suburbs. It is produced by the Ile-de-France-Centre studios. Each edition is broadcast live from one of the suburbs facing difficulties such as unemployment, drugs and social exclusion. The programme aims to 'show problem neighbourhoods from the inside and to look at the issues raised through the eyes of the different people who live there'. It tries to pinpoint what has gone wrong as well as highlighting the positive aspects of the neighbourhood and introducing those who are trying to change things for the better.

➤*CONTINENTALES*, produced by the Nancy studios and broadcast every day except Wednesdays and Sundays, is a window on the world, providing a look at how other countries handle news and documentaries.

Very few of France 3's fiction productions feature the daily lives of immigrants. Among the exceptions are:

➤*FRUITS ET LEGUMES* (Fruit and Vegetables), on the air since 25 July 1994, is broadcast Monday to Friday at 1.30 pm. The 26 × 30 mins sitcom was the idea of Henri de Turenne and Akli Tadjer and is produced by Cinétévé. It aims to entertain and to 'offer a positive model' of an immigrant family who run a corner grocery shop. *Fruits et légumes* is a follow-up to *Sixième Gauche* (Sixth Floor on the Left), a comedy series about three generations of an immigrant family of Algerian origin and their relations with their French neighbours (the same cast appears in both series). The 50 episodes of *Sixième Gauche*, broadcast in 1990, aimed to 'combat racism with humour'. It was the first time a French comedy series had featured an immigrant family.

❸ **Arte – La Sept**, the cultural channel, attempts to show the full range of European culture. It aims to be open-minded and tolerant towards other people's ideas and ways of life.

Documentaries and international cinema are the spearhead of Arte's schedules. Often the films shown have won awards at festivals but have not been widely screened. The 'theme evenings' that are another characteristic of the channel are organized in turn by Germany, Belgium and France: for example *Etranges étrangers*, organized by the Belgian company RTBF and shown on 14 November 1993 (see the chapter on Belgium), *L'Impasse algérienne*, organized by France and broadcast on 23 June 1994, and the German channel SDR's *Arab Dream*, shown on 13 March 1994.

La Sept has coproduced several documentaries for Arte:

➤*BEURS*, made by Ange Casta, was coproduced with the National Broadcasting Institute (INA) and Euros Production and broadcast by La Sept on FR3 on 14 December 1991. It tried to put forward a positive image of *beurs*, second-generation North Africans who form part of a new, mixed-heritage culture but who are often associated with violence and problem neighbourhoods. A professional dancer, a music festival organizer and a boxing champion were featured in the programme.

➤*JUAN GOYTISOLO, GEOGRAPHIE DE L'EXIL*, was coproduced with TIP-TV and made by Pierre Aubry. Juan Goytisolo is a Spanish novelist living in exile who describes himself as 'Spanish in Catalonia, 'afrancesado' in Spain, a Latin in North America, a Christian in Morocco and a wog everywhere'. Broadcast on 9 September 1991, the documentary received the prize for the best personality portrait at the International Art Film Festival in Montreal.

➤*LETTRES D'EXIL*, broadcast on 26 May 1992, is the work of Bohrane Alaouie and shows Lebanese people living in exile in major European cities.

Arte's magazine programmes include:

➤*TRANSIT*, a weekly broadcast launched in late September 1992. Peter Wien, Daniel Leconte and Daniel Cohn-Bendit have devoted several editions to the problems of racism, xenophobia and integration. On 19 October 1993, for instance, Yasmina, Kader and Kemal, immigrants in Belgium, France and Germany, were asked to air their views on fitting into a foreign society.

❹ **TV 5**, which sets out to broadcast the best of French-language television, shows leading documentaries and magazines from France, Belgium, Switzerland and Canada. The channel also features magazines that reflect the multicultural societies of Africa and the Arab world. Some examples are:

➤*OBSIDIENNE*, produced by AITV (Agence d'Images et de Télévision) and the overseas department of Radio France.

➤*REFLETS, IMAGES D'AILLEURS*, produced by African television companies with Belgium's RTBF and the ACCT (Cultural and Technical Cooperation Agency). Its features and reports invite viewers to discover the African continent.

➤*ORIENT SUR SEINE*, a weekly magazine coproduced with the Institute of the Arab World in Paris (IMA) and featuring artists from Arab countries who live and work in France.

❺ **TF1**, the private channel, emphasizes programmes for a mass audience; variety shows, reality shows and other forms of entertainment have pride of place. Although documentaries have practically disappeared from the channel's schedules, news and general-interest magazines such as *Reportages* and *52 sur la Une* still tackle the subject of immigration from time to time. The issue also crops up occasionally in drama:

➤*NAVARRO* is a detective series made by different directors. Practically every other episode is set in an ethnic neighbourhood in or near Paris. On 11 February 1993 'Les enfants de nulle part' ('Children from Nowhere'),[1] which went out at 8.45 pm, was set against the background of riots that took place a few months earlier in temporary accommodation provided for *Harkis* (Algerians who fought on the side of the French during the Algerian war of independence).

❻ **M6**, also privately owned, offers some alternative programmes aimed at a younger audience.

➤*RAPLINE*, presented by Olivier Cachin, features a large proportion of multicultu-

---

1 The original title, *Fils de Harkis* (*Sons of Harkis*) was changed at the last minute.

ral music, particularly rap and music produced in poor neighbourhoods in France and worldwide.

➤*CULTURE PUB*, a magazine which looks at advertising in different countries, has often dealt with the subjects of immigration and ethnic minorities in Europe and the United States.

➤*ZONE INTERDITE*, Patrice de Carolis' monthly magazine, has been on the air since March 1993. It takes a fresh and incisive approach to the more controversial social issues.

➤*LA FAMILLE RAMDAN*, a 40-part series, is something of an exception on French television in that it was written by North Africans and that almost all the characters are North Africans. Broadcast at 7.30 pm on Sundays from October 1990, the story concerned a North African family living in Paris, with French friends and neighbours playing a minor role. In most of the episodes, the family conflicts that form the centre of the action could equally well arise in any French family.

La famille Ramdan was devised and coproduced by Vertigo, a company set up by Aïssa Djabri and Farid Lahouassa, both of whom are from Algerian backgrounds. Although M6 was the only channel to consider the series, it demanded major changes to the original idea and insisted that the more experienced company IMA Production be brought in as coproducer. The final version of *La famille Ramdan* was much more 'Frenchified' than its authors had planned. Could M6 have missed an opportunity to encourage greater understanding of another culture? The series was sold in Sweden, The Netherlands and North Africa.[1]

❼ **Canal Plus**, the encoded channel devoted mainly to cinema films and entertainment, also has ambitions to be the channel of documentaries and magazines. It either coproduces programmes of this kind or buys them from other countries.

➤*LA VAGUE BLANCHE* (The White Wave), broadcast in January 1991 as part of the magazine *24 heures*, concerned immigrants from Eastern Europe – a 'white wave' which now represents 10 per cent of all immigration to France. A film crew from the CAPA agency followed a group of such immigrants around offices and hostels in Paris. The newcomers, who had white-collar jobs in their home countries, seemed doomed to live on the streets because there was no room for them in French society.

➤*URSS-AFRIQUE, VOYAGES D'AMOUR*, tells the story of young Russian women who met and fell in love with Africans studying in the Soviet Union. The documentary, made by Brigitte Delpech and Karim Miské and produced by Taxi-Vidéo

---

1   See Alec Hargreaves' article, '*La famille Ramdan*: un sitcom pur beur', in *Hommes et Migrations*, No. 1147, Paris, October 1991.

Brousse, showed that their visits to Africa and their coffee- coloured offspring gave rise to clashes with different societies and with state bureaucracy. It was shown in August 1992.

►*MOMO*, a film made for television by Jean- Louis Bertucelli, takes an affectionate and humorous look at the problems of youngsters living in working-class suburbs through the encounter of a police chief and a teenager from a North African family. Coproduced with Alya Productions and France 3, *Momo* was broadcast in December 1992.

►*CHRONIQUE D'UNE BANLIEUE ORDINAIRE*, coproduced with Iskra and the National Broadcasting Institute (INA), is a documentary made by Dominique Cabrera and broadcast on 8 January 1993. Inhabitants of a high-rise apartment block due for demolition were asked to relate memories of their past, their families and their neighbours.

Satellite, cable and local channels

Satellite television

Cable and local channels are still spreading slowly in France compared to other European countries, but sales of dish aerials that allow foreign channels to be received by satellite really took off in 1993 and 1994 – and immigrants were among the most enthusiastic buyers.

Eutelsat's four satellites and Intelsat's two offer about 50 channels between them, including two Italian, two Spanish, one Portuguese, one Polish, ten Turkish, two Greek, one Egyptian and one Tunisian. Most are not encoded, especially those from North Africa and other Arab countries. Moroccan television (RTM), for instance, has been broadcasting 12 hours a day since 12 February 1993 via the Eutelsat II F3 satellite, which covers the whole of Europe, North Africa and the Middle East. Algerian national television has been using the same satellite since 20 August 1994, and Tunisian television (RTT) and Egypt's ESC (Egyptian Satellite Channel) since autumn 1992. MBC, a pan-Arab channel owned by a group of Saudis, broadcasts from London on another Eutelsat satellite. Five million Arabic-speakers living in Europe are now able to receive these channels.

Ten Turkish channels are also available in France by satellite[1] The first, which started broadcasting in February 1990, was the official TRT. Two years later the various private channels in Turkey gained access to different satellites and soon overtook TRT in popularity. All tastes are catered for, from the mainstream and

---

1   See the section on Turkish channels in the chapter on Germany.

religious channel TGRT to the slightly saucy Show TV and the kitsch musical channel Télé On. What they have in common is that Turkish programmes make up a large proportion of their schedules, with very little American content. This obviously appeals to Turkish immigrants who are missing their mother country, but it has another, more subtle effect, as *Satellite TV* magazine pointed out in June 1993: 'The countries of origin fear that integrating immigrant children into French society means they will be swallowed up by French culture and will lose all contact with their homelands. These channels exert significant pressure because their news broadcasts are strictly controlled by the authorities and purged of any controversial content...'

In May 1994 about 600,000 dish aerials were estimated to be operating in France and sales of 150,000 a year were reported, mostly to immigrants.

Cable television and local channels

Cable television, on the other hand, is making slow progress in France. There were only 1,014,705 subscribers in late March 1993, compared to 13.5 million in Germany and 9 million in the Benelux countries (Belgium, the Netherlands and Luxembourg). Even the number of would-be subscribers was down on the previous year. To counter this trend, the Association of Cabled Cities has asked cable operators to make the Arabic-language, Turkish and Portuguese channels broadcast by Eutelsat available on cable. In 1994, Canal France International was carrying out a feasibility study on plans for an Arabic-language channel along the lines of TV 5 that would be broadcast on cable.

❶ **Planète,** One of cable's success stories is Planète, the popular documentary channel launched in September 1988 via the Télécom 2B satellite and whose main shareholders are La Générale d'Images, Canal Plus and La Lyonnaise de Communication. Planète, which broadcasts 16 hours a day, aims to enable viewers to discover and understand the world around them. Its schedules quite often feature magazines and documentaries on the subject of immigration and other cultures, most of them bought from other channels.

Two local channels worthy of mention are Canal Nord and 2M Cable.

❷ **Canal Nord** began broadcasting in 1985, initially to the northern part of Amiens, which is home to a large proportion of immigrants. Managed by the organization CARMEN, it has gradually increased its coverage to three neighbourhoods of the city with a total of 6,000 households. Individual homes are hooked up to the large aerials on apartment blocks which receive the channel. Canal Nord is financed by the city council, the DRAC (an organization for culture in the regions) and CARMEN, none of which has a controlling share nor the right to say how the channel should be run. It puts out about six hours of programmes three or four times a year, usually three days running, reporting on the life of the neighbour-hoods.

In November 1991 Canal Nord helped to start up a similar local channel in the city of Beauvais, Télé Saint-Jean.

❸ **2M Cable** was a mainly Arabic-language channel operating in the sister cities of Roubaix and Tourcoing, near the Belgian border, from October 1989. Most of its programmes were provided by Morocco's second channel, 2M Internationale, which is itself a mixture of several channels around the Mediterranean. The schedule included fiction, entertainment, educational programmes, cartoons and news magazines, but no religious programmes or newscasts. Although studio discussions in the magazines were sometimes in French, most of the programmes were in literary Arabic with no subtitles – which might have been a problem for the older generation who learned French at school, or for youngsters who have grown up in France.

From April 1990 2M Cable also broadcast to the Paris suburb of Mantes-la-Jolie from 9 am to midday on Sundays. From October 1991 it went on the air once a week in Epinal, eastern France, as part of another local channel, Images Plus.

Financial difficulties forced 2M to stop broadcasting in October 1993. France Télécom Câble took over its slot, transmitting a selection of six foreign channels to Roubaix-Tourcoing, Mantes- la-Jolie and Epinal.

❹ **VidéoPole**, a mini-experiment has been carried out in Albertville, south-east France, in 1994. The cable operator VidéoPole, a subsidiary of the French electricity company EDF, launched an 'oriental selection' of channels in April 1994. This comprises four Arabic channels (MBC of Saudi Arabia, RTM of Morocco, RTT of Tunisia and ESC of Egypt). Nearly half the Arabic-speaking families in Albertville are believed to have subscribed to this experimental network. Fear of damaging the French ideal of integration could be what has stopped other such channels from being launched, although they are much in evidence in other European countries.

4

INITIATIVES

❶ **THE PRESENCE AND REPRESENTATION OF IMMIGRANTS AND ETHNIC MINORITIES ON FRENCH TELEVISION** is the name of a survey commissioned from the Centre of Information and Studies on International Migration (CIEMI) by the Audiovisual Contacts Association (ARA). Eleven researchers, coordinated by journalist Ahmed Boubeker, looked at about 750 programmes – a total of 555 hours – on all the French channels from 5 pm to midnight from 16 to 30 October 1991. Their work was not restricted to news but covered all categories of programme: fiction, entertainment, game shows, music, videoclips and even advertising.[1]

❷ **THE THREE WORLDS ASSOCIATION AND MEDIATHEQUE.** Since 1980 this organization has concentrated on organizing intercultural contacts using audiovisual techniques. It has an information centre and a database that enables rapid searches to be made by country, director, theme, and so on. The Mediathèque, which specializes in distribution in France, has about 100 recent films available for hire to organizations, teachers and television and cable programme planners. It also publishes videocassettes and is currently looking at new ways of distributing them in France's overseas departments and territories and in the rest of Europe.

In 1992 the Three Worlds Association brought out a booklet listing films and videocassettes available to teachers and group leaders, *L'intégration des personnes immigrées – 101 films*. An updated version was published in 1994.

❸ **THE INSTITUTE OF THE ARAB WORLD (IMA)**, was founded in Paris by France and about 21 Arab nations. France contributed 50 per cent of the cost. The purpose of the Institute is to enable French and other European citizens to discover, understand and appreciate the Arab world, its culture and civilization.

The institute organized the Second Arab Cinema Festival in June 1994. The competition brought together the best films of the past two years, making them available to a wider audience. Later a selection of films toured suburban neighbourhoods.

Another biennial event, the Images of the Arab World Festival, was organized in October 1993 for documentary films and television programmes about the Arab world. It provided an opportunity for professionals from Arab and European channels to get together, share their experiences and buy one another's programmes.

❹ **THE VIDEO FRATERNITY FESTIVAL**, organized by the International League Against Racism and Anti-Semitism (LICRA), is scheduled to take place at the Paris *Videothèque* on 21 and 22 January 1995. The films shown and discussions held will be open to the public. The aim of the festival is to 'identify and highlight recent audiovisual creative works on the theme of human rights, fraternity and tolerance, and against racism and anti-Semitism'. Prizes will be awarded to the best amateur and professional films in the categories: fiction, documentary, fiction-newcomer, documentary-newcomer.

---

1 See Antonio Perotti, 'Immigrations et télévision, conclusions d'une enquête', in *Migrations-Société*, 18, CIEMI, Paris, November-December 1991.

GERMANY

Total population (on 1/1/92):
80,569,000

Foreign population:
5,882,300
7.3 per cent of the total
population

Distribution by country of origin:
Turkey	1,779,600
Former Yugoslavia	775,100
Italy	560,100
Greece	336,900
Poland	271,200
Austria	186,900
Spain	135,200
Netherlands	113,300
United Kingdom	103,200
United States of America	99,700
Iran	97,900
Portugal	93,000
Romania	92,100
France	88,900
Morocco	75,100

Source: SOPEMI, *Trends in International Migration*, Paris, OECD, 1993 (based on Statistiches Bundesamt figures).

GERMANY

1

IMMIGRATION HISTORY

Since the Second World War, West Germany has taken in about 15 million people – mostly of German origin – who had been forcibly moved or expelled, or who had emigrated. To these must be added 5 million people counted as foreigners. In 1991, Germany allowed in 250,000 refugees, five times as many as France,[1] and in 1992, 500,000 asylum seekers entered the country (compared to only 30,000 in France) along with 150,000 citizens of East European countries with Germany ancestors.

Article 16 of the Federal Republic of Germany's basic law, which states that from 1949 'people suffering political persecution have the right of asylum', was adopted in memory of the 800,000 Germans who found refuge abroad during Nazi rule. This clause has made Germany the leading industrialized country in taking in refugees since the collapse of the Berlin Wall, and also puts it ahead of the other traditional countries of immigration. Germany has attracted about half the asylum seekers allowed into western Europe[2] (most of them Yugoslavs, Romanians and Kurds).

Three major phases of immigration can be distiguished in Germany since 1945: those who had left the country (Umsiedler) and refugees arrived between 1945 and 1955; guest workers (Gastarbeiter) came mostly from 1955 to 1973 (when the word 'immigration', formerly rejected, gradually came into use); and the current phase, typified by the changes that have taken place since reunification.

The economic and social integration of refugees and people who left Germany during the war is generally agreed to have been completed by the mid-1950s. Most

---

1 Philippe Bernard, 'Allemagne, refuge forcé', *Le Monde*, Paris, 1 January 1992.
2 Lorraine Millot, 'Allemagne, terre d'asile fragile', *Libération*, Paris, 9 August 1991.

of these came from the East, fleeing the Soviet Army and changes to the Oder-Neisse border: the Sudetenland, eastern Prussia, Pomerania and Silesia, as well as the Soviet-occupied zone that had become East Germany. They were joined by a large number of *Volksdeutsche* (people of German origin), particularly from the Balkans, and by Germans from the Volga region who had been deported to Kazakhstan by Stalin.

Between 1960 and 1969, international agreements covering the employment of *Gastarbeiter* were signed with Spain, Greece, Turkey, Portugal, Morocco, Tunisia and Yugoslavia, as they were in most European countries. The theory of rotating labour proved difficult to enforce in practice and was officially abandoned in the early 1970s. West Germany then began a slow process of integrating its 'guest workers' by suspending recruitment in those countries where labour had tradition-ally been hired and by extending the permits of those workers already in the federal republic. However, West Germany continued to deny that it was a 'country of immigration'. It was only on 4 May 1983 that the government announced the move from a *Gastarbeiter Politik* to an *Ausländer Politik* (policy on foreigners).[1]

The current situation is complicated by the way in which German nationality may be acquired. This is fairly restricted because Germany does not recognize the *jus solis* in force in some European countries that gives anyone born there the right to citizenship of that country. Nor does it allow dual nationality. Only those with German ancestors have the right to apply for German nationality, according to the legal principle of *jus sanguinis*, because the German nation is still based on the idea of belonging to an ethnic or organic community, a single people. This idea leads on to the notion of descendance: even those whose families have lived outside Ger-many for several generations continue to form part of the *Volk*.[2]

Nonetheless, reunification has introduced a degree of flexibility into the naturali-zation of foreigners living in Germany. The former law of 1965, which replaced the regulations introduced by the Nazis, gave civil servants the right to decide whether foreigners were 'harmful to the interests' of West Germany, and to expel those that fell into this category.

The new law, which was voted on 26 April 1990 and came into force on 1 January 1991, makes naturalization easier for young foreigners born in Germany. They are required to have at least eight years of residence, to have attended school for four years and to give up their original nationality. Adults living in Germany for more than 15 years have the same right. The principle of changing the Constitution to restrict the right of asylum was finally accepted when the Social Democrat Party,

---

1   Dominique Schnapper, *L'Europe des immigrés*, Ed. François Bourin, Paris, 1992.

2   Dominique Schnapper, *op. cit.*

the current opposition, gave way to demands from Chancellor Helmut Kohl's Christian Democats.

After the new law came into force on 1 July 1993, the number of requests for asylum fell by half. But this did nothing to stop attacks on refugee centres, despite massive anti-racist demonstrations. Violence was used against the Turkish community, the largest group of foreigners in Germany since the economic boom of the 1960s who had been living in relative harmony with the Germans.

Racist attacks caused a deep moral crisis and controversy continues between the supporters of *jus sanguinis* and those demanding reforms of immigration policy as well as a change in the law on naturalization to allow Germans to hold dual nationality.

2

THE BROADCASTING SCENE

The reunification of Germany led to a reorganization of the broadcasting system which is now virtually complete. An agreement signed with the Länder on 1 August 1991 laid down the broad outline. East German television ceased definitively on 31 December 1991; Deutscher Fernsehfunk (DFF), which had covered the five Länder with its two channels DFF 1 and DFF 2, no longer exists. In their place, two new regional channels were set up, both belonging to the Arbeitsgemeinschaft der Offentlichrechtlichen Rundfunkanstalten (ARD); the main public channel, Ostdeutscher Rundfunk Brandenburg (ORB) serves the Berlin region and Mitteldeutscher Rundfunk (MDR) covers the Länder of Saxony, Thuringen and Saxony-Anhalt. The fifth new Länder, Mecklemburg, picks up Norddeutscher Rundfunk (NDR), whose headquarters is in Hamburg.

Alongside this reorganization, the public channels are losing clout as the private channels gain ground.

One major difference remains between the east and west of the country: in the former federal republic 67 per cent of homes are cabled whereas in the five new Länder the figure is only 6 per cent.

Public channels

❶ **ARD** (or DFS: Deutsche Fernsehen), established in 1952, links the Länder's 13 broadcasting companies (11 that existed in the Federal Republic and the two new ones)[1] and offers them national programmes. ARD is financed mainly from the

---

1 WDR, HR, BR, SR, SDR, SWF, NDR, RB, SFB, Deutschlandfunk (DLF), Deutsche Welle (DW),

licence fee but is being harder hit by falling advertising revenues than the other public channels. These have plunged to half what they were five years ago and now make up around 5 per cent of the total budget. ARD's financing seems to be suffering the economic consequences of reunification and of competition from the private channels.

ARD broadcasts a national schedule (ARD 1) during the morning and from 6 pm. Early afternoons are reserved for a joint schedule proposed by ARD and the second public channel, ZDF (Zweites Deutsches Fernsehen), and regional programmes fill the 4 pm to 6 pm slot. Total annual broadcasting time is more than 4,000 hours (plus 600 hours of joint ARD/ZDF broadcasts). The morning and evening schedules are worked out with ZDF to ensure that they do not clash. ARD is a mainstream channel giving priority to news and factual magazines, which make up 37 per cent of its schedule. Entertainment is also important: fiction occupied 32 per cent of programmes in 1991, including 15 per cent serials and 13 per cent made-for-television films, children's programmes 9 per cent and sport 5 per cent.

ARD's third network, ARD 3, launched in 1953, is made up of general-interest regional programmes: Bayerischer Rundfunk (BR), Hessen 3, Hessischer Rundfunk (HR), Mitteldeutscher Rundfunk (MDR Fernsehen Mecklembourg), Nord 3 (N3), Norddeutscher Rundfunk (NDR), Radio Bremen (RB), Sender Freies Berlin (SFB), Ostdeutscher Rundfunk Brandenburg (ORB), Südwest 3 Saarländischer Rundfunk (SR), Süddeutscher Rundfunk (SDR), Südwestfunk (SWF) and West 3 Westdeutscher Rundfunk (WDR). Nord 3 and West 3 are also broadcast by cable and satellite and can therefore be picked up in other regions. They give priority to news (they have their own production teams) and entertainment, but with a more cultural bias than ARD 1. In 1991, 62 per cent of regional programmes were devoted to news (newscasts and magazines) and 14 per cent to fiction (apart from children's and young people's programmes). In the reunified Germany, ARD now has seven channels: BR, Hessen 3 (HR), MDR Fernsehen Mecklembourg, Nord 3 (NDR, RB, SFB), ORB Fernsehen, Südwest 3 (SR, SDR, SWF) and West 3. Nord 3 and West 3 are also broadcast by satellite and can therefore be picked up in other regions.

In 1991, before the former East Germany's broadcasting was reorganized, ARD 1 was the most popular channel, watched by 27.3 per cent of viewers. Its lead fell slightly in 1992 (23.8 per cent in June 1992, for all Länder). In 1991 ARD 3 had an 8.6 per cent share of the total audience, falling to 6.1 per cent in June 1992.

The cultural channel Eins Plus, owned by ARD and broadcast by satellite, is received on cable by 37 per cent of German homes. Its schedules concentrate on

---

ORB and MDR.

cinema films, theatre and music, and it has a restricted audience (1.4 per cent of the market in June 1992).

❷ **ZDF**, the second public channel, was established in 1963. Like ARD, it gets most of its income from licence fees. In 1991 it broadcast as many hours as ARD 1 (4,980 hours, plus 600 hours of joint schedules). Like the first channel, it aims to provide mainstream programmes but solely for a national audience, giving precedence to news and magazine programmes (which made up 40 per cent of the schedules in 1991) and fiction (33 per cent). ZDF is also Germany's second most popular channel, attracting 25.3 per cent of viewers in 1991. This had dropped to 22.4 per cent by June 1992 in the face of competition from private channels.

❸ **3 SAT**, launched in 1984 and broadcast by satellite, is also part of ZDF. The Austrian and Swiss public channels provide some of its capital as well as supplying programmes. The schedules therefore offer a mix of ZDF's programmes and those of Austria's ORF and Switzerland's Deutsche und Rätoromanische Schweiz (DRS), a total of 3,760 hours in 1991. News and magazines took up 30 per cent of the programmes on offer, sport 6 per cent, cultural programmes 14 per cent and fiction 20 per cent. It still attracts only a fringe audience.

❹ **ARTE**, the Franco-German cultural channel,[1] was launched on 30 May 1992. It has a French arm in Paris, Société d'édition de programmes de télévision (La Sept), and a German arm in Baden-Baden (Arte Deutschland TV, a subsidiary of the public channels ARD and ZDF), both of which send programmes to the head office in Strasbourg. Nine million cable homes in Germany can receive Arte's pro- grammes. It is also broadcast by the German satellite Kopernikus, the French satellite TDF 1, and, in France, on the terrestrial wavelength formerly occupied by La Cinq.

Private channels

The private broadcasting sector is gaining ground at the expense of the public sector in Germany. The first private channels, Sat 1 and Radio Television Luxem- bourg (RTL), are thriving and are out of the red. There should be nine privately owned channels in 1994. Capital in the private broadcasting sector is being con- centrated into two sets of groups: Bertelsmann and the Luxembourg Broadcasting Company (CLT) on the one hand, and Springer and Leo Kirch on the other. The private channels are also available by cable.

❶ **SAT 1**, set up in 1985 by the press, and in particular the Springer group, was taken over two years later by Leo Kirch, who had become the majority shareholder

---

1 See the chapter on France for more details.

with 43 per cent of the capital. Axel Springer kept only 20 per cent. Since 1987 Sat 1 has been broadcast by land-based transmission as well. It puts out 19 hours of programmes a day, mostly fiction (47 per cent, including 21 per cent of made-for-television films and 23 per cent serials, and excluding children's and young people's programmes) and news (20 per cent, including magazines). Coming on the market after RTL Plus, Sat 1 obtained 10.4 per cent of the total audience in 1991 and its share had increased to 13 per cent in May 1992.

❷ **RTL TELEVISION** (formerly RTL Plus) began broadcasting from Luxembourg by satellite in 1984 to be relayed by cable networks. It later moved to Cologne and is now Germany's most widely watched private channel, with 14 per cent of the total audience in 1991 and 16.8 per cent in 1992, the Länder of the former East Germany included. CLT holds a majority share of the capital (46 per cent) and UFA Film holds 39 per cent. Like Sat 1, RTL Television offers 19 hours of programmes a day, dominated by fiction (50 per cent, including 30 per cent of serials). News takes up 15 per cent of the schedules.

❸ **RTL 2**, 24 per cent of which is owned by CLT, 24 per cent by Bauer Verlag and 24 per cent by Tele München Fernsehen, has been on the air since 1993. It concentrates on programmes for young people.

❹ **PRO 7** came on the scene in 1989. Thomas Kirch, Leo's son, owns 48 per cent of the capital and Gerhard Ackermanns 50 per cent. Its nine hours of daily programmes, broadcast by cable only, give precedence to fiction (73 per cent of programmes in 1991, including 33 per cent made-for-television films and 36 per cent serials). Pro 7's viewing figures have overtaken those of Tele 5, attracting 3.7 per cent of the total audience in 1991 and reaching 6.3 per cent in August 1992, the former Eastern Länder included.

❺ **TELE 5** was initially called Music Box. Silvio Berlusconi started buying up the channel's capital in 1987 and now holds 33 per cent. The rest belongs mainly to Axel Springer (25 per cent) and the Kirch group (25 per cent). Tele 5 broadcasts round the clock on cable, offering mainly films and serials (26 per cent), children's programmes (27 per cent, dominated by fiction) and news (11 per cent).

In 1991 Tele 5 was only attracting 2.5 per cent of viewers, but the figure was up to 5.4 per cent by June 1992 and it seems to be one of the more dynamic private channels.

❻ **PREMIERE**, launched early in 1991, is an encoded channel available only to subscribers and 37 per cent owned by the French Canal Plus, which operates on a similar basis. UFA Film holds another 37 per cent and the rest of the capital is owned by Teleclub/Kirch. Premiere is broadcast by satellite to the German cable networks.

3

CHANNEL POLICIES

German broadcasting law explicitly states that the media should promote understanding between peoples.

Magazine programmes for immigrants

The German public broadcasters were the first to make magazines for foreigners. At the moment only channels in what used to be West Germany, which have undergone numerous alterations as a result of changing national immigration policy, offer this type of programme.

❶ **ZDF** began broadcasting magazine programmes in foreign languages, with German subtitles, in 1963.

➤*NACHBARN IN EUROPA* (Neighbours in Europe), started in 1963 with the aim of combating prejudice, encouraging tolerance and providing a bridge between immigrants and their country of origin, while at the same time helping them to integrate into German society. In the early days, programmes for foreigners were seen largely as a way of dealing with homesickness.

Six separate magazines, either fortnightly or monthly, taken from programmes produced by foreign channels, were broadcast as part of *Nachbarn in Europa*:

Cordialmente dall'Italia (Greetings from Italy), started on 1 November 1964, broadcast on Saturdays, 26 programmes a year.

Aqui España (Spain Calling), started on 31 July 1966, broadcast on Saturdays, lasting 45 minutes, 26 programmes a year.

Jugoslavijo dobar dan (Hello Yugoslavs), started on 1 January 1970, broadcast on Sundays, 26 programmes a year.

Turkiye mektubu (Letter from Turkey) and *Kalimera* (Hello), both started in 1973 and broadcast on Sundays, 13 programmes a year.

Apo tin Ellada (From Greece), started in 1973, broadcast on Sundays, 13 programmes a year.

Portugal, minha terra (Portugal, my country), started on 14 April 1979, broadcast on Sundays, 13 programmes a year.

German immigration policy was gradually altered from 1975: most guest workers would stay in Germany and their families would be allowed to join them. It was against this background that a practical advice programme, *Wir bitten um ihre Aufmerksamkeit* (Thank You for Your Attention), was launched in June 1975.

Features on work and residence permits, looking for an apartment, training opportunities, the right to hold meetings and German customs were written by German journalists from ZDF, translated and presented by foreign journalists and used in the programme in the language of the country of origin. In March 1978 this programme gave rise to another, *Informationen aus der Bundesrepublik Deutschland* (News from West Germany).

In 1979 *Nachbarn in Europa* went weekly and was broadcast on Saturdays. It was still intended for people of six foreign nationalities, split into two groups: Yugoslav, Greek and Spanish; Italian, Portuguese and Turkish. A total of 45 minutes was devoted to each group once a fortnight.

From 1 October 1982 the magazine took on a more uniform appearance, with a new presenter linking the parts supplied by different countries. The introductions, comments and explanations were given in German. The new name of the programme was *Nachbarn in Europa: Informationen und Unterhaltung für Ausländer und Deutsche* (Neighbours in Europe: News and Entertainment for Foreigners and Germans). From 1 January 1988 music was included in the broadcasts, along with a diary of cultural events, a feature on sport from southern Europe and a weekly look at news from the countries of origin.

In agreements signed between 1985 and 1987 by ZDF and its six television partners, Elleniki Radiophonia Tileorassi (ERT-Athens), Radio televizija (RT-Zagreb), Radio Audizioni Italia (RAI-Rome), Radio Televiso Portuguesa (RTP-Porto), Türkiye Radio Televizyon (TRT-Ankara) and Televisión Española (TVE-Madrid), covering cooperation on *Nachbarn in Europa*, their objectives were defined as follows: 'The programme is intended for both Germans and foreigners. It aims to contribute to better understanding of foreign minorities by Germans, while maintaining links with their home countries through features about their cultural past and news of current events in those countries.'

From October 1989, each nationality had ten minutes of airtime per programme, divided up as follows:

- National news: short news reports about the most important events involving the home countries, written by ZDF journalists.

- Film slots lasting 30 to 50 seconds on five or six other topics covering the political, economic, sporting and cultural life of the countries over the previous two weeks. These were provided in finished form by the six national television companies.

- News about Germany, given in each of the six foreign languages and

167

dealing with politics (policies on foreigners, integration, economic and social policy and the labour market) as well as sport and culture.

The whole of the magazine, subtitled in German and broadcast from 11 am to 12.35 pm, was aimed at the six different nationalities as well as Germans.

Since 1 January 1992, when ZDF's new schedules came into force, *Nachbarn in Europa* has radically changed its format and content. The changes were introduced because of the reunification of Germany, the emergence of a second generation who speak German better than their parents' language and who have assimilated German culture, and the presence of other foreigners (especially from Poland and the former Soviet Union). In addition, it was difficult to integrate the slots provided by the foreign partners, which varied greatly in quality, style and journalistic staffing, into a uniform programme concept. Hans Heinz Röll, then in charge of *Nachbarn in Europa*, commented: 'For a 92-minute programme on Saturday mornings, viewers were getting something that was too long, which led to a falling audience.'

Nachbarn in Europa was split into two programmes: *Nachbarn – ein Magazin für Ausländer und Deutsche* (Neighbours – a Magazine for Foreigners and Germans) and *Nachbarn in Europa – Informationen und Berichte in Fremdsprachen* (Neighbours in Europe: News and Features in Foreign Languages). Both are produced by 12 full-time journalists and about 40 freelances (half German, half foreign).

►*NACHBARN* (Neighbours), which lasts 45 minutes, is broadcast on alternate Fridays at 1.45 pm and repeated at 9 am on Saturdays. It is in effect a new programme, entirely in German, and aimed at both Germans and foreigners. It highlights the problems and prospects of Germans and foreigners living together through items on social, cultural and economic life, and is anxious to take into account the new immigrants from the former East European countries. *Nachbarn* experiments with all the different formats used in television magazines: news items, reports, features, interviews and discussions. Bekir Gensch, who was badly disfigured in a fire at a Turkish hostel in Solingen in May 1993, was interviewed in December 1993 when he came out of hospital, and there were several reports on the subsequent demonstrations of support that attracted thousands of Germans, and the 'chains of light' that were formed. Bernd Fischer, head of *Nachbarn* since January 1994, wants to stress 'the positive side and depict the multicultural life that has sprung up in many sectors of society'.

►*NACHBARN IN EUROPA* (Neighbours in Europe) lasts an hour and is broadcast on Saturdays at 8 am. The new format features three 15-minute reports contributed by the foreign partners, with German subtitles: Greek, Italian and Portuguese one week alternating with Croat, Polish and Turkish the next. The programme also includes five minutes of news about Germany written by ZDF journalists.

TVE-Madrid has stopped taking part in the project because its programme *España Internacional* can now be picked up by satellite in central Europe. Poland started contributing in July 1992 – *Oto Polska* (This is Poland) is produced in partnership with Telewisja Polska – and cooperation with other East European countries was planned from September 1994. Since the war in Yugoslavia began, ZDF has been broadcasting a programme in the Croat language in cooperation with Hrvastska televizija (HTV Zagreb).

❷ **ARD** has also been broadcasting magazine programmes for immigrants, since 1965, but these are slightly different from those offered by ZDF.

➤*IHRE HEIMAT – UNSERE HEIMAT* (Your Homeland – Our Homeland), produced and broadcast by WDR, was initially intended to be a daily 10-minute programme with German subtitles, focusing on each of the immigrant communities in turn: Italian, Greek, Spanish, Turkish and, since 1969, Yugoslav. Unlike *Nachbarn in Europa, Ihre Heimat – Unsere Heimat* did not use features produced by television companies in the home countries. A network of ARD foreign correspondents contributed political and cultural reports, making for a rather more objective viewpoint. In 1990 the programme went weekly, broadcast at 11 am on Sundays and incorporating reports filmed in Portugal.

➤*BABYLON* took over from *Ihre Heimat – Unsere Heimat* in April 1993, broadcast in the same time slot by West 3. Still produced by the political and social staff of WDR in Cologne, it is also received by Hessischer Rundfunk (HR) and Suddeutscher Rundfunk (SDR). The programme is aimed both at foreigners living in Germany and at ethnic Germans, dealing first and foremost with the social and cultural situation of minorities in Germany and how they can best be integrated, but also showing reports on the home countries along the same lines as *Ihre Heimat – Unsere Heimat*.

Babylon is split thematically and linguistically into three sections: the southern countries of the European Union (Italy, Spain, Greece and Portugal), central Europe (the former Yugoslavia, Poland, Russia), and Turkey. Reports are shown in the language of origin with German subtitles, while the programme presenters speak German (translations appear on the screen in the other languages). Aysim Alpman, one of the four foreign journalists who introduce *Babylon*, won the Civis Prize in 1993 for her apposite comments on the arson attacks at Solingen.

➤*MONITOR ITALIA* has been produced for over ten years by Bayerischer Rundfunk (Bayern 3) in cooperation with Italy's RAI and the ARD office in Rome. It is a magazine of news, sport and entertainment, broadcast in Italian with German subtitles, and is targeted at the Italian community in Bavaria. Lasting half an hour, it goes out at Saturday lunchtime on Bayerischer Rundfunk.

Mainstream programmes

Apart from occasional programmes intended to make the German public aware of anti-racism demonstrations, the public channels regularly offer a look at other cultures in documentaries, films, serials, and children's programmes

❶ **ARD** The increase in attacks on immigrants since the autumn of 1991 has given rise to a number of broadcasts. They include:

➤*ZUM BEISPIEL BERLIN* (Berlin, for instance), a WDR production broadcast by ARD on 12 March 1992, was made up of four reports about racism in Berlin.

- Felix Kuballa filmed a social worker in the suburb of Marzahn trying to deal with a group of skinheads;

- Gerd Monheim investigated racism at a football club in Oberliga, Turkiyemspor, in Berlin-Kreuzberg;

- Yoash Tafari interviewed the official responsible for foreigners at the Berlin Senate;

- Peter Schran followed a police unit specializing in the fight against violence for two nights.

The reports won the 1992 Civis Prize in the news category.

Programmes like this are mushrooming: discussions on racism are organized practically every day on radio and television and in businesses and schools.

For many years some children's programmes have tried to encourage an interest in other cultures. One example is:

➤*DIE SENDUNG MIT DER MAUS* (The Programme with the Mouse), produced by the children's programme unit of the regional channel WDR, has been broadcast by ARD twice a week since 1976. From the beginning it used foreign languages to make children aware of other cultures. Each programme, using cartoons and features to present a series of games and quizzes, is presented in a different language: Italian, Turkish, Serbo-Croat, Greek, Portuguese and so on. *Die Sendung mit der Maus* was awarded the Civis Prize in 1991.

The fiction shown during prime time does not always take account of the multicultural society Germany has become.

➤*LINDENSTRASSE* (Lime Street) is a family series broadcast on ARD and repeated on West 3. Based on Britain's long-running *Coronation Street*, it is made by WDR and the Geissendörfer Film und Fersehgesellschaft (GFF), a production company owned by H-W Geissendörfer. Decried by critics, adored by viewers, *Lindenstrasse* attracted about 30 per cent of the audience when it was launched on 8 December 1985 (the 1991 average was 24.4 per cent, which represents 8.5 million households). It is shown on Sundays from 6.40 to 7.10 pm and was scheduled to continue until 1994.

Lindenstrasse raises issues and problems of everyday life, such as separation, Aids, Nazis and neo-Nazis, drugs, dropouts, the integration of foreigners and all kinds of family conflict. The problems of foreigners living in Germany is not a focal point and roles for foreigners only emerged recently. *Lindenstrasse* now has 61 actors and actresses, nine of them foreign roles: a Greek couple and their son, an Italian married to a German woman, a Vietnamese man, a Polish woman, a French woman and her father, an adopted child of Peruvian origin with Mexican nationality, and a black South African.

Geissendörfer, who produces the series, describes it as follows: '*Lindenstrasse* is a mirror of society and must also be play the role of critic, provide information and viewpoints, and demonstrate freedom of speech, while at the same time denouncing taboos, scandals and shortcomings in German society. Minorities appear in the series in the same way as Germans'.[1] In fact only some minorities are used and it is striking that there are no Turks – by far the biggest group of foreigners on German soil . . .

❷ **ZDF** The Channel's July 1963 guidelines specify that it must take care 'to provide an objective, overall view of multicultural life by presenting the history of the German people and the wide variety of ethnic and cultural groups in Germany'.[2] This concern is clearly shown in ZDF's children's programmes.

➤*KARFUNKEL* is a series of 30-minute stories, each written and produced by a foreigner living and working in Germany. First broadcast between November 1991 and February 1992, the programme is aimed at children aged six to ten. Producer Bärbel Lutz-Saal said it tried to emphasize interethnic cohabitation and the wealth of intercultural relations that can develop between German children and those of foreign origin. Each programme has its own theme and its own heroes, although three minor characters appear throughout the series. Encounters between children of different cultures are tackled in a comic or dramatic context, mixing humour,

---

1 Geissendörfer, 'Wie Kunstfiguren zum Leben erwachen' (How characters come to life), in *Rundfunk und Fernsehen*, No. 1, 1990.

2 Guidelines for the programmes of ZDF, 11 July 1963 (ZDF charter).

compassion and imaginativeness, based on the sort of everyday experiences youngsters are liable to have: a German boy pretends to be a Kanak and finds out how differently people treat him; a friendship grows up between two children – one Russian, one German – whose grandparents were enemies during the war; a young Kurd who has just arrived from a village in Anatolia, and who speaks neither German nor Turkish, is taken in by a German family.

All these programmes were made in Berlin, a city well known for its openness to all cultures. Bärbel Lutz-Saal explained: 'It is not a question of trying to resolve conflicts, as adults might expect, but of trying above all to show what is worthwhile in other people, to stimulate children's natural curiosity about the world around them and to create a process of identification'. She added: 'Film speaks the international language of feelings. The natural use of different languages makes the programmes more authentic.' The initial broadcasts allowed the programme makers to check that the dialogues in Kurdish, Russian, Eritrean and South American languages – deliberately not subtitled – had been perfectly understood by young viewers, both Germans and immigrants.

The episode entitled *Ich bin ein Kanake* (I am a Kanak) won the 1992 Civis Prize in the fiction category.

In view of the popularity of *Karfunkel* on television and when it was shown in schools, ZDF repeated the series in 1993. It also produced another 12 episodes that took into account racist violence in Germany and the arrival of new immigrants. This second series was broadcast in 1994, and another series of six episodes is planned for 1995.

➤*DAS KLEINE FERNSEHSPIEL*, started in 1962 and headed by Eckart Stein, is one of the most innovative programmes on European television. It aims to be a laboratory for experimenting with multicultural programming that may cover fiction, documentaries, videoclips or poetry, and includes contributions from film makers and journalists from all over the world. This unstructured 'niche', as Eckart Stein calls it, is now broadcast 38 times a year at 11 pm. The programme is open-ended, its length depending on what happens to be available. All types of contribution are welcomed, including the many films about minority rights and people in search of an identity. Some examples are:

Drachenfutter (The Dragon's Nosh), a 69-minute film made by Jan Schütte and broadcast at 9.15 pm on 19 October 1988, tells the story of two luckless friends – one Chinese, one Pakistani – who want to open a restaurant in Hamburg.

Transit levantkade, an 82-minute story based on archive film, draws a parallel between immigrants who arrived on a canal bank in Amsterdam in 1926 and the squatters who live there today. Made by Rose Marie Blank, it was broadcast at 11 pm on 19 March 1991.

Yasemin, a 90-minute film made by Hark Bohm, is a love story involving a Hamburg Romeo and a Turkish Juliet and the subsequent clash between their different worlds. Broadcast by ZDF at 8.10 pm on 4 February 1991, it received the Golden Ribbon and the prize for best actress in the 1989 German film awards, followed by the Civis Prize in 1991.

66 war ein gutes Jahr für den fremden Verkehr (66 was a Good Year for Tourism), a 66-minute documentary made by Amit Goren, gives the director's view of the past, present and future of an immigrant Israeli family, with scenes in Alexandria, Tel Aviv, New York and Los Angeles. It was broadcast at 11 pm on 30 June 1992.

Mitten ins Schwarze (Among the Blacks), a 69-minute documentary made by Moise Matura, describes the situation of African asylum seekers in Germany. It was broadcast on 21 September 1993.

Like ARD, ZDF has shown many programmes about recent racist attacks and the subsequent demonstrations of support for immigrants. On 25 August 1992 one report about the city of Rostock, by Thomas Euting and Dietmar Schumann, was included in the magazine *Kennzeichen D*, which deals mainly with issues concerning the former East Germany. The ZDF camera crew had been inside a hostel for asylum seekers in Rostock, surrounded by groups of skinheads trying to set fire to the building, and had filmed the panic of Vietnamese refugees as they waited in vain for the police to turn up. This startling report won the IG Metall union's media prize at Augsburg in October 1992 and was shown again by Arte on 9 October 1992 in *Transit*, a magazine produced by Daniel Leconte and Peter Wien.

The films of Tewfik Baser, Ali Özgentürk and Erden Kiral (both fiction and documentaries) – coproduced with WDR, ZDF, sometimes Britain's Channel 4 and partly with Turkish companies – were revelations when they first appeared. This young school of Turkish directors has over the past decade developed a genuine alternative cinema in Germany. Some of their films have been broadcast on German television. In July 1990 Roland Schneider wrote in a special issue of *CinémAction*: 'The dynamism of documentaries puts together ethnological reporting with the experience of life in Germany...Unlike the *beur* (second-generation North Africans) phenomenon that emerged in France among second-generation immigrants, this trend looks from the outside at an environment experienced from the inside'.

Cable, satellite and local channels

The cable, satellite and local channels provide a few programmes open to other cultures. The Turks have several of their own channels and the Offene Kanale (open channels) represent an interesting departure that allows any inhabitant of Germany to express an opinion backed up by modern broadcasting techniques.

❶ **ARTE.** The Franco-German channel's theme evenings have included:

➤*FREMDE BLICKE* (Looking at Others), produced by Claus Josten and the ZDF, went out from 8 pm to midnight on 10 September 1992. The programme was introduced by Roshan Dhunjibhoy, a Pakistani television journalist living in Cologne, Ali Yurhagül, a Turk working for the Greens in the European Parliament, and Brigitte Granzow, a German radio reporter and writer. The evening featured *Saal der Verlorenen Schritte* (The Waiting Hall), a 52-minute documentary by Benno Trautmann, *Seriat*, a documentary of 1 hour 52 minutes by Marlies Graf-Dätwyler and Urs Graf, and *Die Ohnmacht* (The Failure), a 35-minute film by Karim Traidia.

On 7 January 1993 Arte broadcast the Frankfurt anti-racism show that had attracted thousands of young people the previous month. More than 30 German rock musicians took part.

❷ **ARD 3** has taken a special interest in cinema films produced by French *beurs*.

➤*DIE WUT ZU LEBEN* (Passion for Life), an 83-minute documentary produced by NDR/N3 in 1991, deals with relations between *beurs*, the suburbs of Paris and dormitory towns seen through the eyes of the *beur* film makers of the 1980s, especially Medhi Charef, one of the founders of the movement with his *Le thé au harem d'Archimède*, made in 1984. Others followed the same path: Rachid Bouchareb, Abdelkarim Bahloul and Farid Lahouassa, for instance, described with realism tinged with stinging humour the breakup of family structures, life in the suburbs and the tragedies of everyday racism. Made by Jochen Wolf, *Die Wut zu Leben* was broadcast on 27 April 1991 on NDR, then on 12 December 1992 on Arte.

On the initiative of Jochen Wolf, NDR also showed a series of about 20 long and short *beur* films on N3 between April and September 1991 – the first time this had been done by any European channel.

❸ **3 SAT**, ZDF's satellite cultural channel, scheduled a Yiddish Film Festival between 21 February and 27 March 1992, including documentaries. Yiddish-Polish coproductions were also featured. The emphasis was on anti-Semitism and problems arising from emigration and immigration. The films included: *Es war nicht Spiel, es war Leben* (That wasn't a Game, it was Life), produced by the Moskauer Jüdische Akademische Theater, *Jüdisches Glück* (Jewish Happiness), *Der Dibbuk* and *Tewje, der Milchmann* (Tewje the Milkman).

➤*FREMDE HEIMAT* (Foreign Homeland), broadcast on Remembrance Sunday 17 November 1991 from noon to midnight, was also the idea of Eckart Stein. He explained that the programme was '12 hours about exile, a sort of follow-up to my

Berlin day on the French channel FR 3 on 8 June 1987 and obviously a calling card, a laboratory for the theme days on the European channel Arte...Television is a place of communal remembrance like no other, a multicultural medium in a world where more and more people are living in exile, where every day there are more and more immigrants.' Stein had collected documentaries, films and features, added original material and punctuated the result with three discussion groups entitled *Weggehen* (Leaving), *Dableiben* (Staying) and *Züruckkehren* (Coming Back).

Fremde Heimat was awarded a special Civis Prize in 1992 for its originality and quality.

❹ **OFFENE KANALE**. The German constitution, which guarantees everyone living in Germany freedom of speech, was the foundation for the Offene Kanale (Open Channels) started in 1985. These local radio and television stations were entirely financed from public funds and gave anyone with something to say the chance to express their views on the air.

An Offener Kanal is a sort of free-access community channel designed to encourage the emergence or revival of direct democracy, allow people who are normally excluded from society to have a say and foster dialogue between the various social groups. It has been defined as 'a local broadcaster whose radio and television programmes are not produced and edited by paid staff but are made up of individual contributions from citizens wishing to communicate with their neighbours via the media'. The channel is open first and foremost to people living in the Land in question – which therefore includes immigrants – apart from professional broad-casters, political parties and local authorities.

The open channels are a direct result of the installation of cable networks. The first cities to launch pilot cable projects were Berlin Ludwigshafen/Mannheim, Munich and Dortmund, and the first open channel started in Ludwigshafen on 1 June 1985, followed shortly afterwards by another in Dortmund. As the idea spread, the Federation of Open Channels was established in Bonn. In late 1991 there were eight open radio and television channels in the 11 old Länder and three in the five new Länder.

An open channel is governed by a statute drafted by the regulatory authority of the Land in question, which grants it a radio wavelength or television cable channel available to any person or group of people, either free of charge or in exchange for a contribution to expenses (depending on the particular Land). Fully equipped studios and a team of technicians are provided. There are no editors, no schedules and no directives about the content of the programmes. Advertising is banned. The planning and production of the programme are therefore left entirely in the hands of the person or group responsible. The Offene Kanale are financed from the licence fee through the regulatory authorities of the various Länder.

Let us take the Berlin open channel as an example. With 13 technicians, two studios, three cutting rooms and six mobile units, it broadcasts on cable every day from 4 pm to midnight – more than 87,000 hours in 1992. About 75 per cent of the programmes are not in German, but in Turkish, Serbo-Croat, Pakistani, Sri Lankan and Polish. Despite the way the programmes are split up, the number of viewers can reach 50,000 a day. Director Jurgen Linke said: 'The importance of the Offener Kanal lies mainly in the experience people acquire in becoming the producers of their own programmes while having access to a local communication network'. Since its launch in 1985 the channel had only been taken to court once, he added.

Nonetheless, freedom of speech has its darker side: Turkish Moslem fundamentalists and German neo-Nazis are also allowed to express their views on the open channels, which are on principle not subject to any control.

Several Turkish channels can be received on cable and satellite:

❺ **TRT-INT** (the Turkish state channel) is aimed at Turks living abroad. It broadcasts from 6 pm to midnight on weekdays and from 5 pm to half past midnight at weekends, offering a mix of news, features, music and serials. The channel describes itself as a provider of information rather than entertainment. All programmes are in Turkish, with no subtitles. TRT-Int has been broadcasting since 28 February 1990 via the Eutelsat 1 F4 satellite to all the Länder of the former West Germany and to Berlin, and can also be picked up in Bulgaria, Turkey, Switzerland, Belgium, the Netherlands, Denmark, France and London. At the end of 1991 the channel was granted a licence and its own channel for Germany, on condition that it produced 30 per cent of its programmes there. As the company has no studios abroad, crews are sent from Turkey and the resulting film is edited in Ankara. TRT-Int can be received by 72 per cent of Turkish households in Germany, according to its press office, (50 to 55 per cent, according to the Media Port Berlin survey), 77 per cent by cable (Media Port Berlin says 60 per cent) and 23 per cent by satellite. Eight million German households also have access to the channel.[1]

Apart from the TRT monopoly, several unofficial commercial channels have emerged. The following can be received by cable in Berlin and have a significant audience in the Turkish community:

❻ **TD1** (Türkisch Deutsch 1) has been broadcasting since 1978, starting as a pilot project, and now has the most airtime in Berlin. For a long time its programmes

---

1   A telephone survey conducted by Media Port Berlin between 6 pm and 11.30 pm from 12 to 20 June 1992.

only went out in the evening and were repeated during the morning. Current schedules sometimes include live broadcasts (music, serials, many of which are bought from other Turkish broadcasters, magazines, children's programmes, sport and phone-in programmes). The audience is estimated at 160,000.

❼ ATT (Avrupa Türk Televizyonu), the smallest, also started as a pilot project. It broadcasts for two hours a day (from 4 to 6 pm) on the TD1 channel, offering reports in German and Turkish as well as some pirated programmes. Its own programmes are often of poor quality. ATT relies on advertising for its income and coproduces advertising features with its customers.

❽ BTT (Berlin Türkiyem Televizyonu) From two hours of Turkish programmes a week in November 1986, BTT now puts out six hours a day, mornings and afternoons, and occasionally in the evening. Serials, videoclips and cartoons are the standard fare and the two main presenters are the station's owners.

❾ TFD (Türkisches Fernsehen in Deutschland), launched in 1989, is subsidized by the Islamic organization AMGT, which supports the Turkish Salvation Party. Its programmes are mostly religious and the woman presenter is dressed according to strict Islamic rules. The sociopolitical claims of the broadcasters come through clearly in the way the programmes are written and edited. TFD also offers a review of the Turkish press, satirical features and variety shows. Like the other private channels, it carries a lot of local advertising for Turkish shops and services. TFD and TRT-Int are the only cable channels that enjoy financial security. TFD was planning to start broadcasting by cable to North Rhine-Westphalia in 1993.

Apart from TFD, all the privately owned Turkish channels in Berlin pirate programmes from other broadcasters (about 90 per cent of the music videos, for instance), claiming that this is the only way they can survive.[1]

❿ TELE 10, TELE ON, SHOW TV and TGRT are just four of the ten or so private Turkish channels available by satellite in western Europe. Their viewing figures are believed to be higher than those of the state channel TRT-Int. Their strong point is heavy emphasis on local programmes and relatively little American material. All tastes are catered for, from the kitsch music channel Tele On to the spicier Show TV, popular for its soft porn programmes and quiz shows. The latest of these channels, TGRT, is offering mainstream programmes with a large proportion of religious broadcasts. Available via the Eutelsat 2 F3 since April 1993, it belongs to IHLAS Holding, a financial group based in Istanbul. The company has plans to launch a Turkish satellite.

---

1   Media Port Berlin and the Centre of Turkish Studies of the University of Essen.

4

INITIATIVES

❶ **THE CIVIS PRIZE**, created in Cologne in 1988 and the first of its kind in Europe, is given to radio and television programmes that encourage better understanding between Germans, foreigners and cultural minorities in Germany. It is awarded jointly by the Freudenberg Foundation, the German government's official responsible for matters regarding foreigners and ARD, represented by the regional channel WDR.

In November 1992 the following prizes were awarded: in the news category, *Zum Beispiel Berlin* (Berlin, for instance), produced and broadcast by WDR and made by Felix Kuballa, Gerd Manheim, Yoash Tafari and Peter Schran; in the entertainment and serials category, the report *Junge Ausländer in Deutschland* (Young Foreigners in Germany) made for *100 Grad – das Junge Magazin* (100 Degrees – The Young Magazine) by Ille Simon, produced and broadcast by Rias TV and Deutsche Welle Berlin; in the fiction category, *Ich bin ein Kanake* (I am a Kanak) by Thomas Draeger, one of the films for children in the *Karfunkel* series on ZDF. A special prize was awarded to the *Fremde Heimat* (Foreign Homeland) theme day, made by the staff of ZDF's *Das Kleine Fernsehspiel* and broadcast on 3 SAT on 17 November 1991.

In November 1993 the jury, chaired by writer and film director Ralph Giordano, awarded the following prizes: in the news category, *Heiterblick, Roma in Sachsen* (Romanies in Saxony), made by Kerstin Mempel, produced and broadcast by MDR on 12 March 1993; in the entertainment category, *Scheibenwischer* (Windscreen Wiper), a humorous, sarcastic programme produced by SFB, written and directed by Dieter Hildebrandt, and two series of 50-second anti-racist spots, *Wie gegen Rassismus* and *Kumpel Anton*, shown daily on RTL since December 1992. Special prizes went to WDR for the documentary *Wer Gewält sät ... Von Brandstiftern und Biedermännern* (On Fires and Gentlemen), made by Gert Monheim after the arson attacks at Rostock in which foreigners were killed (broadcast on 28 January 1993), and to ARD for *Kommentare zum Brandanschlag in Solingen*, a discussion about a similar attack in Solingen between Fritz Pleitgen, Klauz Bednarz and Aysim Alpman of WDR and Georg Hafner of HR.

❷ **TV SPOTS**. Hessischer Rundfunk decided to broadcast a series of spots on 23 October 1991 during the programme *Holgers Waschsalon*, under the patronage of Cornelia Schmalz-Jacobsen, the government official for matters concerning foreigners. The spots, on the theme 'Xenophobia, not here' and lasting approximately 35 seconds, were made by four Frankfurt advertising agencies (Young and Rubicam, Saatchi and Saatchi, Ogilvy and Mather, and Leipziger and Partner). The slogans included: 'In 178 countries, we Germans are foreigners. Let's not act as if we were alone in the world', 'Foreigners out?', 'Stop race hatred', 'Germany: no place for hatred and violence; Germany: a place for people?', 'Xenophobia, not here', 'You're not a foreigner? Then maybe it's you we're after: People who wear glasses out! Left-handers out! Fat people out!' The spots were broadcast on the third channel, ARD and ZDF, between 8 November 1991 and 3 February 1992 and the campaign ended with a special programme on Hessischer Rundfunk, *Mob gestoppt?* (Has Race Hatred Been Stopped?).

All the media (television, radio, the press and a poster campaign) took part in the operation, which was run by Daniel Cohn-Bendit in Frankfurt and in about 230 other major German cities. Among the political parties, trade unions and companies that offered support were the Social Democratic and Free Democratic groups in Parliament, the ecologists, the IG Metall union, the DGB union, the Hesse Land authority and the Agrippina insurance group.

Reactions to the campaign were many and varied. Philippe Dewitte, editor of *Hommes et Migrations*, described it as: 'An extremely violent advertising campaign, run along the same lines as what it is supposed to be attacking, sometimes playing on people's guilt, and which leaves one wondering if, in the end, it may not be double edged.'[1]

The idea of television advertising spots was taken up by several channels, both public and private. ARD's Berlin channel, SFB, broadcast a series of extremely caustic spots, especially during its programmes for young people, which attracted a lot of attention. RTL, which has broken all audience records in Germany, launched its own campaign in November 1992. This included the showing three times a day from 3 December of 50-second anti-racist spots ordered from various German advertising agencies with the backing of the Artistic Directors' Club and the communications union BDW. This campaign, convincing in its call for tolerance and not without humour, was broadcast throughout 1993 and received a Civis Prize.

SFB also put out a series of spots making scathing attacks on racism in its young people's programme *Moskito*. One of these, a two-and-a-half minute film called 'Letter to a Skinhead', about a skinhead who gets into trouble with his guardian angel, was taken up by several foreign channels.

❸ **EUROPA TOLERANCE**, a television prize against racism, was organized by the Council of Europe and the ARD regional channel Südwestfunk in Baden-Baden. Open to both amateur and professional film makers, it was to be awarded in October 1994 to the best video about violence against foreigners and minorities. The films, seeking to further tolerance and no more than three minutes long, had to be

---

1   *Hommes et Migrations*, No. 1151, February–March 1992.

understandable without translation within Europe. They were to be judged on their originality, power of persuasion and technical quality by an international jury of media professionals. The award, intended to make people aware of the problems of racism, paved the way for a campaign against intolerance launched in December 1994. Thirty-two Council of Europe member states supported the campaign at the Vienna summit in October 1993.

HUNGARY

Total population (on 1/1/91):
10,365,000

Foreign population:
123,000
1.2 per cent of the total population

Distribution by country of origin:
The number of Romanies is estimated
at 500,000. Other figures not
available.

Sources: INED, *Population et Sociétés*,
No. 261, October 1991; SOPEMI,
Trends in International Migration,
Paris, OECD, 1992.

Children of Apocalypse. Photo: Hunnia Filmstúdió

HUNGARY

1

IMMIGRATION HISTORY

The division of Europe after the First World War under the terms of the Treaty of Trianon reduced Hungary to two-thirds of its former size, leaving Hungarian minorities in Czechoslovakia, Romania (Transylvania), Yugoslavia, Ukraine and even Austria. These communities have been integrated to varying degrees, as can be seen from Hungary's current tense relations with Romania or the problems suffered by the Hungarian minority in the Balkans conflict. About 3.5 million ethnic Hungarians live in neighbouring countries.

The 1956 crisis led to two waves of Hungarians fleeing the country: the first after the uprising of October 1956, the second after the Soviet invasion that quelled the revolt a month later. Many refugees went to the United States and Canada; next popular were Germany and Austria, with which Hungary has historic ties.

Following the collapse of communism in 1989, Hungary opened its borders to the west and lifted the restrictions on people entering and leaving the country. Those who have chosen to emigrate recently – mainly to the OECD countries – have done so for a mixture of economic, ethnic and political reasons. Meanwhile, people of other nationalities have been coming to Hungary for a variety of reasons: East Germans and Romanians seeking a better life, refugees fleeing the Balkans conflict, citizens of the former Soviet Union, Hungarians returning from Ukraine and Hungarians who had earlier left the country for political reasons. Moreover, there has been an increase in the number of transmigrants on their way to western Europe. The Hungarian government is thinking of closing its borders to all its East European neighbours, especially Romania (the two populations are strongly interwoven).

With rising unemployment, immigration has led to growing tension among Hungarians. An immigration committee set up in August 1991 was asked to make policy recommendations and draft a law on cultural integration, education and social services for immigrants.

In 1993, after long discussions between the six parliamentary groups, the Minorities Bill was finally drawn up. It has a strategic purpose: to set an example to other countries, given the large numbers of Hungarians living abroad. It is important to point out that the bill was the idea of the authorities rather than the result of pressure from minority groups themselves, who, on the contrary, seem reticent about having a status that sets them apart. The bill gives far-reaching powers to local authorities because most minorities live in small towns and villages. They already have the right to be taught in their own language and to use it in dealings with the local authorities. A joint national body to represent minorities is also planned, to be known as the Minorities Assembly. The bill, which has not yet been voted on by parliament, comes up against two major problems: first, it is based on the principle of uniting minorities at national level when in fact they are scattered all over the country, and second, the budget of 2 million forints is not enough to carry through the government's undertakings.

'Act Against Hatred', an organization set up in 1992 along the lines of SOS Racisme in France, is gaining ground in Hungary. By the end of 1993, more than 300,000 people had signed the organization's appeal for a society free of exclusion. According to the movement's leaders, the main problem in Hungary is neither racism nor anti-Semitism, but the social exclusion of Romanies, the disabled and the unemployed.

The 12 officially recognized ethnic minorities make up 10 per cent of the population at most. In descending order of size, they are Romanies, Germans, Slovaks (100,000), Croats, Romanians (25,000), Poles, Serbs, Slovenians, Greeks, Bulgarians (3,000), Armenians (3,000) and Ruthenians.

2

THE BROADCASTING SCENE

Even before the demise of communism in 1989, Hungarian broadcasting had witnessed major upheavals due to the changing political landscape. As early as 1987 foreign satellite channels were authorized and major cities were being cabled.

In July 1989 the government, in agreement with the opposition, introduced a moratorium on broadcasting and ruled that new laws should be drafted. However the moratorium only covered land-based broadcasting, so it did not prevent the launch on 11 October 1992 of the country's first satellite channel, Duna 7, which is aimed at Hungarians abroad.

The broadcasting deadlock was finally broken in July 1993, when a law on local frequencies was adopted by the government on the basis of a Press Law dating from 1986, and bids were called for. A committee was set up by the Ministry of Culture and Education to decide which companies would be granted six-year licences. Preference is to be given to those that broadcast programmes produced locally, and foreign participation is limited to 49 per cent.

A recent national survey showed that 55 per cent of Hungarians own a television set and can pick up foreign programmes.

Public channels

MTV (Magyar televizio) has two national channels. In 1992 its budget was divided between licence fees (60 per cent), advertising (25 per cent) and state subsidies (15 per cent). In 1993/94, 50 per cent of revenue came from advertising. As it seems likely that the two channels will be privatized, they are already competing for viewers. Each has its own advertising department. Foreigners keen to launch other channels have already come forward. In addition to the big European names (the French companies Hersant and Bouygues, Germany's Bertelsmann group and Italy's Silvio Berlusconi), Britain's London Weekend Television has put in a bid.

The law is expected to lay down quotas for programmes of Hungarian origin and for cultural broadcasts.

❶ **MTV First Channel**, formerly known as MTV1, was started in 1953 and broadcasts 14 hours a day. Its schedule is aimed at a wider audience than that of its sister channel. In 1991, news and news magazines occupied 31 per cent of airtime, fiction 18 per cent, cultural programmes 13 per cent and children's programmes 11 per cent.

❷ **MTV Second Channel**, formerly known as MTV2, was launched in 1965 and broadcasts 12 hours a day. From 6 am to 9 am, its frequency is used by a private television company, Nap- TV ('nap' means sun), which only offers foreign programmes. The Second Channel's own schedule includes news and news magazines (25 per cent), fiction (20 per cent), sport (11 per cent – more than MTV First Channel), cultural programmes (11 per cent), music (9 per cent), variety programmes (7 per cent) and children's programmes (6 per cent).

The public channels estimate that their audience is divided 66 per cent/34 per cent in favour of MTV First Channel. Hungarian Gallup, which takes account of all the channels available, puts the figures at 53 per cent for MTV First Channel, 30 per cent for MTV Second Channel and the remainder for foreign channels picked up by satellite.

Private channels

❶ **NAP-TV** broadcasts each morning on MTV Second Channel's frequency as a sort of warm-up for the privatization of the state channel. Launched in 1989, it is 50 per cent owned by the Rupert Murdoch group and only broadcasts to the Budapest region.

Since the summer of 1989, another private channel, run by Hungarians, has been broadcasting in the Lake Balaton region. Originally known as Balaton Channel, it has since been renamed Siofok TV.

Hungary's 800,000 or so cable subscribers receive an average of eight to twelve channels. These include local channels financed by city authorities and foreign channels (such as Superchannel, MTV Europe, TV5, CNN and RTL Plus). Kabelcom, a company owned by United International Holdings, a Hungarian group, and the American group Time Warner, has been responsible for the rapid spread of cable. In 1991 Kabelcom became central Europe's first encoded channel, offering three films every evening.

3

CHANNEL POLICIES

Broadcasting was one of the priorities for the government that came into power in May 1990. The bill drawn up in December 1991, which lays down fundamental regulations governing public service television, states in article 12: 'Public broadcasters are required to inform viewers in a full, regular and objective manner about external and internal events that are worthy of interest ... They are required to put forward a range of viewpoints, include those of minorities.' Article 13 states:

> The programmes provided by public broadcasters must respond to the needs of viewers living in the reception area by making available information with a view to education and training useful to the public, by showing cultural values and artistic work, by publicizing scientific results ... Particular attention should be paid to Hungarian and universal cultural values and to the cultural values of national and ethnic minorities living in Hungary. Public broadcasters are required to broadcast regularly in their reception area programmes in the languages of national and ethnic minorities. Public broadcasters should provide ample airtime for religious communities.

185

Hungarian minorities living in neighbouring countries near the border are able to pick up the First Channel. Since October 1992, those able to receive cable or satellite broadcasts have also been able to watch Duna 7, the Hungarian satellite channel launched and financed by the Hungarian Television Foundation, a private cultural organization entirely funded by the government. However, very few expatriates have access to cable networks or dish aerials, whereas in Hungary some 800,000 households are cabled, so the future of Duna 7 would appear to lie within rather than outside the country's borders (Yves-Michel Riols, *Le Monde*, 24 November 1992).

Magazine programmes for immigrants

❶ **MTV Second Channel** broadcasts programmes intended for Hungary's Serb, Croat, Slovenian, Slovak, German, Romanian and Romany minorities, all including a news section as well as cultural features. The focus is on the lives of minorities in Hungary rather than on what is happening in their countries of origin. The programmes are made in Hungary and each magazine has its own production crew composed of both Hungarians and professionals from the minorities concerned.

The weekly, fortnightly or monthly broadcasts last 25 minutes and go out on Saturday mornings between 9 and 11.30. All are made in the relevant minority language with Hungarian subtitles. Most are produced in Hungarian television's regional studios in the south and west of the country – areas that have the highest concentration of minorities. The exceptions are the Serb and Romany magazines, which are made directly by Hungarian television's minorities programme department (KKMI).

➤*HRVATSKA KRONIKA* is a weekly magazine for the Croat minority, produced by the regional studios in Pecs, southwest Hungary. It is made up of several regular features, including a newscast, and reports on topics such as architecture, music and literature.

➤*SRPSKI EKRAN* (Serb Screen) is a similar magazine produced for Serbs by the KKMI. It has been broadcast fortnightly since September 1992.

➤*SLOVENSKI UTRINKI* (Slovenian Screen), for Slovenians, has been broadcast fortnightly since 1 May 1992. It is produced by the regional studios in Szeged, southern Hungary.

From 1978 to 1992, a single programme entitled *Del-Szlav Magazin* (South Slav Magazine) was produced for the three above groups.

➤*NAŠA OBRAZOVKA* (Our Screen) is a weekly magazine for Slovaks started in 1982. Produced by the Szeged studios, it includes features, cultural news and folk song and dance, all introduced by a female presenter.

➤*ECRANUL NOSTRU* (Our Screen), the Romanians' weekly magazine, is also produced by the Szeged studios. It has been on the air since 1981. In 1992 its audience was estimated at two million (the Romanian minority in Hungary plus inhabitants of the area near the border with Romania).

➤*CIGÁNY MAGAZIN*, for Romanies, has been produced by the KKMI since 1 September 1992. The programme has had a new title since the start of 1993, *Patrin – üzenet – Vorba*. All three words mean message: Patrin and Vorba in different dialects of the Romany language and üzenet in Hungarian.

➤*UNSERE BILDSCHIRM* (Our Screen), the German minority's magazine since 1978, is produced by the regional studios in Pecs.

➤*DREHSCHEIBE EUROPA* (European Revolving Stage) is a 30-minute programme produced by Deutsche Welle and broadcast once a fortnight. Aimed at German-speaking communities throughout Europe, it was broadcast on MTV First Channel until 31 May 1992. The programme is off the air at the moment but is expected to return on the Second Channel in its original format – in German with Hungarian subtitles.

➤*RONDO* is a new half-hour magazine launched in January 1994. Broadcast on Saturdays at 10.30 am, it is intended for Hungary's Greek, Polish, Bulgarian, Ruthenian and Armenian minorities. Short reports feature each group in turn.

Mainstream programmes

Some programmes have started to deal regularly with the problems faced by minorities and foreigners, from different points of view. A few are listed below.

➤*ALPOK-ADRIA MAGAZIN* (Adriatic Alps) is a 20-minute magazine in Hungarian broadcast on alternate Sundays by MTV Second Channel. The programmes are put together by an editorial committee of representatives from the public television companies of Italy, Austria, Croatia, Slovenia and Hungary. At meetings held every three months, the committee selects which of the wide range of features submitted by the different national companies are to be used in the magazine. It is not intended specifically for minorities.

➤*HÖMERÖ* (Thermometer), an MTV First Channel programme produced and presented by Henrik Havas, looks at topical social and political issues. It goes out on Saturdays from 3 pm to 4 pm. The theme of the first broadcast on 21 March 1992 was foreigners living in Hungary and people wishing to enter the country. In the studio to discuss the subject were István Morvai, secretary of state at the interior ministry, Marton Ill, director of the Martin Luther King Association, Ferenc Kúnszabó, author and editor of the right-wing weekly *Hunnia Journal*, Pal Bodor, chairman of the Hungarian Journalists' Association, Lajos Tamás, who works for the minorities section of the Fidesz (young democrats') party, Boldizsár Nagy, a jurist specializing in international issues, Endre Sik, who works for the Institute of Political Science, and foreign students living in Hungary. The debate covered the current situtation, legislation, refugees, what laws should be introduced, the status of foreign students, xenophobia, immigrant workers, and so on. Other guests were invited to comment on the points of view put forward.

➤*CHILDREN OF THE APOCALYPSE*, a documentary in two hour-long parts, traces the wanderings of two young musicians fleeing the former Soviet Union. In Budapest, Yuri meets an English girl, Maggie, and goes to live with her in England. They have a child and plan to move to another country. Sergei stays in Budapest and marries a Hungarian woman. The documentary shows two young men attracted by western Europe, trying to escape from poverty, but it is also the story of many young people at a crucial moment in their history, the collapse of the communist world, with Hungary at the crossroads where the two civilizations meet. *Children of the Apocalypse* was made by Ibolya Fekete and coproduced by Hunnia Filmstudio, an independent company, and MTV. It was shown in 1991 and 1992 on the Second Channel.

➤*HABORÙ* (War), a 27-minute documentary broadcast on 29 January 1992 on the Second Channel, shows the current tension between foreign minorities and the extreme right. Produced and directed by Mihaly Gaal-Kovacs, it took as its starting point a fight between skinheads and black students living in Hungary at the Kobanya-Kispest underground station in Budapest. Such clashes have become increasingly common, but it was the first time a black student had been killed. The events added to the spiral of violence as the students planned self-defence while the skinheads prepared for revenge.

ITALY

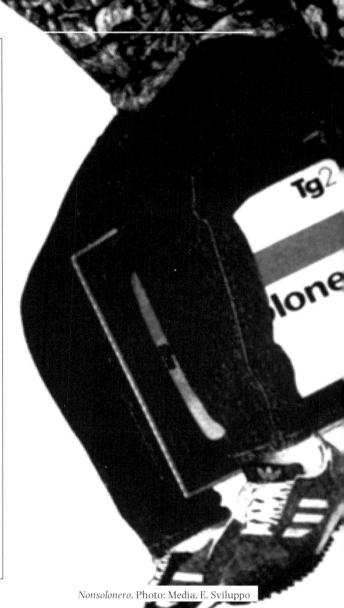

Total population (on 1/1/92):
56,859,000

Foreign population:
896,800
1.58 per cent of the total population

Distribution by country of origin:

Morocco	90,600
United States of America	60,900
Tunisia	47,600
Philippines	41,100
Germany	40,300
Former Yugoslavia	34,700
United Kingdom	27,900
Senegal	27,800
Albania	27,000
France	25,100
Egypt	22,700
China	22,000
Poland	19,300
Switzerland	18,700
Greece	17,500
Brazil	17,300
Argentina	15,100
Spain	14,700
Romania	14,000
Sri Lanka	13,900
Ghana	12,900

Sources: Presidenza del Consiglio dei Ministri – Osservatorio Immigrazione; SOPEMI, *Trends in International Migration*, Paris, OECD, 1993 (based on Italian Interior Ministry figures).

Nonsolonero. Photo: Media, E. Sviluppo

ITALY

1

IMMIGRATION HISTORY

Between the late 19th century and the start of the Second World War, some 26 million Italians crossed the Atlantic to try their luck in the United States. Since then many more have emigrated to other parts of Europe, causing scars in the national psyche that linger today, especially in southern Italy. The 1950s saw an internal population shift – the migration of southerners to seek work in the more prosperous north.

Italians are used to having large numbers of foreigners in their country, both because of the strong tourist tradition and because Italy's geographical position makes it an obvious staging post.[1] It was only from the 1970s that foreigners with more meagre resources began to be noticeable in Italian society.

Immigration by people from the south and south-east Mediterranean and from African countries like Senegal and Mali was not the result of the labour needs of major industry. They came seeking seasonal work in agriculture and small factories: temporary or part-time jobs in the informal economy which resulted in a wave of illegal immigrants.

Between 1989 and 1990, the number of foreigners with a residence permit practically doubled. In December 1989 the government decided to grant working papers to 223,000 illegal immigrants from outside the EU, allowing them to register as job hunters. The main nationalities that benefited from the move were Moroccans (50,000), Tunisians (29,000), Senegalese (17,000), Filipinos (14,000), Yugoslavs (12,000), Chinese (10,000), Egyptians (7,500), Ghanaians (6,500), Poles (5,500), Bangladeshis (3,500) and Pakistanis (3,200).

---

1 Perotti, Antonio, & Thépaut, France, 'Les Caractéristiques du débat sur l'immigration dans le contexte italien: Revue de presse', *Migrations-Société*, 11, September/October 1990.

The decree of 30 December 1989, which sanctioned the permits, passed into law on 28 February 1990. Known as the Martelli law (its sponsor, Claudio Martelli, was then deputy prime minister), it also established emergency measures covering requests for political asylum and regulating the entry and residence rights of people from outside the EU. The biggest operation of its kind in Europe for 20 years, the law launched a major debate in the media which soon spread throughout the country, just as regionalist movements like Umberto Bossi's Northern League were starting up.

In 1991, with the collapse of the totalitarian regime in Albania imminent, Italy was confronted with a sudden influx of Albanian refugees. Many had been attracted by the image of a well-off and welcoming Italy projected by Italian television.

The 1992 elections led to the abolition of the Immigration Ministry. On 15 December 1992, following a wave of racist and anti-Semitic attacks in several central and northern cities, the Cabinet approved a decree making the perpetrators of racist and anti-Semitic acts liable to the same penalties as mafiosi and terrorists. The decree, aimed in particular at members of skinhead gangs, punished racist propaganda with prison sentences of from two to six years.

Meanwhile, a new immigration bill is being prepared on the initiative of the authorities in major cities like Rome, Milan, Bologna and Genoa. It would make it easier to expel illegal immigrants, introduce a new type of work contract for seasonal and temporary jobs and bring in a series of measures to help legal immigrants, especially concerning education, health and social security.

Some local officials are calling for a further, restricted, amnesty for illegal immigrants in regular employment. In June 1993 a statutory order was issued allowing immigrant workers to enter the country for seasonal work for a maximum period of six months.

It should be stressed that in Italy it is often the local authorities who are responsible for dealing with immigrants. Several regions, enjoying a large degree of autonomy from the central government, have introduced their own programmes setting up reception centres and other services for foreigners. But the most effective work is probably being done by volunteers, and the role of the Roman Catholic Church is also important.

According to the head of the Roman Catholic organization Caritas, Monsignor Luigi di Liegro, it was because of a restrictive interpretation of the Martelli law, which was intended to stem the flow of immigration, that Rome filled up with Asians, Africans and East Europeans who were *forced* into a position of illegality. Current data show that there are some 800,000 immigrant workers in the Italian capital with valid working papers; to this figure should be added between 200,000 and 800,000 illegal workers.

Meanwhile tighter border controls in France and Germany, as well as European citizenship policy, have prompted Italy to toughen its immigration policy, especially on obtaining an Italian passport. Applicants now have to have lived in the country for ten years, compared to only five years previously.

At the same time, violence against immigrants has been rising and there have been an increasing number of attacks on immigrant hostels. This mounting aggression coincided with the spectacular collapse of the Christian Democrats and the Socialist Party in 1993 in favour of the neofascist Italian Social Movement and the federalist Northern League. In 1994 the general election was won by Freedom Alliance, a right-wing coalition of media magnate Silvio Berlusconi's Forza Italia, the Northern League and the National Alliance.

2

THE BROADCASTING SCENE

The arrival in power of Silvio Berlusconi led to severe upsets in the operation of public service television. The new prime minister, owner of the most powerful communications group in Italy, selected most members of his government from his former colleagues at Fininvest. One of the new government's first acts, in July 1994, was to refuse to approve the RAI's provisional budget for 1995, combined with a plan designed to help Italian public television out of its current financial difficulties. This led to the resignation of the RAI directors, who were immediately replaced by a new set close to the majority. Against this tense background, it is impossible to predict what direction public television is liable to take. Rumours abound, one being that the RAI's three channels would be restructured according to three distinct themes. Whatever the truth of this, the situation is unlikely to become clear during 1995, due to the fall of Berlusconi's precarious coalition government.

Italy was the first European country to witness the appearance of private television on a massive scale: the number of stations peaked in 1981. After this unsettled period, the media scene seems to have been stablilized by the Mammi law of August 1990, which officially recognized the public channels of the RAI on the one hand and the private channels run by Silvio Berlusconi (Italy's prime minister from May to December 1994) and his company Fininvest on the other. Italy now has 12 national channels (three of them state-run) and 831 local television stations.

Public channels

The RAI (Radio Audizioni Italia), the state-run radio and television authority, has three channels financed mainly from the licence fee.

❶ **RAI 1**, launched in 1954, broadcasts 18 hours a day. Like RAI 2, it has managed to boost its viewing figures through shrewd scheduling policies concentrating on broadening its appeal, despite competition from the private channels. Of the 7,000 hours of programmes broadcast in 1991, 26 per cent were devoted to news and sport. Next most important were quiz and game shows (15 per cent), films (12 per cent) and made-for-television films (10 per cent).

In 1991 RAI 1 was Italy's most popular channel, attracting 22 per cent of the total audience. In May 1992 the figure had slipped to 18 per cent.

❷ **RAI 2**, started in 1961, is also a mainstream channel but has a stronger identity than RAI 1. Broadcasting 17 hours a day, it offers mainly fiction (26 per cent) and films (17 per cent), as well as news (12 per cent), quiz and game shows (8 per cent) and sport (7 per cent). In 1991 RAI 2 broadcast a total of 7,117 hours and its market share was 19 per cent.

❸ **RAI 3**, both a national and a regional channel, came on the scene in 1979. It broadcasts 13 hours a day (a total of 5,452 hours in 1991), offering films (18 per cent), sport (17 per cent), news (16 per cent), quiz and game shows (10 per cent) and documentaries (10 per cent).

RAI 3 has the smallest audience of Italy's six main channels: 8.9 per cent of market share in 1991 (8.5 per cent in June 1992).

Private channels

Nine privately owned television channels are authorized to broadcast nationally, including the three biggest Fininvest channels, Canale 5, Italia 1 and Rete 4 – collectively known as Rete Italia.

❶ **CANALE 5**, launched by Berlusconi in 1980, broadcasts 20 hours a day (7,900 hours in 1991). Its schedules concentrate on fiction, which takes up more than a third of airtime in the form of films, made-for-television films, soaps, serials and cartoons. The channel also features variety programmes (20 per cent), quiz and game shows (16 per cent) and news (17 per cent).

Canale 5 was Italy's third most popular channel in 1991, with 16.5 per cent of the total audience, and looks set to overtake its state-sector rivals soon.

❷ **ITALIA 1** was sold to Fininvest by the Rusconi publishing group in 1983. It places even more emphasis on fiction than Canale 5, devoting three-fifths of its schedule to films, made-for-television films and cartoons. News (13 per cent), sport (8 per cent) and variety programmes (7 per cent) fill the rest. Broadcasting 8,700 hours a year, Italia 1 attracted 11 per cent of market share in 1991 and 13 per cent in June 1992.

❸ **RETE 4** was taken over from the Mondadori publishing group in 1984. It broadcasts 7,700 hours a year, also with a heavy bias towards fiction. Its speciality is Brazilian soaps (*telenovelas*), which occupy 42 per cent of the schedule. Other programmes include films (19 per cent), made-for-television films (15 per cent), variety programmes (8 per cent) and news (7 per cent). In 1991 Rete 4 had 10.5 per cent of the total audience (12.6 per cent in June 1992).

Three other authorized private channels try to compete with the Fininvest channels, but it is an unequal struggle. Videomusic shows mostly videoclips, Rete A concentrates on soaps and serials, while Tele Monte-Carlo specializes in sport. There are also three pay channels, Telepiú 1, 2 and 3, which at the moment are controlled by Fininvest.

3

CHANNEL POLICIES

Magazine programmes for immigrants

❶ **RAI 2**. *Nonsolonero*, linked to RAI 2's news department and broadcast by the channel, was the first and only programme devoted entirely to the problem of helping immigrants settle into Italian society. Started in 1988 for a two-month trial period, it was decided to continue the programme after a survey by the Auditel company showed that its audience had peaked at 5 million viewers (the average was 33 per cent). Until October 1991, *Nonsolonero* was broadcast on Sundays at 1.30 pm, just after the lunchtime newscast; subsequently it went out at the same time on Thursdays. In 1993, the programme did not start up again in October as planned. It was only in mid-March 1994 that *Nonsolonero* came back on the air, running until mid-June. The magazine was produced by a smaller team and was broadcast at 5 pm on Thursdays.

According to the head of RAI 2's news department, all the additional programmes that came under its wing, such as *Nonsolonero*, were being scrapped from September 1994 and would not be replaced. The reason given is that such initiatives are now out of date. But as xenophobia becomes an increasingly acute problem in Italy, does this mean that public service television has lost interest in the subject?

➤*NONSOLONERO* (Not Only Black), was a 15-minute weekly programme initially intended to deal with problems between developed and developing countries. Growing hostility towards foreigners influenced the content of the magazine, which subsequently turned its attention to the theme of immigration and racism, looked at from an analytical viewpoint. No particular type of audience was targeted; rather it was hoped that a broad range of Italians would be made aware of the issues at stake. *Nonsolonero*'s main objective was not to provide information that might be useful to immigrants but to involve as many viewers as possible in the debate on interethnic cohabitation while giving an accurate reflection of society and relations with different cultures.

The decision to have a Cape Verdean woman introduce the programme was significant: she had a multiple role in helping to produce the magazine and acting as a mediator – as regards both image and content – between the Italian public and immigrant communities. She also happened to be the first black woman programme presenter in Italy.

Each edition of *Nonsolonero* was made up of several reports, either on general topics or relating to a recent event, plus a regular feature acting as backup to the main theme, a news bulletin, a culture and music slot and a feature on the latest books concerned with immigration and racism. Priority was given to aspects of the subject that are neglected in regular news programmes and aspects that were liable to be distorted or that tended to get lost in news stories. Experts on immigration issues and immigrant communities themselves were consulted by the programme's editors in deciding which subjects should be covered in greater depth.

The way the various sequences were filmed took advertising spots as its model, deliberately putting across a series of brief, concise messages. The reason for this was not just that time was restricted, but also in order to capture and hold the viewer's attention and to make the maximum impact. The programme's slogan, 'Let's get to know them', emphasized the cultural contributions made by immigrant communities.

The main themes during the 1990-91 season were the social and cultural lives of foreigners in addition to their basic rights to housing, employment, and physical and moral integrity. Of the 42 reports broadcast during 30 programmes, most were concerned with the Arab world: covering both the lives of immigrants in Italy and the situation in their countries of origin. Part of the reason was the events leading up to and following the Gulf War, which gave rise to increased hostility and wariness towards people of Arab origin. Other topics included foreigners' housing problems, discrimination and violence, employment (reports on people who had found work, either in Italy or abroad, with special emphasis on jobs for women), education for children of foreign origin (mixed schooling and experiments in intercultural teaching methods in a few Italian and European schools), immigration from Eastern Europe (the most controversial and problematic being from Albania) and the treatment of immigrants and refugees arriving in Italy. Although only three features were devoted to sport and entertainment, these took up a fair proportion of airtime (one was about modern African music). Life in Italy was obviously mentioned a great deal (especially urban areas where the problems facing immigrants are most acute), but there were also many references to a wider European context.[1]

Nonsolonero's audience often reached 35 per cent of viewers each week (an average of five million people), making it one of the most popular television magazines in Italy. Its success meant that the producers received many telephone calls from immigrants seeking practical advice.

Mainstream programmes

The issue of immigration quite often crops up in news and general-interest magazines.

➤*SAMARCANDA* (Samarkand) takes its title from the city in Uzbekistan, an important stopping-place on the Silk Route, where people of several different races and religions meet and mingle. This current-affairs magazine, broadcast by RAI 3 at 8.30 pm on Thursdays, has shown several reports on illegal immigration since it started in 1986. *Samarcanda* sometimes attracts five million viewers and between November 1991 and May 1992 clocked up 19 per cent of audience share. Each programme lasts three hours and is made up of filmed reports, studio debates and live link-ups with outside locations. In 1991 the question of immigration came up four times, including reports two weeks running on Albanians in the Adriatic city of Bari and a discussion with former immigration minister Margherita Boniver. In 1992 the programme tackled the issues of immigrant workers in southern Italy and racism in poorer parts of the region. *Samarcanda* unfortunately went off the air in 1993 after the programme manager resigned.

➤*MIXER*, RAI 2's popular wraparound news magazine, has been running for ten years. It includes live interviews, reports on current events and impressive documentaries and specials. Documents dealing with racism and immigration are regularly presented in the magazine, which is on the air every week in different time slots including prime time, and in various formats.

---

1   Marinella Belluati. *Immagini di immigrazione. L'informazione giornalistica sui rapporti interetnici.* (Thesis for the Faculty of Political Science, University of Turin, directed by Professor Carlo Marletti.)

➤*IL CORAGGIO DE VIVERE* (The Courage to Live), a weekly magazine broadcast by RAI 2, concentrates on problems in Italian society. Launched in February 1991 and initially broadcast from 10.15 pm to 11.30 pm as part of a Saturday night variety show, the programme was favourably received by viewers, with an average audience of 2.5 million. On 17, 18 and 19 April 1992, the channel started a special feature, *Sessantadue ore per la vita* (Sixty-two Hours For Life), in which people facing a daily struggle against illness, violence and social exclusion speak out and share their experiences. The 24 February 1992 edition, alternating filmed reports and studio debate, was devoted to the living conditions of immigrants in southern Italy.

➤*PUMMARO*, the first full-length film dealing with the issue of immigration in Italy, was coproduced in 1989-90. The title comes from the Neapolitan dialect word for tomato. Directed by actor Michele Placido, the film was on the cinema circuit for a short time in September 1990 and broadcast on RAI 2 in the autumn of the following year. It tells the story of a young Ghanaian, just out of medical school, who goes to Italy to look for his long-lost brother. His journey begins in the south of the country where, like many immigrants, he finds work picking tomatoes.

Local channels

❶ **TELEREGIONE**, a Rome local channel, has been showing a weekly 50-minute programme, *Una strada a colori* (Street of Many Colours), at 8.40 pm on Wednesdays since 1990. The magazine is composed of two or three reports introduced by a Filipina presenter speaking Italian. A popular Italian journalist, Carlo Mazzarilla, often adds his own comments. The topics covered are of direct concern to foreigners: legal problems, education, health and women's issues.

❷ **ANTENNA VESUVIO**, the Neapolitan local channel, broadcasts a 30-minute news programme in English, French, Arabic and Spanish, *Bianco, nero e a colori* (Black, White and in Colour). On the air since 1991, the programme goes out live at 9.30 pm on Wednesdays and is repeated on two other weekday evenings at 11.30 pm.

4

INITIATIVES

❶ **THE NONSOLONERO FESTIVAL** is organized annually with the association Medias by Massimo Ghirelli, one of the team in charge of the magazine. It has been held in Rome and Milan since 1989. He presents an international selection of video programmes made by television channels or independent producers and chosen according to themes discussed during roundtables.

For example the fourth festival, held in Milan from 22 to 26 June 1992, dealt with the following themes: North Africa in Italy, the courage of being a woman, the colour of children, identity on paper, immigrants arriving in big cities, cities as the crossroads between Utopia and violence. The films chosen to illustrate them came from Italy, Tunisia, Senegal and Morocco. The festival also offers participants the opportunity to discover cooking from North and sub-Saharan Africa, China and the Philippines.

In 1994, on account of the political upheavals in Italy and the difficulties faced by *Nonsolonero* magazine, a scaled-down version of the festival was held in Milan in June.

❷ **CONFERENCE ON JOURNALISTS AND THE NEWS. COMMUNICATION ACROSS THE MEDITERRANEAN** was organized by Arci Cultura e Sviluppo and sponsored by the Italian foreign ministry. It took place in Rome on 30 June and 1 July 1992. The aim of the conference was to bring together communications experts from Europe, North Africa and the Middle East in order to find practical opportunities for professional exchanges between the two sides of the Mediterranean and to offer fresh proposals for cooperation in the news sector. One of the themes of the second day, in a roundtable chaired by Massimo Ghirelli, looked at possibilities for television cooperation in the region. Those taking part included Vittorio Panchetti, the RAI's director of international relations, Belhacene Zerouki, head of Algerian public television (ENTV), Kamel Cherif, head of international relations with Tunisian radio and television (RTT), Mohamed Tricha, head of Moroccan radio and television (RTM), and film director Gillo Pontecorvo.

❸ **GUARDANDO ALL'ITALIA: INFLUENZA DELLE TV E DELLE RADIO ITALIANE SULL'ESODO DEGLI ALBANESI** (Looking at Italy: the influence of Italian radio and television on the flight from Albania) is a book published by the RAI in 1991 and edited by Piero Dorfles with the assistance of Giovanna Gatteschi. Through a combination of investigative journalism and sociological research carried out by the RAI's public opinion service, it sought to determine to what extent the flight of Albanians to Italy was the result of the image of Italian society conveyed by radio and television in the previous few years, and to what extent this image corresponded to reality.

❹ **THE FESTIVAL DEI POPOLI** in Florence (International film festival of social documentaries), which covers political, social and anthropological topics, devoted its anthropological section to immigration in 1993.

THE NETHERLANDS

Total population (on 1/1/92):
15,184,000

Foreign population:
732,900*
4.8 per cent of the total population

Distribution by country of origin:

Turkey	214,800
Morocco	163,700
Germany	46,900
United Kingdom*	41,800
Belgium	23,900
Italy	17,200
Spain	16,900
Former Yugoslavia	15,100
Indonesia	8,509
Portugal	8,700
China	6,540
Ghana	5,214
Vietnam	5,127
Greece	5,200

* Including Hong Kong.
There are 228,722 people of
Surinamese origin in 1991.
There are 75,722 people of Caribbean
(Aruba) origin and 40,000 people of
Moluccan origin in 1991.

Sources: SOPEMI, *Trends in
International Migration*, Paris, OECD,
1993 (based on figures from the
Centraal Bureau Voor de Statistiek –
CBS).

De laatste Kantraki. Photo: Swinkels Producties

THE NETHERLANDS

1

IMMIGRATION HISTORY

The Netherlands has a long tradition of both emigration and immigration – and also of tolerance. At the time of the Reformation, the Dutch began taking in refugees from all over Europe who were fleeing their homelands for both economic and religious reasons.

Before the Second World War, 95 per cent of the foreigners living in the Netherlands were Europeans. Subsequently two main groups of immigrants can be identified. The first group came from the former colonies, mainly for political reasons. Some 280,000 immigrants came from Indonesia between 1946 and 1962; many of them had Dutch nationality and therefore the right to settle in the Netherlands. In 1951 about 125,000 Moluccans, former soldiers in the Dutch army, arrived with their families. People started leaving what was then Dutch Guyana in 1954 and when the colony became independent Surinam in 1975 their numbers increased dramatically. Until 1980 they had the choice of either nationality, and almost all opted for Dutch citizenship.

The second group of immigrants, who came more for economic reasons, started to arrive in the mid-1960s. In order to balance the large number of Dutch citizens emigrating to Canada, Australia and New Zealand (480,000 between 1946 and 1972), the Dutch government encouraged workers from developing countries, mainly Turkey and Morocco, to come to the Netherlands.

Although immigration was theoretically stopped after the 1973 oil crisis, it continued on a smaller scale, especially as families reunited. Thus, between 1985 and 1989 the Moroccan community grew by 25 per cent and the Turkish community by 13 per cent. Most of these immigrant workers live with their families in the four biggest Dutch cities, Amsterdam, Rotterdam, The Hague and Utrecht, all of which are important industrial centres. In addition 220,000 Surinamese – more than half the population of Surinam – now live in the Netherlands.

Today half the children attending primary school in the Netherlands are not Dutch nationals.

For a long time the Netherlands had a federalist immigration policy, with separate sets of rules and different ways of dealing with each group. This encouraged the formation of minority groups and respect for cultural difference. The Dutch view of ethnic minorities forms part of the broader concept of a society supported by pillars, in which coexistence between the various social groups is supposed to overcome cultural and religious divisions. Immigrants were regarded as another pillar in a country that values tolerance.

According to the Dutch, the immigrants, people from the colonies and guest workers on the German model were only in the country for a limited period. The Indonesians were called repatriates or Indonesian Dutch, the Moluccans were regarded as temporary refugees and the Surinamese were supposed to come to the Netherlands to study and then return home. Foreign workers were seen as 'rotating'.

The state therefore provided foreigners with substantial welfare benefits, especially housing aid and health care, and did everything possible to help them preserve their social and cultural identity. Lessons in the languages of origin were introduced in schools to prepare the children of immigrants to return to their own countries, and there was no pressure on them to learn Dutch.

The emergence of Moluccan terrorism in the 1960s, backing demands for fairer treatment for Moluccans, sent shock waves through the Netherlands. For the first time the Dutch became fully aware that the immigrants were there to stay and that young immigrants did not have sufficient command of the Dutch language to find employment.

In 1981 a new integration policy incorporating the idea of 'preservation of a separate identity' was introduced. It was based on a report by a special commission set up to advise the government on immigration, the Wetenschappelijke Raad Voor Het Rejeringsbeleid (WRR). The new policy had two main objectives: to reduce the socioeconomic gap between immigrants and Dutch nationals and to ensure equality of opportunity in an openly multi-ethnic society.[1]

1 The law of 1 January 1985 states that immigrants must take part in 'multicultural communal life' and not 'adapt unilaterally to a dominant social and cultural model'. Dutch nationality law, updated in 1985, is a model of integration whereby children born in the country automatically acquire Dutch nationality.

The right to vote and to stand in local elections was granted to immigrants in 1985 but it had very little practical impact. Many immigrants, especially Moroccans, do not bother to vote. In Sweden, which has similar laws, the rate of participation by foreigners is significantly higher.

Despite the steps taken to assist foreigners socially and economically, unemployment among immigrants continued to rise; it stood at 40 per cent for Turks in 1989, compared to 13 per cent for Dutch nationals. In that year the government ordered the WRR to produce a new report, which emphasized the need to provide training and jobs for adults, make the Dutch language compulsory in schools and simplify the naturalization process.

Although there has been criticism from politicians, Dutch anti-racist legislation seems to have been relatively effective and its symbolic value is in any event widely recognized in a country with strong traditions of political pluralism. The racial tensions that have become apparent all over Europe have not in the Netherlands led to violent riots. In the May 1994 general election, the extreme-right parties won only 2.5 per cent of the vote in the four biggest cities, but a series of racist attacks did take place during the summer of 1993. They are thought to have been the work of a few individuals rather than the result of a coordinated campaign; according to the police, the Dutch extreme right is 'badly organized' and has no established links with its counterparts in other countries. What the Anne Frank Foundation calls a 'moral taboo' still prevents the Dutch from admitting openly to racism, but the general attitude towards foreigners is deteriorating and the subject of immigration occupies an ever-larger place in politics. In September 1993 the government approved stricter criteria for foreigners joining members of their families already in the Netherlands, just as Parliament was voting in favour of further restrictions on political asylum.

2
THE BROADCASTING SCENE

Public channels

Television in the Netherlands is organized in an original way, with airtime divided between a total of 34 national organizations. A law passed in November 1986 and brought into effect two years later formalized the relationship between the broadcasting authority NOS (Nederlandse Omroep Stichting) and the organizations, as well as the method of financing, with two-thirds of revenue coming from licence fees and one-third from advertising. The NOS looked after the third public channel itself and allocated airtime on the other two (generally, two days per organization). The main organizations are AVRO, KRO, NCRV, VARA, VPRO, TROS, EO and VOO, which provide about 80 per cent of broadcasts. The other 25 include 13 Christian organizations grouped as the Interkerkelijke Omroep Nederland (IKON), an Islamic organization, and a group of three educational organizations.

The rapid success of private television – RTL 4 and the other cable channels have within a few years conquered 50 per cent of the market – has given the organizations serious cause for concern, and led the Ministry of Well-Being, Health and Cultural Affairs to prepare new legislation in an attempt to improve the competitiveness of the public channels.

The law, passed in February 1994, states that the three state channels should each try to obtain equal shares of the market. In order to achieve this, the organizations are required to work together more closely on each channel and the channels are also expected to cooperate to a greater extent. A department of the NOS has been turned into an autonomous body, the NPS (Nederlandse Programma Stichting – Netherlands Programme Association), to coordinate these efforts. The NOS will be responsible for news broadcasts and sport on all three channels and will supervise cooperation agreements between them. The new system, which also lifts the ban on private channels broadcasting within the Netherlands, is due to come into effect from 1 January 1995.

❶ **NEDERLANDS 1** (Ned 1) was established in 1953. Its broadcasting time, from mid-afternoon to midnight, will be divided between KRO (Catholic), NCRV (Protestant), AVRO (Liberal) and the NOS. The organizations' political and religious views have tended to come through in the programmes. Ned 1 attracted 20 per cent of the total audience in 1991.

❷ **NEDERLANDS 2** (Ned 2) was started in 1968 and broadcasts at the same times as Ned 1. Airtime is to be shared between TROS (neutral, mainstream), VOO (neutral, children's programmes), EO (Evangelical) and the NOS. Ned 2's market share in 1991 was 22 per cent.

❸ **NEDERLANDS 3** (Ned 3) has only been broadcasting since 1988. On the air from 5 pm to 11 pm, it will be shared in 1995 by VARA (Socialist), VPRO (Liberal and progressive), NPS (neutral) and the NOS. Its market share was around 12 per cent in 1991.

The ultimate objective of the new law is for the organizations to merge completely within ten years.

Private channels

❶ RTL 4. Only a short time ago, the creation of private television channels was still illegal in the Netherlands. The Luxembourg channel RTL 4 got round this with satellite broadcasts relayed by cable – which is in accordance with EU legislation. Taking a resolutely commercial approach, RTL 4 quickly became the most popular channel; although it has only been broadcasting in Dutch since September 1990, it has already won 30 per cent of the market. Its main shareholder is the Compagnie luxembourgeoise de télédiffusion (CLT), which owns 37 per cent, along with the publishing group Verenigde Nederlandse Uitgevers (VNU).

❷ RTL 5. Expecting stronger competition now that commercial television has been officially legalized in the Netherlands, RTL launched another channel in late 1993. Aimed at young people and a more intellectual audience, it schedules more documentaries and fewer games, and hopes eventually to win 10 per cent of the market.

Ninety per cent of Dutch homes are cabled and 7 per cent of viewers watch Belgian, Flemish and German channels. Other cable channels – including the encoded Filmnet and the interactive Free Choice TV – account for 12 per cent of the audience.

3

CHANNEL POLICIES

In 1991 a document on the role of the media in a multicultural society published by the then Minister of Well-Being, Health and Cultural Affairs, Hedy d'Ancona (now a member of the European Parliament), was debated in the Dutch parliament. The media has an important part to play in helping ethnic minorities to integrate and in giving a positive image of immigrants, Ms Ancona said. While she did not wish to force broadcasters to act in a particular way through legislation, she hoped they would come up with suggestions for new programmes, encourage greater participation by immigrants and stress this aspect of Dutch culture in training programmes. The minister promised to provide the funds needed to implement these measures.

Hedy d'Ancona was also behind the February 1994 law on the media, which gave a new body, the NPS, a specific role regarding minorities.

The NPS is responsible for 650 hours of airtime a year – the same as the eight existing major organizations. It is expected to devote 20 per cent of this time to culture in the broadest sense, 20 per cent to the arts (in a narrower sense) and 20 per cent to programmes for ethnic and cultural minorities. The remaining 40 per cent should be used for news and debate on current affairs, educational programmes for young people and programmes that do not appear in the other organizations' schedules, but which are nonetheless vital in order to give a balanced image of the social, cultural, religious and spiritual diversity of the Netherlands.

In determining the overall percentage of airtime to be devoted to minorities, the minister assumed that the NPS programmes for them would be targeted at specific groups.

Magazine programmes for immigrants

❶ **NOS/NPS/Ned 3**. In accordance with the new law, under which its schedules are to be taken over by the NPS, the NOS will broadcast programmes for certain target groups on Nederland 3, alongside mainstream programmes. When these programmes are intended for first-generation immigrants, they will be in the immigrants' original language.

➤*HET ALLOCHTOON VIDEO-CIRCUIT* (The Immigrants' Video Circuit) is a documentary magazine broadcast by the NOS in cooperation with social organizations on Tuesday afternoons, usually in Arabic, Berber, Turkish or Chinese. Covering widely varied aspects of life in the Netherlands, the programme is aimed at small target groups which it would otherwise be hard to reach. A video shown during the programme often forms part of a wider information campaign. After the initial broadcast, the videos are offered to the cable networks of large cities and made available to interested groups at cost price. More than 125 magazines, each lasting 30 minutes, have been broadcast over the past five years.

Subjects dealt with have included how to use medicines, parental involvement in schools, immigrants returning to their home countries, retirement homes, violence against women, sterility, drug dependence, AIDS, racism, homeworkers, love, divorce, and Moslem schools.

Het Allochtoon Video-Circuit has also devoted series of programmes to longer items. 'Islam in the Netherlands', which traced the appearance of the religion in the Netherlands, analysed the various forms and examined the reactions of Dutch people to the phenomenon, took up eight editions. 'Children in Close-Up', in 12 parts, followed the different stages of child development from birth to age four, explaining when and how parents can intervene. Currently in preparation is 'Netherlands for Beginners', a 12-part series due to be shown in January 1995, which is intended to help people who have just arrived in the country get used to Dutch society.

In 1994, less programmes were shown in Arabic and Turkish, and immigrant journalists, directors or producers complain at no longer working for NOS.

➤*TANTE FATMA'S SPREKERSHOEK* (Aunt Fatma's Speakers' Corner) is a 10-minute programme broadcast, produced by Najib, on Sundays, after the afternoon film. 'Aunt Fatma', installed in the oriental market of the town of Beverwijk, gives passers-by the chance to air their views on television. The market is one of the busiest meeting places for first-generation Turks and Moroccans in the Netherlands.

Mainstream programmes

The various channels schedule news magazines and documentaries on minorities fairly regularly.

❶ **NOS/NPS/Ned 3**. From 1 pm to 4 pm on Sundays has been chosen as the slot for showing mainstream programmes during the 1994-1995 television season. The following will be broadcast every week:

➤*BINNENLAND* (Internal Affairs) examines the behaviour and attitudes of the Dutch when they meet immigrants, especially in towns. People of widely differing cultures and backgrounds appear in the series. The aim of the programmes is to encourage both sides to describe how they feel, especially on the sensitive aspects of their relations. The reasons for friction and tension are tackled frankly. The format has been slightly modified to allow time for studio discussions after the main part of the programme.

➤*CLOSE-UP* is devoted to personalities of foreign origin, highlighting important moments in their existence through live or pre-recorded interviews with people who know them. The aim of the programme is to present the subjects as unique individuals who do not conform to the stereotypes of foreigners put forward by some politicians.

Along with the Sunday afternoon film, *Binnenland* and *Close-Up* make up a 'multi-cultural afternoon' on the third channel. The films are chosen with a view to familiarizing a wide audience with the 'melting pot' that the Netherlands is becoming – along with western Europe in general. They are expected to have a clear storyline and sympathetic main characters with whom viewers can easily identify. It is hoped that this approach will reinforce the struggle against racism. As far as possible, the films are grouped into series on the same country or theme, showing life in parts of the world that many of the 'new Dutch' come from, such as the Caribbean, the southern Mediterranean, the Far East, the Arab world and other Moslem countries.

➤*OOST, WEST EN DE REST* (How Beautiful is my Country). Opinion polls have shown that foreigners often feel they would like to show the Dutch the beauty of their country of origin. With this in mind, the NOS is preparing this six-part series which will be broadcast by the NPS on Ned 3 in 1995. Individual immigrants are chosen to accompany a film crew to their home country and help to select images for the programme. The series aims to revive the interest of Dutch viewers in the backgrounds of foreigners living in their country.

❷ **OTHER ORGANIZATIONS**. Apart from the NOS/NPS, other organizations such as VPRO, VARA and AVRO produce documentaries and discussion programmes for and about minorities. The most significant are:

➤*MARCO POLO*, produced by VPRO, a weekly magazine in Dutch about minorities in the Netherlands.

➤*IN MIJN VADERS HUIS* (In My Father's House), produced by Anil Ramdas for VPRO, will be shown on Ned 3 in 1995 for the second year running. It gets 'non-western' intellectuals together for a studio discussion of important issues.

➤*SCHREEUW VAN DE LEEUW* (Scream of the Lion) is a popular entertainment programme about Islam produced by VARA. When first shown on Ned 3, it was regarded as revolutionary because it presented Islam as a fully fledged part of Dutch society rather than a curiosity.

➤*PLEIDOOI* (Speech for the Defence), produced by AVRO and broadcast on Ned 1, is a soap about a group of lawyers in the Netherlands, including an Egyptian whose home life is realistically portrayed. *Pleidooi* illustrates a growing trend in Dutch television to use more actors with foreign backgrounds in fiction, without relegating them to stereotyped roles. Ed Klute of the Stichting Omroep Allochtonen (STOA), a non-governmental cooperative of immigrant associations, said: 'This is a slow but steady development that is taking place on the intiative of both the broadcasters themselves and the STOA.'

Programmes about minorities are unfortunately a rarity on Ned 1 and Ned 2, outside of news broadcasts.

Cable and local channels

The Netherlands has one of the highest concentrations of cable networks in the world. From Deventer to Rotterdam, from The Hague to Enschede, viewers have a vast choice of both legal and pirate channels.

Since the 1988 law on the media came into force, local and regional channels have also sprung up all over the Netherlands. The regional channels are run by professionals and financed by a regional licence fee plus advertising. The local channels tend to be run by volunteers and, except in Amsterdam, have limited financial resources.

In 1984 four cable channels for minorities were established in the four main cities of the Netherlands: Amsterdam, Rotterdam, Utrecht and The Hague – the first of their kind in Europe. The Ministry of Well-Being, which partly financed the channels, withdrew its assistance at the end of 1993 and instead gave a grant of 2 million guilders to the Stichting Omroep Allochonen (STOA) to set up a new organization to merge the four channels into one. The grant was given on condition that the city authorities contributed matching funds. The STOA has managed to persuade the four municipalities to sign an agreement creating the organization SOM-MEDIA.

❶ **MIGRANTEN-TV AMSTERDAM** (MTV) has been in existence since 1984 and produces about 50 hours of programmes a year (95 per cent of the schedule) – a mix of news, culture and entertainment. It is aimed at the immigrants of 40 nationalities who make up more than a quarter of Amsterdam's population. The programmes are in immigrants' own languages, mainly Turkish, Arabic and Surinamese, with Dutch subtitles. The channel broadcasts on Thursdays from 11 am, with repeats of the programmes continuing until 2 am the next day. MTV has various objectives: to inform immigrants about the society they are living in, to establish contacts between the first and second generation of immigrants and between immigrants and the Dutch, to make the Dutch more familiar with immigrants' lives in order to combat racism and discrimination, to improve the image of immigrants in the media, to allow immigrants to preserve their own culture and to make it known in the host country, and to inform immigrants on employment and administrative issues. The channel reaches 26 per cent of the city's population, including 88 per cent of the 25,000 Turks, 86 per cent of the 36,000 Moroccans and 70 per cent of the 68,000 Surinamese and people of Caribbean origin. In 1987, when MTV began to use the High-Band system, its annual budget was 1.2 million guilders (US$600,000); by 1992 this had been reduced to 300,000 guilders (US$150,000). Half the channel's resources are provided by the city authorities, a quarter by the Ministry of Well-Being and the rest has to be found through sponsorship and the sale of programmes. MTV has a permanent staff of eight, plus ten occasional contributors.

❷ **MIGRANTEN-TV DEN HAAG**, the channel for immigrants in The Hague, unfortunately went bankrupt in 1993. It used to broadcast two hours a month of the same type of programmes as MTV, in both Dutch and immigrant languages. It was watched by members of the Turkish, Moroccan, Yugoslav, Spanish, Portuguese, Surinamese and Caribbean communities.

❸ **TV MOZAIEK ROTTERDAM**, which closed down at the end of 1993, used to broadcast one hour a month in Dutch and immigrant languages. Half an hour was devoted to subjects of general interest and half an hour to specific items for, in turn, the Turkish, Moroccan, Italian, Yugoslav, Spanish, Portuguese, Greek, Cape Verdean, Surinamese, Caribbean and Pakistani communities.

❹ **MIGRANTEN-TV UTRECHT**, as it was originally called, has been renamed SEGLO and is still struggling to survive with a schedule of one hour per month and a tiny audience.

❺ **SOM-MEDIA** is creating an international network and should deliver in 1995 two hours a week of programming mainly in Turkish, Moroccan and Surinamese which should enable local channels to be on the air again in the near future.

4

INITIATIVES

The Netherlands, due to a large extent to the efforts of the Ministry of Well-Being, has several organizations that are deeply involved in the struggle against discrimination in the media.

❶ **STOA** is a non-governmental cooperative of immigrant associations set up in 1980 and representing more than 20 nationalities. It has two major objectives: encouraging increased participation by immigrants in radio and television programmes for the general public, and making programmes for the various immigrant groups in their own languages. STOA works as a government and media lobby; it is not allocated airtime on any of the television channels. It receives funding from the Ministry of Well-Being for specific annual projects, while further projects are financed by the European Union and other partners. In 1994 STOA had a staff of about ten.

At the request of the Ministries of Well-Being and of Social Affairs, STOA is exploring the opportunities offered by radio and television to provide support for projects involving ethnic minorities. It also advises broadcasting companies with a view to increasing the participation of ethnic minorities in mainstream programmes and is establishing networks for immigrants involved in broadcasting.[1]

❷ **SOM-MEDIA** (Service Organisatie Migranten-Media). In 1993 STOA was ascribed the task of working with the local television channels for immigrants to set

---

1   See Europe Singh, in this volume.

up a national organization to coordinate coproductions and programme buying. This organization, SOM-MEDIA, is expected to find extra material for the channels and compose a schedule that will be attractive to ethnic minorities. The programmes, which may include information, films, entertainment and documentaries, should reflect the interests of the minorities and give Dutch viewers an overview of their opinions and cultures. In addition to programmes already shown by the NOS and other national broadcasters, SOM-MEDIA can purchase material from other European television companies. This extra material is supplied to the local channels in the form of ready-to-broadcast tape.

❸ **ADO** (Anti Discriminatie Overleg) is an independent organization founded ten years ago by immigrant associations, journalists, film makers and press officers anxious to combat the extreme right and all forms of discrimination. The first five years of its existence were devoted to setting up the various activities it continues today. Since 1987 ADO has been concentrating on improving the image of ethnic minorities and immigrants projected by the media. In 1991 it set up an advice service for journalists, students and academics involved with the representation of minorities in the media. Joop Lahaise, who is in charge of the service, said Dutch journalists were aware of their own prejudices and paid increasing attention to the way they handled reports about ethnic minorities. In 199 ADO organized workshops for producers and journalists from the news departments of the NOS, RTL, the regional channel KRO Radio Brabant and the Belgian Flemish channel BRTN. ADO is also involved in the work of the One World Group of Broadcasters and the North-South Centre of the Council of Europe to launch a European campaign against xenophobia late in 1994.

Alongside these activities, ADO introduced a Media Prize in 1987, to be awarded in alternate years to the press and broadcasting. The prize, worth 10,000 guilders, rewards journalists and producers whose work contributes to a better understanding of foreigners, or to improving their image. So far all the winners have been Dutch, although there is also a prize for promising young journalists and producers which may be awarded to foreigners.

In 1994 the ADO Media Prize for broadcasting went to the IKON production Vesuvius, presented by Cees Grimbergen as part of his special programme on young Moroccans in the Netherlands. Often the victims of discrimination, these youngsters are frequently regarded as the group with the highest incidence of crime and social problems. Rather than deny their difficulties, Vesuvius set out to show that such problems are inherent to Dutch society as a whole. In this way, the programme broke with the traditional approach of 'us versus them'.

A special award entitled the Media Prize of the City of Amsterdam was introduced in 1993 to reward particularly striking programmes. Worth 2,500 guilders, it first went to Paul van de Leeuw for his humorous and innovative report on Islam for the programme *Schreeuw van de Leeuw* (Scream of the Lion).

Programmes like these are indicative of changing attitudes among programme planners, whether of Dutch or foreign origin, who no longer try systematically to present a positive image of immigrants or to impose a 'white' viewpoint.

ADO is also planning to introduce a European award in collaboration with the Civis Prize in Germany, the Human Rights League in France, the Media Prize for a Harmonious Society in Belgium and the Commission for Racial Equality 'Race in the Media' awards in Britain. The new award will be called the Iris Prize.

❹ **NVJ** (Nederlandse Vereniging van Journalisten). Members of the Dutch journalists' union with foreign backgrounds have started a working group that organizes workshops and seminars on the image of immigrants in the media. The group urges newspapers and broadcasters to provide training for immigrants and helps journalists from immigrant families to find work in the mass media.

The Netherlands often acts as host to conferences on the relations between immigrants and the media.

❺ **IMMIGRANTS, THE MEDIA AND CULTURAL DIVERSITY**. This conference was organized by the Council of Europe with the Dutch Ministry of Well-Being, Health and Cultural Affairs in Noordwijkerhout in November 1988. It made a number of interesting proposals on how to improve the image of immigrants in broadcasting.

❻ **PUBLIC BROADCASTING FOR A MULTICULTURAL EUROPE** (PBME). This European conference was also held in Noordwijkerhout, in November 1992. It was organized by the BBC, the Luton College of Higher Education's Centre for Educational Opportunity, the STOA and the NOS. The 150 people from seven countries (United Kingdom, Netherlands, France, Germany, Belgium, Sweden and Denmark) who took part included broadcasting professionals, representatives of immigrant groups and members of European and national governmental and non-governmental organizations.

The aims of the conference were:

  – to determine the role and social responsibility of public broadcasters in a multicultural Europe (how immigrants should be portrayed on television, for instance);

  – to set up a European public broadcasting working committee to encourage multicultural scheduling and equal employment opportunities for immigrants in European broadcasting;

- to draw up guidelines to help the public media avoid giving a negative image of ethnic minorities;

- to make high-quality programmes that would foster harmonious relations between the various ethnic and cultural groups;

- to establish a network of immigrant workers and organizations involved in public broadcasting.

After the PBME conference, a European organization was formed to work for the fulfilment of these objectives and a member of the European Parliament said he would request funding for this purpose. The European Broadcasting Union's television programmes committee said it planned to draw up a code of conduct on equal opportunities and the portrayal of immigrants.

The main focus of the conference debates was how much remains to be done before radio and television provide a true reflection of the whole of European society. Participants thought that drama and serials should more accurately represent multicultural society, and that quiz and game shows should include people of different ethnic origins. News broadcasts and magazines should not stress the problems of immigrants; rather they should mention them only as an everyday part of society with their own contribution to make. Programmes made especially for minorities should become a permanent and integral part of the channels' schedules.

A steering committee composed of representatives of the leading European public channels was set up to start a database on all the organizations involved, launch a biannual magazine to keep track of progress and to organize a European conference every two years to give independent producers the chance to meet public broadcasters. The steering committee was also made responsible for running workshops and awarding a European broadcasting prize.

The biannual magazine in English, *Spectrum*, was launched early in 1993 and transnational workshops were set up to discuss topics like equal opportunities, radio and racism, the proposed code of conduct and the database (see the article by the PBME's secretary, Europe Singh, earlier in this book).

❼ **THE NEXT FIVE MINUTES** was the name of a conference organized by the Paradiso Foundation of Amsterdam from 8 to 10 January 1993 to discuss local television, alternative broadcasting and pirate channels. Several workshops focused on the role of 'tactical television' as opposed to 'strategic television' as a thread in the social fabric and a means of combating racism and xenophobia.

❽ **EBU HILVERSUM CONFERENCE**. The European Broadcasting Union's educational programmes working group organized this conference, which was the idea of secretary Armin Veihl, from 17 to 19 May 1993. Chaired by Jos Tuerlinckx of the Flemish BRT network and hosted by the NOS, it provided a forum for the exchange of short multicultural and antiracist programmes between public broadcasters and the screening of documentaries on the same theme. The conference has become an annual event.

NORWAY

Total population (on 1/1/92):
4,287,000

Foreign population:
147,800
3.5 per cent of the total population

Distribution by country of origin:

Denmark	17,400
Sweden	12,000
United Kingdom	11,500
Pakistan	11,300
United States of America	9,600
Vietnam	6,800
Iran	6,600
Sri Lanka	5,700
Turkey	5,500
Chile	5,400
Former Yugoslavia	4,800
Germany	4,300
India	3,400

Source: SOPEMI, *Trends in International Migration*, Paris, OECD, 1993 (based on the Norwegian Central Statistics Office).

Vet du hvem Tung er? Photo: NRK

NORWAY

1

IMMIGRATION HISTORY

Norway began to take in people from the third world, especially Pakistanis and Indians, in the late 1960s to cope with its labour requirements. In theory, immigration has been suspended since 1975 except for citizens of other Nordic countries. The labour market situation and more restrictive policies have led to a slowdown in immigration, from 18,400 people in 1989 to 15,700 in 1990.

Refugees and people seeking asylum (12,019 in 1991) and those coming to join members of their families already in the country make up the majority of immigrants from countries outside western Europe (mainly Pakistan, Vietnam, Iran, Chile, Turkey and Sri Lanka).

Although the 1991 law on foreigners restricts family reunification and work and residence permits, it also allows a greater proportion of asylum seekers to remain in Norway for humanitarian reasons. In 1991 most of these came from Yugoslavia, Sri Lanka, Somalia and Ethiopia.

In 1990 the number of naturalizations (4,700) was double the average recorded between 1980 and 1987. Refugees can be naturalized after seven years' residence in Norway.

According to police estimates, Norway has around 4,000 to 5,000 illegal immigrants, most of them from North Africa and Eastern Europe. Immigrants from the third world are worse hit by unemployment than Norwegians and people from other industrialized countries (15 per cent compared to 4.4 per cent in 1990). A degree of hostility seems to be emerging towards third world immigrants, especially those seeking asylum. The success of three small political parties espousing anti-immigration policies in the 1991 local elections has added to the fears of some immigrants. Norway is also facing claims from 20,000 nomadic Sami people

(Lapps), of whom 40,000 have already adopted a settled lifestyle and are being integrated into Norwegian society.

To sum up, government policy is aimed at integration and peaceful coexistence in a multicultural Norwegian society. Anti-racism campaigns and equal opportunity reforms are being introduced.

2

THE BROADCASTING SCENE

The state television channel run by Norsk Rikskringkasting (NRK, the Norwegian broadcasting authority) has recently been facing competition for the first time. Private broadcasting began with the emergence of TV 2, launched in September 1992, and the arrival of cable has given Norwegians access to foreign stations, particularly Swedish television.

Public channel

❶ The **NRK** has only one channel, despite discussions in parliament aimed at starting a second. The NRK's new status, adopted in May 1988, gave it greater independence, making it more like an autonomous foundation than a state monopoly. The reform was accompanied by internal restructuring of the channel to make it more competitive.

Advertising is banned and licence fees provide 80 per cent of NRK's income. Part of the remainder comes from a tax on sales of equipment. A mainstream channel broadcasting 3,227 hours a year (15 hours a day), NRK puts the emphasis on news (27 per cent of newscasts and news magazines), sport (16 per cent), fiction (17 per cent) and programmes aimed at children and young people (12 per cent). With its direct competitor TV 2, NRK's main competition comes from foreign channels and cable; it still attracts the lion's share of viewers. Its market share did, however, fall from 80 per cent in 1991 to 64 per cent in April 1992.

Private channels

❶ **TV 2**, based in Bergen, has been broadcasting since September 1992 and can be received by 70 per cent of Norwegian households. Its revenue comes from advertising, which is on the increase thanks to promising viewing figures, despite some official restrictions and competition from cable channels with aggressive marketing policies.

Its main shareholders are the Norwegian publishing group Schibsted, the Vital Forsikring insurance group, the Gutenberghus media group and Nordic Television

Norway.

With six hours of broadcasts a day, TV 2 aims to compete with NRK in the fields of news, magazine programmes and sport.

❷ **TV NORGE** and TV 3 are among the most go-ahead cable channels. The former, available to 50 per cent of households, is owned mainly by the Orkla group and Scandinavian Broadcast Systems (SBS) and attracts 7 per cent of the total audience. It provides 45 hours of programmes a week during the evenings and shows mainly entertainment (40 per cent), sport (25 per cent) and serials (15 per cent).

❸ **TV 3**, the Scandinavian channel, is also broadcast by satellite and reaches 40 per cent of households. It attracts 10 per cent of the total audience.

❹ **TV 4** belonged to the Swedish channel of the same name before being sold to a group of Norwegian investors.

3
CHANNEL POLICIES

The state channel NRK does have its own policy on programmes for minorities. Nonetheless, in June 1991 it stopped broadcasting the only specific magazine produced for them since 1988. In 1993/94 only public and privately owned radio stations had regular programmes made by and for immigrants, in their own languages.

Magazine programmes for immigrants

➤*MØTESTED NORGE* (Encounters in Norway) was a 40-50 minute cultural magazine. During its first year it was broadcast on Mondays at 8.30 pm, then at 6.45 pm, before the main evening news. Aimed at spreading knowledge of foreign cultures, it was composed chiefly of reports made by the channel about immigrant artistes living in Norway: dancers, musicians, writers, painters and actors.

Intended for an audience of Norwegians, immigrants, refugees and asylum seekers, *Møtested Norge* was presented jointly by the producer, Egil Teige, in Norwegian, and by Pakistani journalist Farhat Naaeem Khokhar in Urdu. Interviews were conducted in Norwegian, Urdu or English.

Both for financial reasons and because viewing figures were low, the channel management decided to take the magazine off the air in June 1991, putting Egil Teige in charge of producing occasional programmes on immigrant cultures. The first such programme, *Veivalg* (Choosing the Way), a mix of reports and live sequences, was broadcast over Christmas 1991 and showed the festivals and rituals of Jews, Moslems and Buddhists. The second, which went out on 17 May 1992, the Norwegian national holiday, was entitled *Fest for frihet* (Freedom Festival) and invited guest artistes from Kurdistan, Côte d'Ivoire, Kenya, Vietnam, Norway, Pakistan and Iran to celebrate freedom together. *Trondheim midt i verden* (Trondheim, Centre of the World), broadcast in June 1992, was about the Trondheim Festival of Immigrant Cultures.

In August 1992 Egil Teige was awarded the Union of Pakistani Workers' prize for his work.

Mainstream programmes

Norwegian television occasionally broadcasts documentaries, films and serials featuring immigration and racism.

➤*NORGE, MITT NORGE?* (Norway, for Norwegians only?), broadcast by NRK at 6.40 pm on 27 October 1989, before the evening news, is one of the most interesting documentaries made on the subject. Produced by Media Service A/S and directed by Jan Robert Jore, this 39-minute programme initially set out to report on the quiet life of a refugee in a small Norwegian town. But following the violent demonstrations against Norway's official policy on refugees that broke out in Arendal before filming started, the programme became an account of the truth behind the protests. It was awarded prizes for best documentary of 1990 at the Nordic Panorama and at the Norway Short Films Festival, and has been widely distributed in Norwegian schools along with back-up documents.

The work of the company Kaleidoskopet, which specializes in multicultural programmes, has included:

➤*MARIAS VALG* (Maria's Choice), produced by Hildur Ferksaug and broadcast on NRK at 10 pm on 18 January 1991. This 19-minute documentary tells how 16-year-old Nassir, working day and night in a bar to support his family, meets Maria, an unemployed Norwegian girl.

➤*RULLETRAPPEN* (The Lift), a 30-minute documentary also produced by Hildur Ferksaug. Broadcast in September 1991, at 7 pm, it showed how immigrants were being integrated into Norwegian society: Derick from Surinam; and Trinidad, her husband and son from Indonesia.

➤*KJENT MEN UKJENT* (Known Yet Unknown), seven 20-minute programmes, is also the work of Hildur Ferksaug. Broadcast by NRK in 1993, it offers a series of portraits of immigrants following successful careers but still unknown to most Norwegians.

The first film dealing with racism in Norway was made for the cinema in 1966:

➤*AFRIKANER* (The African), a full-length film directed by Barthold Halle, tells of a love affair between an African man and a Norwegian woman. After being shown in several cinemas, it was broadcast by NRK in 1970.

➤*FREDELANDET* (The Homeland), composed of four 90-minute episodes, was made by Jarl Emsell Larsen and Ulf Breistrand. Produced by NRK's fiction department and broadcast in April 1991, it attracted attention at the Prix Italia awards in October of that year. The action takes place at two different periods: in Oslo during the 1970s, when Norway was becoming aware of the problems of immigrant workers, and in a west coast village in the late 1980s. The main character is Rakel, who was born in the village and has a daughter of mixed race. In the 1970s Rakel, young and idealistic, is working in Oslo as part of a programme to help immigrant workers when she falls in love with a Pakistani who has had an accident at work. When she learns that he is married and that his wife and children plan to join him in Norway, and then finds out she is pregnant, Rakel returns to her home village to try and forget.

Programmes for children and young people

Until NRK was reorganized ahead of the launch of TV 2 in September 1992, the children's programme department drew between 75 per cent and 83 per cent of younger viewers. Ada Haug, leading a team of 30, tried to give prominence to multicultural issues and young immigrants were often among the children presenting the programmes. With a view to making children aware of other languages, the multicultural broadcasts were shown in the original language, with Norwegian subtitles.

➤*KOLOLI BARNA* (The Kololi Children), a serial of five 10-minute episodes, was filmed in The Gambia and broadcast at 6.15 pm on Saturdays in September 1992.

➤*VET DU HVEM...ER?* (Do you know...?), a series of 16×20-minute programmes, made in 1986-1987 by Chris Foss for children aged four to seven was re-broadcast in 1992. It is based on the true stories of four immigrant children: Tung, a Vietnamese refugee who arrived in Oslo in 1984, aged four, Angela, from Chile, Amadou, from the Gambia, and Nadia, from Pakistan. Four programmes were devoted to each child.

The idea was to follow the children from getting up to bedtime, sharing their joys and sorrows and showing that these were much the same as those experienced by Norwegian children. 'The aim of the series was to emphasize what all youngsters have in common rather than to point out their differences, and thus to help Norwegian children identify with the young immigrants, whatever their cultural differences', Ada Haug explained. The scripts were written in close collaboration with the children themselves and their families, based on their own experiences. The series went out at 6 pm, which was thought to be the best time for families to watch and discuss the programmes together.

Programmes for the Sami people

NRK Sami Radio, a department of NRK, produces a monthly magazine made by and for the Sami people (Lapps). It deals in particular with the status of the Sami language and with Lapp culture, both traditional and modern, with the nuclear threat, problems concerning the environment and pollution, and the dispersal of the Sami people across the Nordic countries. The programme has been in existence since February 1990, when NRK Sami Radio was given a regular broadcasting slot, and has had two titles:

➤*CSV*, after the title of a Sami poem about the diverse merits of the Sami people (the same initials have been used as a political slogan in their struggle for their rights, and especially during the 1981 dispute over the Alta/Kautokeino nuclear power station).

➤*ARRAN*, the title since November 1991, is also symbolic, referring to the hearth in the middle of a Sami tent. The programme is produced jointly by Sami Radio and SVT Sami, a department of Swedish television, with each country contributing one or more reports. There are two presenters, one Swedish, one Norwegian. The 30-minute magazine is broadcast one Saturday a month from November to April at about 11 am – a total of six programmes a year – in Norway, Sweden and Finland, where the Finnish channel Yleisradio also has a Sami department. *Arran* is subtitled in the language of the country where it is scheduled.

➤*SAMI MANIAD TV* is a fortnightly children's programme, also broadcast since February 1990 by NRK Sami Radio. It goes out in the Sami language, without subtitles. Made up of reports, videoclips and cartoons, the programmes aim to make children aware of the situation of minorities.

SPAIN

Total population (on 1/1/92):
39,085,000

Foreign population:
360,700
0.92 per cent of the total population[*]

Distribution by country of origin:

United Kingdom	50,100
Morocco	49,500
Germany	28,700
Portugal	25,400
France	20,000
Argentina	20,000
United States of America	13,200
Italy	11,700
Netherlands	9,700
Philippines	8,000
Venezuela	6,900
Belgium	6,700
Dominican Republic	6,600
Peru	6,500

[*] Not counting illegal immigrants, of whom there are believed to be at least 294,000 (98,000 Africans, 86,000 South Americans, 67,000 Asians, 50,000 Moroccans, 38,000 Portuguese and 35,000 Filipinos in 1991).
N.B. The Romany population, many of whom now have a settled lifestyle, is estimated at 670,000, with a large community in Andalusia in 1991.

Sources: SOPEMI, *Trends in International Migration*, Paris, OECD, 1993. IOE, Situation et problématique des immigrés en Espagne, in: Jacqueline Costa-Lascoux & Patrick Weil (Eds) *Logique d'Etat et Immigration*, Kimé, Paris, 1992.

Linea 900. Photo: TVE

SPAIN

1

IMMIGRATION HISTORY

For more than 100 years, Spain was a country from which people emigrated. It was only during the 1970s that it began to take in foreigners on a significant scale, and it was not until 1990 that immigration became a political issue – 20 years later than in other European countries. There are nearly 400,000 immigrants in Spain. To this figure must be added about 300,000 illegal immigrants, 80 per cent of whom come from third world countries.

Although the government claims that it recognizes immigrants' rights and is trying to establish an immigration policy, in practice not much is happening. Economic immigrants from poor countries suffer openly ethnic discrimination; many could be described as social outcasts. Surveys in the field have revealed growing xenophobia against both black Africans and North Africans – a phenomenon actively cultivated by the media. A recent opinion poll in Spain showed that 62 per cent of those questioned associated immigrants with criminals.

At the moment Spain has accepted European Union guidelines on immigration as outlined in the Schengen agreements, giving priority to the needs of the Spanish labour market and taking account of the recession that has persisted since 1984.

In 1991 Spain decided to give working papers to some 104,000 people (mostly Moroccans) who were illegally employed or self-employed. At the same time, on 15 May 1991 the government introduced an entry visa for North Africans to bring Spain into line with EU norms. Immigrants of Spanish origin were exempt from the visa requirement under the Peace and Friendship Treaty signed in 1863 between Spain and its former colonies, which gave them the same rights as Spanish nationals to live and work in Spain.

All matters concerned with immigration, emigration, the right of asylum and legislation on residence permits and employment of foreigners come under central government, and can on no account be delegated to local authorities. In May 1992, in order to alleviate the lack of coordination between the various ministries that deal with immigration (interior, foreign affairs, labour and social security), the Spanish government set up an Interministerial Committee for Foreigners, whose task is to coordinate the work of the ministries, formulate general principles and draft laws. The committee has spawned four subcommittees to handle visas and international cooperation; general conditions affecting foreigners; employment and immigrant flows; and integration of immigrants and refugees.

Since 1993 the governments of Spain and Morocco have strengthened cooperation to provide stricter border controls and combat illegal immigration.

2

THE BROADCASTING SCENE

Over the past few years the gradual creation of regional channels under the control of the powerful regional authorities and the launching of three private channels have severely dented the viewing figures and finances of Radiotelevisión Española (RTVE) and its two public channels, which until recently had a monopoly. Nowadays most Spanish households can receive between five and eight different channels.

Public channels

As Spain has no licence fee, TVE 1 and TVE 2 get most of their income from advertising. In 1989, before the private channels started up, it was still providing about 90 per cent, with the state making up the rest. The public channels have not made a profit since 1990 and are now receiving much less by way of subsidies than the regional channels.

❶ TVE 1, a mainstream channel established in 1956, tries to compete with the private channels on their own ground by putting the accent on entertainment. In 1992 its schedules were offering 45.8 per cent fiction and 25 per cent variety programmes. News represented 13.6 per cent and children's programmes 9 per cent. Although TVE 1 is still the most widely watched channel, its position is looking increasingly fragile. Its share of the total audience fell from 52 per cent in 1990 to 43 per cent in 1991 and 33 per cent in May 1992.

❷ TVE 2, the second public channel started in 1965, offers more cultural programmes (14.3 per cent) and sport (18.5 per cent, against only 1 per cent on TVE 1). But entertainment still dominates, with fiction taking up 42.5 per cent of the schedule and variety programmes 13.6 per cent. News occupies 7.9 per cent and children's programmes 3 per cent.

Although it attracted 20.2 per cent of the national audience in 1990, TVE 2 has also been hard hit by competition from the private and regional channels. In 1991, with 14 per cent market share, it slipped back into third place behind TVE 1 and Tele Cinco. By June 1992 TVE 2 was still in third place but its share of the audience had risen slightly to 17.5 per cent.

There are six state-run regional channels:

❸ **ETB** (Euskal Telebista), the Basque country's television, was set up in 1983 with two channels. On average, ETB 1 and 2 attract 11 per cent and 16 per cent respectively of the regional audience. ETB 1 offers 30 per cent fiction, 24 per cent sport, 21 per cent variety programmes and 12 per cent news. ETB 2 puts more stress on fiction (43 per cent) and on news (23 per cent), also showing variety programmes (19 per cent), sport (6 per cent) and cultural programmes (5 per cent).

❹ **CCRTV**, Catalan television, was launched in 1984 and also has two channels. TV 3, offering mostly fiction (50 per cent), news (20 per cent) and variety programmes (17 per cent), attracted 39 per cent of the average regional audience in 1991. Canal 33's regional market share was 10 per cent.

❺ **RTVG**, which covers the Galicia region, was launched in 1985 and now attracts 26 per cent of the average regional audience. Its schedule is composed mainly of news, fiction, magazine and variety programmes.

❻ **RTVA**, Andalusian television, was launched in 1989. Its Canal Sur drew 43.7 per cent of the average regional audience in 1991. The schedule includes fiction (46 per cent), variety programmes (20 per cent), news (13.5 per cent), sport (9 per cent), children's programmes (5 per cent) and culture (4 per cent).

❼ **RTVM** was started in the Spanish capital in 1989 with the channel Telemadrid. In 1991 the average regional audience was 21.6 per cent. On offer were fiction (49 per cent), variety programmes (22 per cent), news (19 per cent) and sport (6.5 per cent).

❽ **RTVV**, covering the region of Valencia, was launched in January 1990. Its Canal 9 broadcasts 126 hours a week and attracted about 41.8 per cent of the regional audience in 1991. Its schedules offer soaps and serials (25 per cent), cartoons (20 per cent), films (20 per cent), news (15 per cent), sport (10 per cent), documentaries (5 per cent) and educational programmes (5 per cent).

Private channels

❶ **ANTENA 3**, launched in January 1990, at first counted the newspaper ABC among its shareholders. The takeover by businessman Mario Conde, who is linked to the ZETA press group of Antonio Asensio and Rupert Murdoch, was expected to lead to changes in scheduling. In early 1992 programmes were still largely Spanish in flavour and aimed at a family audience, offering 38 per cent fiction, 27 per cent variety programmes, 16 per cent news and 12 per cent children's programmes. In June 1992 Antena 3 was attracting 14 per cent of the total audience, putting it behind Tele Cinco.

❷ **TELE CINCO**, started in 1990, is 25 per cent owned by Italian prime minister and media magnate Silvio Berlusconi. Other shareholders have had no choice but to follow his lead in offering entertainment-based schedules with a wide appeal. Early in 1992 they featured fiction (45 per cent), variety programmes (31 per cent), children's programmes (13 per cent), news (6.7 per cent) and sport (3 per cent). The most popular private channel, Tele Cinco nudged ahead of TVE 2 to pick up 20.8 per cent of the total audience in June 1992.

❸ **CANAL PLUS SPAIN**, an encoded pay channel, was launched in September 1990 on the model of its French counterpart, which owns 25 per cent of the capital. In the autumn of 1992 it had 450,000 subscribers. Fiction, and films in particular, occupy 73 per cent of the schedule. Variety programmes take up 9.6 per cent, sport 8 per cent and news 5 per cent.

3

CHANNEL POLICIES

In 1988 the Spanish Emigration Institute noted at the conference on Migrants, the Media and Cultural Diversity organized by the Council of Europe that the programmes of TVE 1 had been broadcast all over Europe by satellite since January of that year. The institute's management started a project to install dish aerials in a number of cities with large concentrations of Spanish people to allow them to receive these broadcasts. TVE-Madrid broadcasts the programme *España internacional* by satellite for the Spanish diaspora, particularly in western and central Europe. For this reason, in July 1992 the channel announced its intention to end its contribution to the German channel ZDF's programme *Nachbarn in Europa* (Neighbours in Europe), part of which was aimed at Spanish people living in Germany.

The Institute pointed out that immigration to Spain was a relatively recent phenomenon: 'This is perhaps why none of the mass media have come up with any specialized coverage intended for immigrants ... The national press, radio and television often report on the way of life of foreign communities. The media sometimes mention foreigners in a negative sense, when waves of xenophobia sweep the country. Generally speaking, the media all condemn this type of attitude. Nonetheless, it should also be said that most Spanish people know nothing about foreigners, and the media have not taken any active steps to encourage multiculturalism.'

Early in 1990, as immigrants' and refugees' living conditions continued to worsen, a group of organizations launched a campaign to encourage the government to give them working papers and help them settle into Spanish society. 'Immigrants have rights too' was the slogan of the campaign, which was covered by the press, radio and television.

❶ **TVE**. At the moment there are no programmes made specifically for immigrants or ethnic minorities living in Spain, although the subject does come up in TVE's schedules. Apart from newscasts, the main forum for discussion of immigration – and especially illegal immigration – has been news magazines. Some examples are:

➤*INFORME SEMANAL* (Weekly News), the oldest such programme, which has been around for more than 20 years. Broadcast by TVE 1 at 9 pm on Saturdays, it is made up of four 15-minute features. Since 1990 *Informe semanal* has scheduled three features on immigration, two of them on illegal immigration. In September 1992 the programme had five million viewers.

➤*ESPIRAL* (Spiral), a monthly magazine, went out on TVE 1 from November 1989 to November 1990. Lasting 20 minutes and combining reports with studio debate, it devoted two editions to the situation of immigrants in Europe (during the Gulf War) and to the problem of illegal immigration to Spain.

➤*LINEA 900* (Line 900) is produced in Barcelona and broadcast on TVE 2 on Sundays at 8.30 pm. This 30- minute magazine is composed chiefly of viewers giving their opinions on current affairs and social trends. At the end of each edition, the presenter announces forthcoming topics and gives a telephone number so that people interested in taking part can call in. Since it was started in 1991, *Linea 900* has only shown one programme on immigration; it included anonymous interviews with Moroccans who had entered southern Spain illegally.

Generally speaking, these broadcasts take a conservative approach, stressing the appalling conditions in which illegal immigrants enter the country. Thousands of Africans risk their lives in an attempt to start a new life in Europe. Those who survive the crossing of the Straits of Gibraltar have to avoid Spain's paramilitary police, who are increasingly vigilant along the south coast, and find work on the black market – where conditions are equally horrifying. Immigrants who are caught are sent back to Morocco – but most swear they will try to return. Only one programme has tackled the subject of 'Afro- Catalans' of the second generation.

❷ **CANAL SUR**, the Andalusian channel, frequently deals with immigration issues in its weekly news magazine, *Los Reporteros*, which is broadcast at 2 pm on Sundays and repeated at midnight. On the air since 1990, the magazine includes three 12-15 minute reports on social, political and cultural events.

In 1993 the magazine featured 'Proxima estacion Zafarraya' (Next Station Zafarraya), which described the reactions of the inhabitants of a small Andalusian village to the arrival of a group of North Africans, and the emergence of a sense of solidarity and friendship. 'Mas legos del paraiso' looked at the problems North Africans had obtaining visas for the 'new European paradise'. ' 'Mafia' China', about Andalusia's Chinese community, tried to explain why this was the only group of foreigners who did not adopt the Spanish way of life. Highly organized, the Chinese 'mafia' managed to get work permits for their members. The programme also showed how the Chinese arrived in Spain, how they lived, their hopes and fears, and the various gangs operating within the community. 'Mercancia hacia el paraiso' was about immigrants from Eastern Europe trying to get on board ships at the port of Cadiz to go to North America. Interviews with stowaways and port officials highlighted the appalling conditions endured by this 'human cargo'.

Andalusia is in the front line of illegal immigration and it is not surprising that the local television channel gives prominent coverage to the subject. Canal Sur also broadcasts features that give Spanish viewers a better idea of African lifestyles – reports on African towns and villages, for instance – and thus a better understanding of the new arrivals.

SWEDEN

Total population (on 1/1/92):
8,674,000

Foreign population:
493,800
5.7 per cent of the total population

Distribution by country of origin:

Finland	115,000
Former Yugoslavia	41,000
Iran	40,000
Norway	36,700
Denmark	27,900
Turkey	26,400
Chile	19,100
Poland	16,100
Germany	12,900
United Kingdom	10,500
Ethiopia	9,600
Iraq	9,300
United States of America	8,500
Lebanon	7,300
Greece	6,000

Source: SOPEMI, *Trends in International Migration*, Paris, OECD, 1993 (based on Statistics Sweden).

SWEDEN

1

IMMIGRATION HISTORY

Until the Second World War, immigration in Sweden was negligible. The first major inflows during the war years brought mostly Danes, Finns and Norwegians – many of whom subsequently returned to their homelands – as well as refugees from the Baltic countries. After the war, immigration assumed larger proportions and expanded to include other nationals from further afield. From an ethnically and linguistically uniform society, Sweden was transformed within a few decades into a multicultural, multilingual nation, home to numerous ethnic minorities. Labour requirements increased significantly after the war and Swedish industry started to hire workers from various European countries. The number of immigrant workers from other Scandinavian countries also rose, especially after an agreement on a single labour market for the region was signed in 1954.

Two further waves of immigration followed. The first, in the mid-1960s, was composed chiefly of workers from Yugoslavia, Greece and Turkey; the second, between 1968 and 1970, brought in 166,000 foreign nationals, 100,000 of them Finns.

After 1967, immigrants from non-Scandinavian countries were required to have work permits, and in theory the flow of immigrant labour from outside the region has dried up since the early 1970s. On the other hand, the number of political refugees has risen steeply. In the mid-1980s, annual immigration stood at around 30,000 people, two-thirds of whom were refugees from outside Scandinavia or relatives of immigrants who already had Swedish residence permits.

At the end of 1991, about 484,000 non-naturalized foreigners were living in Sweden; 42 per cent of them were from other Scandinavian countries, especially Finland. In 1989 some 17,200 immigrants acquired Swedish nationality, bringing the number of naturalized immigrants to 392,000. Nationals of other Scandinavian countries may apply for naturalization after two years of residence in Sweden; other people have to wait for five years. More than 70 per cent of the second generation (children born in Sweden) have Swedish nationality. In practice, foreigners living in Sweden enjoy the same rights as Swedish citizens, such as education and other social benefits.

Various reforms have been implemented since the mid-1960s with the aim of improving the situation of foreigners in Sweden. Free teaching in the Swedish language was introduced in 1965. The following year the government set up a working group to look at issues connected with social integration, and in 1969 the National Immigration Department, Statens Invandrarvek (SIV), was created. Since 1986 there has been an ombudsman to help combat racial discrimination.

Between 1968 and 1974, a parliamentary committee conducted an inquiry into the measures taken to help immigrants and ethnic minorities. In 1975 the Swedish parliament adopted a new policy based on the pursuit of three goals: equal treatment for immigrants and Swedes, freedom of cultural choice for immigrants, and cooperation and solidarity between the Swedish majority and the various ethnic minorities. In order to give immigrants a better opportunity to make their voices heard, the state offered special support to their national organizations, especially for cultural activities: grants for the publication of books in minority languages, funding for public libraries to help them buy foreign books, an increase in government aid to newspapers run by ethnic groups, and publication by the state of a newspaper in nine languages. A large part of these reforms concerned immigrant children: lessons were given in more than 24 minority languages from nursery school until the end of secondary education, while the children were taught Swedish as a second language. Teaching for adult immigrants was also expanded.

The main office of the National Immigration and Naturalization Department is responsible for implementing the intercommunity relations policy adopted by parliament. One of the aims of the programme drawn up in 1975 is to give immigrants a bigger say in politics. The law passed in 1976 gives foreigners who have lived in Sweden for at least three years the right to vote and to stand in local and regional elections. However, only Swedish citizens are allowed to vote in national elections.

Over the past few years Sweden has followed very restrictive policies towards workers wishing to enter the country, while maintaining a liberal attitude towards foreigners already living there.

In this country with a reputation for tolerance, aid to the third world and urging others to do the same, xenophobic and fascist groups have been springing up in recent years, sowing terror among immigrants and refugees. Although the extreme right is still only a minor force in politics, racial attacks in Sweden have been increasing since 1990 and propaganda against foreigners is invading schools and even the hit parade (with the rock group Ultima Thule, for instance).

NB: Sweden also has two internal minorities: about 16,000 Sami people (Lapps) speaking two different dialects, most of them living in the three northern regions, and 40,000 Finns living in the Torne valley who have retained their own language.

2

THE BROADCASTING SCENE

Public channels

Sveriges Television (SVT) is one of the companies that form part of the SR (Sveriges Radio AB) group. SR is not directly controlled by the state but by various organizations (60 per cent), the press (20 per cent) and industry (20 per cent). SVT is financed by licence fees and advertising is banned, although there has been talk of introducing it on the second channel.

The first channel, Kanal 1 (or SVT 1) was launched in 1957, the second, SVT 2, in 1969. They broadcast nine hours of programmes a day, in the afternoon and evening.

❶ **KANAL 1** offers 22 per cent of films and serials, 13 per cent news broadcasts and magazines, 12 per cent children's programmes, 11 per cent sport and 10 per cent entertainment.

❷ **SVT 2**, the other national mainstream channel, broadcasts regional news from ten regional centres. Apart from this, its scheduling is similar to that of SVT 1, with 22 per cent of films and serials, 11 per cent sport, 11 per cent news, 9 per cent children's programmes and 6 per cent entertainment.

The public channels, already facing competition from TV 3, the Scandinavian satellite channel, have everything to fear from the rising viewing figures notched up by TV 4, a new private channel. In 1991 Kanal 1 and SVT 2 still had 38 per cent and 46 per cent respectively of the total audience.

Private channels

❶ **TV 3**, although broadcast by satellite from abroad, has to be considered a Swedish channel, the first to try to break the ban on private television. Launched in December 1987 using the Scansat sateliite, it is owned by the Swedish industrial group Kinnevik and can be picked up by 60 per cent of homes equipped for cable. TV 3's nine hours of daily broadcasts are split between three languages: Swedish, Norwegian and Danish. Its success can partly be explained by the large share of airtime allocated to sport and entertainment, which occupy less space on the public channels. In 1991 TV 3's audience share was 10 per cent.

❷ **NORDISK TELEVISION/TV 4**, broadcasting since September 1990 via the Tele X satellite, obtained a government licence in November 1991. Its land-based broadcasts now cover the whole of Sweden, but TV 4 still uses Tele X as a backup service. Kinnevik, which manages the channel, is also its major shareholder (30 per cent), along with the Wallenberg group.

TV 4 at first tried to woo the government by offering sophisticated programming, but it has now turned to more commercial schedules based on fiction and entertainment. Of the 50 hours of weekly broadcasts, news represents 20 per cent and children's programmes 10 per cent.

3

CHANNEL POLICIES

SR explicitly undertakes to keep in mind the interests of ethnic and linguistic minorities, as stipulated in its covenant with the state, and the number of programmes made and broadcast for these groups has expanded greatly.

A new agreement between the state and SVT, which sets out the obligations of public broadcasting, came into force in January 1993 and is effective until the end of 1996. The Swedish government gave some general indications which were accepted by parliament: SVT *has a major responsibility in spreading the image of a multicultural Swedish society. Moreover, the minority languages department and the immigrants departments must attempt to strengthen understanding between the various ethnic groups and eradicate xenophobia.*

The Swedish public channels follow a general policy based on equality, freedom of choice and interaction, in accordance with their undertakings. On the specific issue of programmes for immigrants, SR can spread responsibility for their production between the various programme companies (radio and television). The overall objective of these programmes is to strengthen the position of minorities in Swedish society by making it easier for them to take part in its development, while retaining their ties with their countries of origin.

Swedish policy on immigration states that immigrants and refugees have the right to choose between adopting a Swedish cultural identity and preserving their original cultural identity. The same choice is reflected in SVT's programmes for foreigners.

Magazine programmes for immigrants

❶ **STV KANAL 1**. Foreign-language programmes for minority groups were introduced on SVT in 1975, in line with parliament's new immigration policy. Twenty-two people are currently working in the SVT immigrants department, eight of them journalists whose mother tongue is Serbo-Croat, Turkish or Greek.

➤*MOSAIK*, a weekly magazine aimed at ethnic minorities, is broadcast on Saturdays from 2 pm to 3 pm on Kanal 1 and repeated on Tuesday evenings. Originally lasting an hour and a half, the length of the programme was cut to an hour early in 1994. The immigrants department (Invandrarredaktionen), headed by Mårten Andersson, has been trying to get the magazine scheduled for a better time slot, so far without success. *Mosaik* was launched in October 1987, after the reorganization of SVT. Regular topics include politics, culture, social affairs and entertainment presented as reports, features, discussions or interviews and introduced by a journalist of foreign origin. Although a few features are bought in from abroad, most are produced by SVT journalists. A typical broadcast includes sequences in Serbo-Croat, Turkish and Greek, with subtitles in Swedish and sometimes in Farsi, Spanish and Kurdish.

Mosaik is watched by immigrants; less often by Swedes. A survey carried out in 1991 showed that 52 per cent of Yugoslavs tuned in every week and 86 per cent saw the programme 'fairly regularly'.

Birgitta Karlström, who is in charge of documentaries and news magazine programmes on Kanal 1, is aware of *Mosaik*'s poor audience rating, which is partly due to its unpopular time slot and its low budget. She is attempting to get these improved and aims to provide better training for *Mosaik*'s journalists by organizing exchanges with journalists from other programme departments.

On Saturdays, ten minutes of news in three languages is broadcast just before *Mosaik*, summarizing the previous week's events in immigrants' countries of origin and issues involving minorities in Sweden.

➤*SPRÅKA* (Talking to the Kids) is a 20- minute children's programme, broadcast 20 times a year at Saturday lunchtimes, also ahead of *Mosaik*. It is aimed at children aged three to eight and has a range of regular features. In 1992, SVT put out three different versions of *Språka*: in Serbo-Croat, Turkish and Greek, with no subtitles. It was planned to replace the Greek by a Farsi version.

➤*GRANNLAND POLEN* (Poland, our neighbour) and *GRANNLAND ESTLAND* (Estonia, our neighbour) are each broadcast four times a year. Lasting 90 minutes and subtitled in Swedish, they include features made in the countries concerned or in Sweden, discussions, Polish and Estonian music.

Like all SVT broadcasts, these programmes can be picked up all over Sweden as well as in much of Denmark, Norway, Finland and Estonia.

Programmes for Finns and the Sami people

The government aims to provide more programmes for Finns and Sami people by granting them priority aid.

Broadcasts in Finnish have their own department within SVT. A five-minute daily newscast goes out on Kanal 1 and a magazine-discussion programme is broadcast on Saturday mornings from 10 am to 11.30 am, with Swedish subtitles.

Since the early 1980s, the regional station SVT 2 Luleå has been producing programmes in the Sami people's language. It makes four to six hours a year of its own programmes, plus coproductions with the Norwegian channel Norsk Rik-sringkasting (NRK) and the Finland's Yleisradio (YLE).

➤*ARRAN* is a series of six 30-minute programmes a year, coproduced with NRK and YLE and broadcast either between 6 pm and 7 pm or after 10 pm.

➤*ANDDE JA RISTEN-JAGI FARUS* (A Year with Anders and Kristina), a ten-part children's serial, was made in cooperation with NRK Sami Radio. The story, taken from a book by the Finnish Sami writer Kerttu Voulabt, describes the adventures of Anders and Kristina as they learn to fish, hunt and look after the reindeer through-out the eight Sami seasons. Sub-titled in Swedish, the serial was broadcast at 6 pm on Saturdays from October 1991, each programme lasting 15 minutes.

Mainstream programmes

Despite a significant level of immigration by workers from southern Europe during the 1950s, 1960s and 1970s, it was only during the 1980s that Sweden began to suffer from cultural clashes and attacks on immigrants and refugees. Various film makers set out to improve tolerance and understanding between peoples through their films.

➤*KOM IGEN GABY* (Try Again, Gaby), a 50-minute documentary, was made in 1990 by PeÅ Holmquist and Suzanne Khardalian and first broadcast by SVT 2 at 8 pm on 17 December 1991. It was repeated at 2 pm a week later, on Christmas

Day. *Kom Igen Gaby* is the story of a Lebanese boy fleeing the horrors of the war in Beirut who winds up in a small village in northern Sweden and finds himself in conflict with his new surroundings. The documentary was shown in cinemas in ten towns and distributed in film and video formats to 400 schools, libraries and political gatherings; it is estimated that within a year about 50,000 people saw the film, which won the Best Film for Young People award in 1990.

➤*VÄLKOMMEN TILL SVERIGE* (Welcome to Sweden), a 20-minute documentary made by Antonia Carnerud and produced by Sweet Movie, deals with the right to asylum.

➤*UTAN ÅTERVÄNDO?* (Never to Return...?), a 75-minute film made by Antonia Carnerud, was broadcast on Kanal 1 on 28 November 1990. It traces the lives and interwoven destinies of two women, one born in Sweden who emigrated to the United States in 1870, and one born in Syria who came to Sweden with her family in 1980. The story highlights the major events in Swedish migration history.

➤*UNSAFE GROUND*, a 58-minute documentary, was made in 1992 by PeÅ Holmquist, Suzanne Khardalian and Jim Downing and broadcast in May 1993 on STV 2. It begins with Thomas, 16, shown demonstrating with a group of skinheads against immigrants. His friend Helge is a member of the Swedish nationalists' youth movement, and both attend the same school as Jack, who was born in Lebanon. During the 1992 summer holidays, the television crew took the three boys to Beirut, leading Thomas and Helge to reconsider their views on immigrants. The documentary was nominated at the Jerusalem Film Festival in April 1993 and at the Ethnographic Film Awards in Paris in March 1994. It has been shown all over Sweden and has provoked much discussion.

Kanal 1, which believes the media must bear a large share of responsiblity for the growth of racism over the past four or five years and is trying to combat the populist stand taken by some Swedes, regularly makes and broadcasts documentaries, factual magazines and debates involving immigrant communities and political refugees.

➤*WAHREIT MACHT FREI!* (Truth Brings Freedom!) is one of the many magazine programmes and documentaries describing the rise of neo-Nazism and anti-immigrant movements in Europe. A painstaking survey, involving more than 100 hours of filming, was carried out over two years for SVT by Mikaël Schmidt and the resulting documentary was shown on Kanal 1 on 18 September 1991. The programme was also broadcast on the French channel Antenne 2's Envoyé Spécial on 12 December 1991, and in a number of other European countries.

➤*STRIP TEASE*, an hour-long current affairs magazine, has been broadcast by Kanal 1 at 8 pm on Wednesdays since 1992. It is made up of two or three reports and takes an incisive look at Swedish domestic policy. Subjects connected with immigration are dealt with frequently.

Satellite programmes

Sweden receives various channels broadcast to the whole of Europe by satellite. One of these is TV 5 Europe, whose schedules include *Sindbad*, a Belgian magazine aimed at immigrants.

4

INITIATIVES

Sweden is one of the few countries where long and medium-length documentaries are shown in cinemas, with the help of grants and distribution networks set up by the film makers themselves. Filmcentrum and Folkets Bio have played a major role in both the production and distribution of documentaries that have won international acclaim. These include films by Agneta Fagerström, such as *Seppan*, made in 1986 and broadcast on Kanal 1 on 21 April 1987, which describes the mix of cultures at a factory in a small Swedish town in the 1950s, and *Ett paradis utan biljard* (A Heaven without Billiards), made by Carlo Barsotti in 1991 and broadcast on SVT 2 on 4 February 1992, which traces the lives of two Italian immigrants during the same period.

SWITZERLAND

Total population (on 1/1/92):
6,875,000

Foreign population:
1,163,200
16.92 per cent of the total population

Distribution by country of origin:

Italy	377,400
Former Yugoslavia	171,200
Spain	115,300
Portugal	101,200
Germany	85,100
Turkey	69,500
France	50,700
Austria	28,900

Source: SOPEMI, *Trends in International Migration*, Paris, OECD, 1993 (based on figures from the Swiss Federal Office of Foreigners).

Temps Présent, chronique d'une expulsion annoncée. Photo: TSR, Peter Fischli

SWITZERLAND

1

IMMIGRATION HISTORY

The buoyancy of the Swiss economy after the Second World War led to an increased and lasting demand for foreign labour. Initially the Swiss regarded the large numbers of foreigners in their country as a temporary phenomenon resulting from the economic recovery.

In the early 1960s the number of foreigners living permanently in Switzerland rose by more than 90,000 a year because of the booming economy and the growing number of workers being joined by their families. The government started to feel the need to restrict the number of foreign workers entering the country, and in 1963 the Federal Council introduced a system of company quotas. Measures aimed at ensuring the integration of foreigners came into force in the form of restrictions on the entry of foreigners from countries described as 'distant'.

In 1970 the company quota system was replaced by an overall quota system aimed chiefly at controlling the number of foreign workers allowed onto the Swiss labour market. This system is still in force today.

Despite the recession of the mid-1970s, 1974 was a record year for the number of foreigners living in Switzerland – 1,064,000. Between 1970 and 1990 seven referendums were held on the subject of strengthening immigration restrictions, all of which were rejected. In 1970 the referendum on the Schwarzenbach proposal to cut the proportion of foreigners to 10 per cent of the population marked a turning point in immigration policy, even though 54 per cent of electors voted against it. The substantial minority in favour forced the authorities to introduce quotas for foreign workers. The Swiss also voted against five subsequent proposals that suggested reducing the proportion of foreigners, and another was rejected after being discussed by the federal parliament. A proposal entitled 'Solidarity – for a new policy towards foreigners', which aimed in particular to abolish the status of seasonal worker, also came to nothing.

The number of foreign workers entering Switzerland has been falling off as their home economies have improved and as it has become easier for them to move around within the European Community. At the moment only workers from Portugal, and to a lesser extent Spain and the former Yugoslavia, are still being hired, mainly as seasonal labour.

Meanwhile, there has been an increase in the number of seasonal work permits converted into full permits. Those who have worked for 36 months during the previous four years are entitled to full permits, which in turn allow them to bring their families into Switzerland.

The Federal Office of Foreigners says that the Swiss economy requires the presence of foreign labour: 'At the moment, one job in four in Switzerland is held by a foreigner'.

At the end of 1993, the federal authorities introduced measures making it harder to obtain political asylum and thus easier to throw out quickly those whose requests are refused. Under the new regulations, foreigners who have entered Switzerland illegally can be arrested and then expelled. On the pretext of fighting crime and expelling those who have committed offences, the authorities are making it increasingly difficult to obtain asylum – a situation that is causing serious concern to the leaders of welfare organizations.

2
THE BROADCASTING SCENE

A dominant feature of Swiss broadcasting is that it is multilingual, and therefore regionally based. Television in neighbouring countries also has a major influence. A law adopted on 21 June 1991 stressed the need to take account of federal structures and linguistic minorities in the organization of broadcasting. It states that concessions may be granted to both public and private channels and confirms the controlling position of the Société Suisse de Radio Télévision (SSR).

Public channels

The SSR has its headquarters in Berne. It is made up of three regional television companies corresponding to the three main language groups: the German Deutsche und Rätoromanische Schweiz (DRS), the Italian or Ticino channel Televisioni Swizzera Italiana (TSI) and the French Télévision Suisse Romande (TSR).

About 70 per cent of the SSR's spending is paid for by the licence fee, with the rest coming from advertising. The 1991 broadcasting law eased the rules on advertising, allowing breaks every 90 minutes, and allowed the public channels to accept sponsors. Despite these reforms and a 25 per cent increase in the licence fee in 1992, the SSR is still short of cash. In order to deal with this problem and to face up to foreign competition, it has introduced a major restructuring programme and revamped its schedules.

The three channels enjoy a large degree of independence and offer mainstream schedules, often broadcasting cultural programmes during prime time.

❶ **TSR**, the French-language channel, was started in 1954. Of the 6,310 hours broadcast in 1990, it concentrated on fiction (40 per cent), sport (13 per cent), cultural programmes (mainly documentaries – 12 per cent), news (9.5 per cent), children's programmes (6 per cent) and news magazines (5 per cent).

That year TSR attracted 36 per cent of the audience in the French-speaking part of Switzerland (40 per cent taking account of viewers in the German-speaking and Italian-speaking cantons). The three main French national channels were watched by another 40 per cent of the French-language audience, while 17 per cent watched other channels.

❷ **DRS**, launched in 1955, covers German- and Romansch-speaking Switzerland. Of the 5,526 hours broadcast in 1990, its schedules included fiction (19 per cent), sport (16 per cent), documentaries (16 per cent), factual magazines (13 per cent), news (11 per cent) and children's programmes (5 per cent).

In German- and Romansch-speaking Switzerland, DRS had 32 per cent of the audience in 1990 (37 per cent for the whole country). The channel faces stronger competition from foreign channels than its French counterpart. German and Austrian broadcasters scoop up a full 62 per cent of the market, including 11 per cent for ARD and 8 per cent for ZDF.

❸ **TSI** was started in 1961. The 4,771 hours broadcast in 1990 were dominated by fiction (29 per cent), followed by sport (22 per cent), news and factual magazines (20 per cent), cultural programmes (12 per cent) and children's programmes (4 per cent).

Private channels

At the moment there are no land-based national or regional channels in Switzerland, although they could be authorized under the 1991 broadcasting law. Six local channels each receive a small share of the licence fee: Canal Alpha Plus (Neuchâtel), Canal 9 (Sierre), Diessenhofen TV, Hasli TV (Zurich), Wil TV and Winti TV. Two pay channels broadcast on cable: Teleclub (in German) and Téléciné (in French, operating in the Lausanne region). Two-thirds of Swiss households are cabled and have access to about 20 channels.

3

CHANNEL POLICIES

How does television choose to reflect the cultural diversity of Switzerland, with its three official languages, four national languages (German, French, Italian and Romansch, plus many dialects) and a substantial immigrant community?

Article 55a, paragraph 2, of the Federal Constitution states that: 'Radio and television ... take account of the distinctive features of the country and the needs of the cantons.' Article 26, headed 'Licence and Mandate', stipulates that the SSR is granted a licence to broadcast both national programmes and programmes intended for the various language regions.

Switzerland has three national channels broadcasting to the French-speaking, German-speaking and Italian-speaking regions.

❶ **TSR**, the French-language channel, puts the emphasis on news coverage for a wide range of viewers. As former head of news Claude Torracinta expressed it: 'TSR is concerned about its own audience, in other words the mass audience.' TSR has decided to draw the attention of viewers to the conditions in which immigrants live in Switzerland. *Temps présent* and *Tell quel*, weekly news magazines broadcast at 8 pm, deal regularly with issues affecting foreigners, refugees and illegal immigrants, and with the right of asylum. A feature on one of these subjects goes out about once a month.

►*TEMPS PRÉSENT*, has been on the air since 1969 and celebrated its 1,000th edition in May 1992. It produces two-thirds of the 50-minute programmes itself and one-third are purchased or coproduced. *Temps présent* attracts around 35 per cent to 40 per cent of the total audience, giving it a market share of up to 60 per cent. It devotes about a third of its investigations to Switzerland, a third to other countries, and a third to general social issues, such as drugs, violence against children, and homosexuality.

With its incisive and critical reporting, *Temps présent* regularly sheds light on the flip side of Swiss prosperity and its view of society is meant to be disturbing. In 1991, for instance, a team from the magazine visited a group of 30 Kurds who had entered Switzerland illegally from Turkey. The programme highlighted the distress that had caused them to leave their home country. Other editions that year dealt with seasonal agricultural workers and the problems of Swiss primary schools, where one in six children is foreign.

On 21 January 1993 *Temps présent* showed a 44-minute film entitled 'Romanies, the pariahs of Europe'. These people have always served as scapegoats and they are still regarded as undesirable wherever they go. In Romania, where they are concentrated, they are the victims of systematic discrimination and persecution. Many tried to escape to Germany, but here too they were driven out by a wave of racial violence. The film, made by Irène Challand and Bertrand Theubet, told the story of a people hounded across Europe.

'Adios Suisse chérie', broadcast on 7 October 1993, followed the return of Spanish people to Spain after 10, 20 or even 30 years living in Switzerland. They left in their thousands, for good, driven by unemployment or general economic instability, thinking life would be easier in their home country. The 24-minute film shows that the journey home proved more difficult that they had thought, studded as it was with separations, heartbreak and lost illusions.

'Le temps des clandestins', broadcast on 17 February 1994, showed the difficult situation facing illegal immigrants from the former Yugoslavia. In 1993, 4,410 of them were arrested at the 'green border' between Italy and Switzerland – most running away from the war, being drafted into the Serb army and extreme poverty. The *Temps présent* crew followed them as they crossed the mountains, were arrested and sent back to Italy, where a chain of assistance had been set up in villages and convents. Made by Nadia Braedle and Nicolas Wadimoff, the 24-minute programme showed that the situation had reached emergency proportions. It also pointed out that if countries like Switzerland are not willing to take in people fleeing war and poverty, they should take steps to combat the causes of emigration from the countries of origin.

In May 1994 'Album de famille' was bought by the TSR news department and shown as part of *Temps présent*. Spanish-Swiss second-generation immigrant Fernand Melgar traced his parents' journey from Andalusia in 1963, when Switzerland encouraged a million workers to come from southern Europe to cope with an acute labour shortage. In 1990 the couple decided to take early retirement and return to Andalusia. In the documentary, they tell their son about the segregation, discrimination and humiliation they had endured which led them in the end to count the days until they could return to Spain.

Temps présent is now broadcast by the French channel TV5 Europe, making it available to 20 million homes by cable and satellite.

►*TELL QUEL*, a 25-minute magazine on the air since 1977, attracts about the same number of viewers as *Temps présent*. It is broadcast on Fridays and lasts 25 minutes. It aims to show life as it really is in Switzerland, and has included reports on topics such as seasonal building workers (70 per cent of whom are Portuguese) and children of illegal immigrants who are deprived of an education.

➤*VIVA*, started in 1987, is a cultural magazine intended for a mass audience. It is shown at 9.40 pm on Tuesdays. One of its features, 'Terres étrangères, Suisse dorée' by Eva Ceccarolli, focused on foreigners living in Switzerland: a Guinean diplomat, a Chilean teacher, a Cambodian shop assistant, a Lebanese librarian and a couple of Zairean evangelists – all contributing the wealth of their different cultures to the host country. This programme was broadcast on 7 April 1992.

➤*LA VIERGE NOIRE* (The Black Virgin) is a six-part series first shown in September 1989. It was coproduced by TSR's entertainment and fiction department with the public channels in France, Austria, Italy and Germany and was also shown in those countries. Each 52-minute episode gives a humorous account of life in a Swiss village. The script was written by Michel Viala and the first two episodes made by Jean-Jacques Lagrange, who subsequently handed over to Igaal Niddam.

The central theme of *La Vierge Noire* is mixed marriages, a common occurrence in Switzerland during the past 15 years. Often the partners are men living in the country who advertise for wives; those who reply are often young African or Mauritian women dreaming of a better life. Several channels helped to finance this 'Euroseries' with the aim of stemming the tide of American productions while confronting an increasingly common phenomenon of Swiss society.

➤*LES GENS D'À CÔTÉ* (The People Next Door), a cross-border magazine, put out a special edition on the theme of foreigners at 8.40 pm on 24 April 1992. The 60-minute live broadcast was also shown on the French channel FR3 in the Rhone-Alpes region. Presented by Jean-Philippe Rapp, it included reports on French and Swiss views of asylum seekers and the integration of immigrant workers, and a link-up between the refugee centre in Broc, Switzerland, and a stadium in Saint-Etienne, France. Studio guests were, in Switzerland, geneticist Albert Jacquard, immigration specialist Nicole Léry, Jean-François Labarthe, head of the Red Cross in Geneva, and in France, writer and researcher Azouz Begag and Joseph-Antoine Bell, spokesman for a sports organization.

On 12 June 1992 another special edition on the theme of people living in border areas was broadcast on TSR and FR3 in the same time slot.

❷ **TSI**'s broadcasts in Italian include four programmes for Italian and Spanish immigrants, two news magazines and two cultural programmes.

Magazine programmes for Immigrants

➤*TELESETTIMANALE*, formerly known as *Ora per voi*, is a news magazine broadcast on Sundays from 11.30 am to 11.45 am, from June to September. In Italian with no subtitles, it alternates reports and studio debates, focusing on the latest developments in Italian immigration (red tape, changes in the law, cultural events, and so on). For example, the 11 October 1992 edition was made up of four reports on foreigners' right to vote, a new trade union in the building industry, a conference in Zurich on Italy in the year 2000, and the steel sculptures of Giuseppe Spagnudo.

►*TG SENZA FRONTIERE*, which follows *Telesettimanale*, is a 15-minute newscast produced by Italian public television and reporting on Italian immigrants to Switzerland and other countries. The 11 October 1992 edition featured the ISI (an extra property tax imposed on Italians living abroad), Italian-Americans and the US presidential elections, and grants for Italian students.

►*GIRO D'ORIZZONTE*, shown on Saturdays at 2.50 pm, is about artistic and cultural events staged by the Italian community in Switzerland. The 30-minute programme goes out from October to June, in Italian.

►*TELE REVISTA* is a magazine of political, cultural and social news for the Spanish community in Switzerland. In Spanish without subtitles, it is broadcast at 11.50 am on the first and third Saturdays of the month from September to June and lasts 15 minutes. Topics tackled include the problems of foreigners in Switzerland, Spain's emigration policy and Spanish cultural events in Switzerland. The 4 October 1992 edition, for instance, reported on foreigners' right to vote, a demonstration in Berne by Spanish organizations protesting against the emigration policy, and a Spanish rock musician, Loquillo, on tour in Switzerland.

❸ **DRS**, the German-language channel, also includes some broadcasts in the fourth national language, Romansch, which is spoken by some 50,000 people, 30,000 of them living in the canton of Graubünden.

►*SVIZRA ROMANTSCHA*, a 45-minute programme broadcast fortnightly, is repeated on TSR and TSI one or two weeks later. The title covers various types of programme. Once a month there is a magazine, *Contrasts*, aimed at a wide audience and including studio discussions and reports. A quiz show, *Pez a cup* (Climb to the Summit), is broadcast six times a year, and *Muschkito* (Mosquito), a magazine for young people in cities with a satirical edge, three times a year. Twice a year *Direct da …* (Live From …) features a typical village of the Graubünden region. *Svizra Romantscha* is broadcast on Sundays from 5.40 pm to 6.25 pm, with a repeat on Wednesdays from 11 pm to 11.45 pm. Except for the live programmes, it is subtitled in German.

Other programmes in Romansch, broadcast only by the DRS, include:

➤*TELESGUARD* is a weekly news magazine about Romansch-speakers, broadcast from 4.40 pm to 4.55 pm on Saturdays and repeated from 1.45 pm to 2 pm on Sundays.

➤*ISTORGIAS DA BUNA NOTG* (Goodnight Stories) is a 10-minute children's programme shown at 5.40 pm on Thursdays.

➤*IN PIED SIN VIA* (A Word on the Way), a religious broadcast, goes out four times a year: Good Friday, Ascension Day, the first Sunday of August and Christmas Day.

The following viewing figures were collected in March 1992 for the 289,000 people aged three and over living in Italian-speaking Switzerland: *Svizra Romant-scha*, 22.5 per cent of market share; *Telesettimanale*, 5.7 per cent; *Tele Revista*, 12 per cent; *Giro d'orizzonte*, 22.1 per cent; *Telesguard*, 12.3 per cent.

4

INITIATIVES

❶ **THE NORTH–SOUTH MEDIA ENCOUNTERS FESTIVAL.** In June 1983 the University Institute of Development Studies in Geneva organized a seminar on the 'New World Information Order'. One of the major outcomes was the observation that there was no forum for professionals from developed and developing countries to show, sell or exchange their films on development, or for professionals, researchers, students and the public to meet and join in the North–South debate, particularly in the areas of news and communication.

The festival was an attempt to provide such a forum. It was organized by the institute in conjunction with the United Nations' Non-Governmental Liaison Service and Infosud, the Lausanne agency for the developing press. TSR supplied the facilities for showing films and the operation was financed by the city and canton of Geneva and the Swiss confederation.

The first festival was held in 1985 and it has since became an annual event. Its aims are to improve understanding about development issues, to encourage the showing of films on these issues, to establish a forum where the heads of television channels, producers and film makers can meet and talk, to try to redress the North–South balance, especially in the field of communication, and to analyse the major trends in development as they emerge.

Television channels from all over the world take part by entering for a competition their best broadcast on development from the previous two years. Documentaries, fiction or cartoons lasting no longer than 60 minutes are all accepted, and may deal either with relations between developed and developing countries or with the divisions within particular societies.

An international jury composed of half communication professionals and half development experts chooses the best programmes and awards three prizes, the Geneva International Television Prize, the Pierre-Alain Donnier Prize (donated by TSR) and the North–South Prize.

The ILO prize for the best film on social justice, awarded in April 1994 by the International Labour Office, went to Fernand Melgar's documentary, 'Album de famille', shown as part of the magazine *Temps présent* and produced by Climage.

❷ **THE EUROPEAN BROADCASTING UNION** (EBU), whose headquarters are in Geneva, has since 1992 organized or taken part in various activities to encourage tolerance and combat racism.

The children's programmes working group was set up to draw the attention of children aged eight to twelve to the problem of racism. Fourteen EBU member channels undertook to make a documentary based on the true story of one or more children who lived in a racist environment, who had been victims of racism or even those who themselves held racist views. In exchange, each channel received free the documentaries made by the others. In 1993 the following channels took part in the project: BBC (United Kingdom), RTBF and BRTN (Belgium), CPB (United States, an associate member), DR (Denmark), MTV (Hungary), NRK (Norway), NOS (Netherlands), ORF (Austria), RTE (Ireland), SBS (Australia, an associate member), SVT (Sweden), TRT (Turkey) and YLE (Finland).

In 1992 the Education Working Group, meeting in Valencia, Spain, took as its main theme 'the challenges of a multicultural society and the fight against racism'. The group decided to draw up a code of conduct to ensure unbiased portrayal of people and events on television, and to provide information and advice to immigrant communities about their civic rights and everyday matters. The group also agreed to fight to increase the number of multicultural programmes, to broadcast more anti-racist programmes and to play an active part in campaigns in this area.

The Education Working Group met again in Hilversum, The Netherlands, in May 1993, and the first exchanges of programmes between state television channels took place. The third meeting was held in Woodnorton, England, with the aim of 'encouraging and facilitating the exchange of documentaries and multicultural magazines'. The following public channels took part: ORF (Austria), ZDF and WDR (Germany), NOS (Netherlands), BRTN (Belgium), Czech TV (Czech Republic), SVT1 and UR (Sweden), BBC (United Kingdom). Three other channels – NRK (Norway), YLE (Finland) and DRS (Switzerland) – were present as observers. The BBC, which chaired the third meeting, is also a founder member of Public Broadcasting for a Multicultural Europe, an organization whose headquarters are in the Netherlands (see the Netherlands chapter for more details). The organization used the meeting to submit a draft code of conduct for EBU members but a final version has not yet been adopted. The next meeting of the education working group is scheduled to take place in Austria in 1995.

UNITED KINGDOM

Desmond's. Photo: Channel 4, Trevor Leighton

Total population (on 1/1/92):
57,998,000

Foreign population:
1,750,000
3.02% of the total population*

Distribution by country of origin:

Ireland	469,000
India	136,000
United States of America	87,000
Italy	86,000
Pakistan	84,000
Caribbean and Guyana	68,000
Central and Eastern Europe[1]	61,000
Western Africa	45,000
Bangladesh	42,000
Germany	41,000
Eastern Africa	40,000
France	38,000
Spain	30,000
Northern Europe	25,000
Portugal	20,000
Other countries	478,000

*People of 'foreign origin' are defined as those retaining nationality other than British and does not include British citizens who are also members of ethnic minority groups.In total, three million UK citizens and residents are of ethnic origin including 1.5 million Asian, 900,000 African-Caribbean and 600,000 others (including 100,000 Chinese).
[1]Including the former Soviet Union.

Source: SOPEMI, *Trends in International Migration*, Paris, OECD, 1993 (based on the Labour Force Survey, London).

UNITED KINGDOM

1

IMMIGRATION HISTORY

The particular history of the British Empire and the Commonwealth has put immigrants to the United Kingdom in a different situation from those in other European countries.[1] Under the terms of the 1948 Nationality Act, any Commonwealth citizen – who is automatically a subject of the Crown just as Britons are – could acquire British nationality after one year of residence in the UK. In fact, Commonwealth 'immigrants' enjoyed the same political and civic rights as people born in the UK, including the right to vote and to stand in local and national elections.

Large-scale immigration to the UK began because of a labour shortage after the Second World War; the UK invited and recruited cheap labour from its colonies. The first immigrants from the Caribbean (especially Barbados) were soon followed by Indians and Pakistanis in the 1960s, then by Bangladeshis in the 1970s.

Racial attacks and discrimination led these minorities to form a black resistance movement, resulting in riots in 1958, and again during the 1970s. In the 1960s and 1970s, as discrimination continued, an assimilation policy was implemented at national level. At the same time a wave of xenophobia and racism gathered, and was given voice by the right-wing MP Enoch Powell in his famous 'rivers of blood' speech. Government responses were two-fold: on one side, successive immigration laws sought to place limitations on entry to the country; on the other, measures were introduced to curb discrimination against minorities and incitement to racial hatred. The 1962 law on immigration from the Commonwealth stipulated that anyone wishing to enter the UK had to have employers' references. In October 1965 the first law against racial discrimination (the Race Relations Act) was

---

1 Because of this, we have modified the layout used for previous chapters.

passed, making discrimination and incitement to racial hatred illegal in public places. In 1968 the scope of the Act was extended to cover discrimination in housing and employment, but this legislation remained virtually a dead letter.

In the same year the Race Relations Board was set up, along with advisory bodies responsible for relations with immigrant communities at district council level. In education, the government's assimilation policy led to a ruling that all teaching in schools should be in English and the introduction of a 30 per cent limit on the number of pupils from ethnic minorities[1] in any one school. However, the shortage of nursery schools meant that most of these children were unable to gain a good command of English at an early age.

The 1971 Immigration Act introduced major modifications:

- The government introduced the concept of patriality as a way of determining a person's right to enter the UK. Anyone with a grandparent (not a parent, as previously) born in the UK or naturalised as a UK citizen is defined as a patrial.

- The right of economic immigrants to stay in the UK indefinitely was abolished.

- Sanctions for illegal immigration were introduced: people entering the UK illegally could be expelled up to five years after their date of arrival (the previous deadline had been 24 hours).

These changes brought the situation of Commonwealth citizens entering the UK without authorisation, in particular black people with no white UK grandparents, closer to that of foreigners.

In 1976 the Race Relations Act was again extended to cover indirect discrimination. The new Commission for Racial Equality was given the right to take cases of racial discrimination to court, although this remained a dead letter until the 1980s.

Meanwhile, as government became increasingly decentralised, local authorities were given wider powers to introduce measures against racial discrimination, and those with large immigrant communities could obtain subsidies. Metropolitan authorities had been set up in major cities, with extensive powers covering education, social services, housing, recreation, public hygiene and equal opportunity.

---

1 The term *ethnic minorities* is used in the UK to describe *non-whites*. The *Asian community* means Indians, Pakistanis and Bangladeshis living in the UK; the *black community* means Africans and people of Caribbean origin – although this classification is disputed, since many Asians also call themselves black.

Only health and the police remained under the direct control of central government.

The principle of equal opportunity was adopted by most local authorities, which introduced measures aimed not only at guarding against discrimination in the hiring of staff, but also at correcting existing imbalances. The impact of such measures was important, as local authorities can often provide a major source of employment for the entire surrounding region; this was the case, for instance, with the municipality of Birmingham.

The 1980s saw fresh waves of uprisings, particularly in run-down inner city areas: Bristol in 1980, followed by London, Birmingham, Liverpool and Manchester in 1981 and 1985. These riots, sparked by the recession, unemployment, racist abuse and discrimination, especially regarding education, largely involved people of Caribbean origin, who tend to have the worst relations with the police, but also some people of Asian origin and working-class white people. Indeed, the riots often began after an incident involving the police.

In 1983 the Home Secretary explicitly rejected the use of the word immigrant: 'It is no longer appropriate to consider ethnic minorities as immigrants. Almost half of Britons originating from the New Commonwealth or Pakistan were born here. Many others were brought up in this country and, for practical reasons, know no other. The United Kingdom is their homeland. They are a part of it. They are here to stay and to play their part in the life of their country.'

In 1986 Margaret Thatcher's government tried to restrict local authorities' room to manoeuvre – notably by abolishing the powerful Greater London Council which had undertaken a number of anti-racist actions. The same attitude was evident from the government's handling of other welfare and social justice issues.

The notions of cultural identity and cultural difference within ethnic minorities have become more important during the 1990s. The struggle for equality of opportunity is coupled with the desire to recognise the different communities' individuality. Ethnic minorities are the object of consultations, negotiations and grants enabling them to set up services for their own communities. Community associations work as pressure groups and exert a significant influence on the course of events at both national and local level.

2

THE BROADCASTING SCENE

From the late 1980s onwards the ruling Conservative party began a programme of far-reaching reform in the field of broadcasting, introducing a number of fundamental changes in the 1991 Broadcasting Act. New franchises for the companies that make up Independent Television (ITV), were awarded in October 1991 and have been effective since January 1993. From the same month, Channel 4 ceased to be financed by contributions from the ITV companies and started managing its own advertising.

The 1991 Broadcasting Act also envisaged the launch of a fifth national channel using spare frequencies reaching up to 70 per cent of the country. The process of awarding a franchise to run the service has been fraught with difficulties. When the service was first put out to tender in 1992 only one proposal was submitted, a radical plan for a network of city-based stations backed by Thames Television, Time Warner and Moses Znaimer, the founder of Toronto's CityTV. However the regulatory authority, the ITC, turned down the bid, claiming that it was not financially viable. A second request for submissions was issued in September 1994.

Britain's main public service broadcaster, the BBC, had also been expected to undergo radical reform, especially given the longstanding hostility of the country's Conservative government, which saw the corporation as given to excessive criticism of government policies.

The replacement of Prime Minister Margaret Thatcher by John Major marked a turn in the BBC's fortunes. Furthermore, by the time debate began over the future of the BBC, the less desirable results of the reform of ITV had begun to emerge. Few wanted to see the BBC change as radically as had the ITV system. The BBC has therefore been allowed to reform itself, and its structure and funding will be left unchanged.

The name of the Independent Broadcasting Authority (IBA, the regulatory body) has been changed to Independent Television Commission (ITC).

Public channels

The BBC channels are financed only from television licence fees. Both advertising and sponsorship are banned.

❶ **The BBC** began experimental television transmissions in 1936, although the main television service (today's BBC 1) effectively began operations after the end of the Second World War. It is a mainstream channel broadcasting from about 6am to midnight, a total of 6,400 hours during the 1990–91 financial year. Imbued with the idea of public service, like its sister channel BBC 2, it is aimed at a family audience. Films and serials are not broadcast during prime time, showing that documentaries can attract viewers too. In 1990–91, fiction, documentaries and magazine programmes made up 36 per cent of scheduling (including 20 per cent of bought-in films and serials), news 18 per cent, children's programmes 13 per cent (including 5 per cent of bought-in serials and cartoons), entertainment 9 per cent, sport 8 per cent ... Taking viewing figures for 1991 as a whole, BBC 1 was the second most popular channel after ITV, with 34% of the audience. This remained practically unchanged the following year (33 per cent in June 1992).

❷ **BBC 2**, launched in 1964, aims to be more culturally oriented than BBC 1, while still showing programmes of general interest. It too is on the air for about 18 hours a day – a total of 6,160 hours between March 1990 and March 1991. Before 6.45 am, BBC 2 broadcasts programmes for the Open University (670 hours a year, or 11 per cent of total airtime). News takes up only 5 per cent, programmes for young people 1.5 per cent and entertainment 3 per cent. More airtime is given to schools programmes (10 per cent), sport (11 per cent), and fiction, documentaries and magazine programmes (42 per cent), half of them bought abroad. Since the channel's audience is more highly targeted, viewing figures are only a third of BBC 1's (9.8 per cent in 1991). In 1992 BBC 2 was still drawing around 10 per cent of viewers.

In 1993–94, the combined audience share for BBC1 and BBC2 was 43 per cent.

The BBC also provides two services aimed at foreign markets:

❸ **BBC World Service Television** was incorporated in 1991, taking over responsibility for BBC TV Europe, established in 1988. This encoded channel broadcasts 18 hours of programmes a day to European viewers, offering a selection of BBC 1 and BBC 2 programmes.

❹ **World Service Television News**, launched in March 1991, is an international service specially produced for foreign viewers.

Originally broadcast via Intelsat VI, these services are now available in Eastern Europe and Asia via Asiasat. They were expected to offer worldwide coverage by the end of 1993.

Private channels

❶ **ITV** was set up in 1955. Based on regions that did not change with the new franchises effective from 1993, it is composed of 15 companies plus the morning channel GMTV. Special mention should be made of Independent Television News (ITN), which is responsible for the famous *News at Ten* programme.

Following the lifting of regulations limiting the concentration of ownership within ITV, a number of mergers have taken place reducing the number of companies within the UK's television system. The mergers are not, however, allowed to override the commitments made by the existing franchise holders, although many of the companies have subsequently cut back their level of production resources.

- London (weekdays): Carlton Television won the franchise which had previously been held by Thames Television (Carlton Television is owned by the Carlton Group and Italy's RCS Group);

- London (weekends): Retained by London Weekend Television, the company was taken over by Granada Television in 1994;

- North West England: Granada Television retained its franchise. Granada is a subsidiary of the Granada leisure and entertainment group;

- North East England: Tyne Tees retained its franchise but has since been acquired by neighbouring Yorkshire Television in a friendly merger between the two companies;

- East Central England: Yorkshire Television remains in control of the franchise area it won back in 1991;

- East and West Midlands: Central Television retained its franchise but was taken over by the Carlton Group in 1994;

- East of England: Anglia retained its licence but has now been taken over by MAI, the principal owner of Meridian;

- Wales and West of England: HTV retained its franchise. A 20 per cent stake in the company was acquired by Flextech, a subsidiary of US cable group Tele-Communications Inc.;

- South West England: Westcountry Television took over the franchise formerly held by TSW. Westcountry shareholders included Associated Newspapers (20 per cent) and South West Water (20 per cent);

- South of England: Meridian Television took over the franchise held by Television South (TVS). Meridian is owned by MAI (65 per cent), Carlton and independent production group SelecTV;

- Central Scotland: Scottish Television retained its franchise. The Mirror Newspapers group acquired a 19.99 per cent stake in the company in 1994 (the maximum allowed under cross-ownership regulations);

– North of Scotland: Grampian Television (unchanged);

– The Borders: Retained by Border Television (in which Granada owns a 20 per cent shareholding);

– Northern Ireland: Ulster Television (unchanged);

– Channel Islands: Channel Television retained its franchise. The company is owned by Channel Hotels and Properties.

The national slot formerly allocated to TV-am has now gone to GMTV (owned by *The Guardian*, LWT, Walt Disney and Carlton).

As before, the ITV companies share many of the same programmes. Even before the new franchises had begun to operate in January 1993, the new companies had agreed to implement a central scheduling system. The new Network Centre now decides 75% of the companies' programme schedule. It is answerable in its operations to a board representing the ITV companies, although it has full autonomy to make decisions on a day-to-day basis. The ITV companies' income is from advertising and overseas sales, and the biggest share goes to the biggest companies: Carlton, Central, Granada, LWT and TVS. Each company also offers between two-and-a- half and ten hours of regional programmes.

In 1991 the ITV companies accounted for 41 per cent of the total television audience, putting ITV in first place. Their share was still around 40 per cent in 1992.

❷ **Channel 4**, with a brief to innovate and cater for minority interests, was established in 1982, and has a semi- public, semi-private status. It is linked to the ITV network but is non-commercial and is aimed at cultural and ethnic minorities. Under the terms of the 1991 Broadcasting Act, Channel 4 must now seek its own advertising resources (it had previously survived on contributions from each of the ITV companies), but the Channel 3 network guarantees it a minimum income in case of difficulties.

Even more cultural than BBC 2, Channel 4 aims above all to be different. It broadcasts 7,000 hours of programmes a year. Fiction takes up 30 per cent (20 per cent of which is cinema films), entertainment 17 per cent, educational programmes 11 per cent, news 9 per cent, magazine programmes 9 per cent, sport 8 per cent and documentaries 7 per cent. Together with Sianel 4 Cymru (S4C), a small Welsh channel which has so far formed part of the same network, Channel 4 obtained 10 per cent of the total television audience in 1992, and was still around 11 per cent in 1993.

The long-established channels are facing increasingly strong competition from the satellite channels of BSkyB – formed when Sky Television and British Satellite Broadcasting (BSB) merged in November 1990. In 1992 channels other than the BBC and ITV/Channel 4 picked up between 5 per cent and 7 per cent of the total audience.

3

CHANNEL POLICIES

The first waves of immigration to the UK coincided with the early days of television and the relationship between ethnic minorities and British television is a long one, starting in the 1960s when the BBC decided to take account of this new audience.

The BBC's response, however, was a piecemeal one, reacting to issues and demands as they arose. However, at the beginning of the 1990s, changing circumstances and shifts in government policy forced the BBC into a thoroughgoing review of its purpose and strategy. This exercise, designed to position the Corporation for the challenges of the coming century has forced the BBC to at least consider the implications of functioning in a multiethnic and multicultural society.

The BBC's strategic document entitled *Extending Choice*, outlines four objectives for the BBC in the coming ten years:

- Informing the national debate;

- Expressing British culture and Entertainment;

- Creating opportunities for education;

- Communicating between the United Kingdom and abroad.

Although multiculturalism is not a primary focus of 'Extending Choice', it does contain indications of the shifts that have taken place in the way that the BBC defines its audience. For example, one of the BBC's objectives (p. 32 of the report) has been defined as reflecting 'the full cultural diversity of country – with regular dramatic contributions from regional and national regional centres and the commissioning of new work by writers and producers from the ethnic minorities'.

The BBC also notes that the context in which it operates is also changing. Broadcasting at the heart of British society, it maintains, is a hard task to perform.

Various forces are at work in the United Kingdom in the 1990s it says. One is the 'fragmentation of society into discrete social, economic, radical and religious groups'.

In the summary of proposals the government also says in its priorities for regional broadcasting that English local services must 'recognize the different religious and ethnic populations and give the country's multiracial and multilingual groups a radio voice in the community'. As an example of this kind of approach it cites the highly successful Asian Network, broadcast on BBC radio stations in the Midlands.

Although the guidelines laid down by the regulatory authority for broadcasting, the Independent Television Commission, do not say that the private channels have any specific obligation towards ethnic minorities, Article 1.4 on 'bad taste and humour' does state:

> There is a danger of offence also in jokes based on different racial charac-
> teristics. Producers need to be sensitive to the possible effect of such jokes
> upon the racial minority concerned, as well as to changes in public
> attitudes to what is and is not acceptable. Even though it may be unlikely
> that matters intended as a joke would constitute an offence ... they may
> nonetheless offend against good taste or decency or be offensive to public
> feeling. Similar considerations apply to the treatment of other, less ob-
> vious and vulnerable, minorities, including older people, homosexuals,
> and minority religious faiths and language groups.

❶ BBC

Although the BBC has to take account of all viewers living in the UK, there are no regulations explicitly forcing it to produce programmes specifically designed for minorities. Nonetheless, public television has set itself the target of having 8 per cent of people from ethnic minorities on its staff, at all levels of the hierarchy. This target has more or less been achieved overall, but unfortunately it is not the higher posts that are occupied by minorities. Nonetheless, it is important to note that the BBC had to defend itself in June 1994 against accusations of over-zealous political correctness: While the BBC said it had a duty to reflect the nation it served, Conservatives MPs said it was uncacceptable positive discrimination to give 6 places out of 13 on the 1994/95 regional News trainee to applicants from ethnic minorities origin.[1]

BBC Multicultural Programme Department

Narendhra Morar, Managing Editor of the BBC's Multicultural Programmes Unit

---

1 'BBC defends stand on jobs for minorities' *Guardian*, London 13 June 1994.

at the Birmingham studios, explains that programmes for minorities have had to be adapted for each succeeding generation: the very first immigrants who arrived in the 1960s, followed by a generation born abroad but educated in the UK, and finally one both born and brought up there. From the mid-1960s, the BBC was showing programmes for Indians and Pakistanis such as *Apna Higbar Samajhye* (Make Yourself at Home) and *Nayl Zindagi, Naya Jeevan* (New Life), in Urdu and Hindi, followed by *Padosi* (Neighbours), for Asian women. These programmes, grouped together in the Immigrant Unit and broadcast early in the morning, had as their main objective to help immigrants to learn English and to teach them about the British lifestyle, helping them to fit into British society without losing their ties with their home countries. Such programmes did not however exist for Caribbean minorities; it was felt that since they spoke English they could watch the BBC's mainstream programmes.

The BBC continued to produce these magazines during the years that followed without really taking account of the changing generations. It was only in 1982, when Channel 4 was set up, that the BBC changed its policy and began producing programmes whose aim was to entertain and not just to educate the public. And the target group was no longer only minorities. This time the aim was to make 'multicultural programmes', in other words programmes aimed at a wider audience. Furthermore, for the first time, a magazine was broadcast especially for the Caribbean community: *Ebony* was a fortnightly 26-minute news magazine, made up of several short reports but sometimes dealing with a single issue. It went off the air in 1988. But it was only in 1987 that a whole new strategy on programmes for immigrants was introduced at the BBC's Midlands offices.

The Asian Unit

The Asian Unit pursued its strategy at four levels:

  – producing a cultural magazine, *Network East*, that included the arts and entertainment;

  – producing a news magazine, *East*, which was broadcast on prime time and became the flagship of the unit;

  – buying drama series;

  – producing and commissioning documentaries.

All these programmes were broadcast on BBC2.

►*NETWORK EAST*, launched in July 1987, is a lively, 40-minute magazine whose coverage includes the arts, fashion, music and sport. It is broadcast on Saturdays at 2.45 pm. It was decided that the programme would be made in English and that contributions in Asian languages would be subtitled in English, in order to reach more people in the Asian community and a wider audience in general. As might be expected, the older generations disapproved of this decision. In 1990 the unit separated the news and entertainment components of *Network East*, leading to the creation of a new magazine, *East*.

➤*EAST*, started in July 1990, lasts 40 minutes and is broadcast at 8 pm on Fridays. It is usually composed of two reports, dealing either with Britain or with the situation in India, Pakistan, Bangladesh and Sri Lanka. Some reports are shown in the original language with English subtitles, the basic rule being to produce the programme in English.

Alongside producing these magazines, the Asian Unit bought its first television serial made in India in 1988. *Shrikant* was shown in the original language with English subtitles. The unit also produced its documentary series, *The Bollywood Story*, which traced the history of Indian cinema in two 60-minute parts.

The African-Caribbean Unit

This new sector, set up in Bristol in 1982 when *Ebony* was launched, was moved to Birmingham in 1985. Three years later *Ebony* was taken off the air because it no longer corresponded to public demand. Attempting to deal with such a wide range of subjects in a single programme meant in-depth coverage was not possible. This was the starting point for a new policy: developing documentaries, magazines based on talk shows and location-based shows. Colin Prescod, then Editor of the Unit, said in 1992: 'At that time, most of the themes dealt with were generated by a sort of social action philosophy'.

In 1992 the documentary series produced covered topics like the situation of black minorities in different European countries (the series *Black on Europe*, for example), and the African continent and the people and movements trying to define and build a new Africa (like *Out of Darkness*, in six 40-minute parts).

At the end of that year the Birmingham Multicultural Unit, hitherto composed of the Asian Unit and the African-Caribbean Unit, moved towards installing a new policy. The two units were merged, with Narendhra Morar as managing editor, with the aim of reflecting the interests of all minorities, not just Asians and Afro-Caribbeans. But the effect of this has been that no new programmes have been produced for other minorities; only programmes such as *Nation*, a late-night discussion programme, and the documentary series *Rumours of Rain*, about the charity Oxfam's work in the Philippines, India and Africa, included other ethnic groups.

In practice, this has yet to have a great impact on the BBC's multicultural output and a number of programmes and strands have continued under the new structure.

Still on BBC 2, a one-hour 50-minute Saturday morning slot entitled *Asia Two*, is devoted to Asian programmes, broadcast as a three month season. The 1993/4 season included the magazine *Network East* followed by an Indian drama or the series *Chanakya*, purchased in India. *Chanakya*, shown in Hindi with English sub-titles, was composed of 47 episodes about the life of Vishnu Gupta, the Machiavelli of Indian politics. *Asia Two* is due to be continued from October 1994 until the end of December.

➤*EAST* was broadcast in February 1994 for ten weeks and will be back on the air in February 1995 for about another ten weeks.

➤*NATION*: This 30-minute weekly discussion series commissioned to the inde-pendent production company Juniper was broadcast in July and August 1993. Subjects tackled ranged from racist attacks to adoptive parents (should they be of the same ethnic origin as the children they adopt?) and whether Britain should intervene to relieve suffering in foreign conflicts such as the war in Bosnia.

➤*ALL BLACK* (series one): This series of seven 30-minute episodes, which looks at the major issues affecting the African-Caribbean community, was shown from the end of July to the beginning of September 1993. Subjects discussed included black boy prostitutes, single black mothers, the national rise in school exclusion among African-Caribbean youngsters, illegal labour, and so on. Because of the choice of the subjects, the programme provoked strong criticism from the black community, who attacked the negative image the programme presented. A series of six more episodes was due to be shown in September-October 1994.

➤*WILL TO WIN* is a series of six 50-minute documentaries produced by the independent company Catalyst Television about blacks who succeed in sport. It was shown on a weekly basis in September-October 1993.

In addition, the unit produced a few music programmes and the movie quiz *Bolly-wood or Bust*. Six 30-minute programmes were shown early in 1994 and the series is to be continued in 1995.

➤*A WHOLE DIFFERENT BALL GAME* looked at culture in various countries through the prism of the national sport: football in Brazil, rugby in South Africa, baseball in Cuba and cricket in India. The four 50-minute programmes were produced by Faction Films and broadcast in July and August 1994.

The programmes described above are not allocated any particular time slot in BBC2s schedules but they always go out during the week on prime time – around

7.30 pm (except for *Nation*, which is broadcast late in the evening) – and aim to reach a wide audience.

In preparation for 1994–95 is a series of six 30-minute documentaries made by Roger Bolton Productions called *Ruling Passions: Sex, Race and Empire*. Using archive film, it looks at sexual relations between the British colonisers and colonised peoples in the Indian subcontinent and in Africa prior to independence. Also forthcoming is *Fancy a Curry*, a series on Indian regional cooking from Indian cookery expert Madhur Jaffrey, and there are even, according to Narendhra Morar, a few drama projects in preparation.

BBC Education

The BBC department responsible for producing educational broadcasts has since 1986 developed a series of programmes about British culture in the broadest sense, stressing its diversity and the contributions made by the black community to British society. Their prime purpose is continuing education and they are shown by BBC2 on prime time – between 7 pm and 9 pm. The programmes are also available on videocassette with an accompanying booklet so that they can be used as a training tool.

➤*MOSAIC*, the overall title of a BBC Continuing Education initiative, started in 1989. The aim of the project was to criticise discrimination against members of the 'visible minority' and to suggest solutions, while encouraging a real debate on cultural diversity, identity and citizenship. Although designed to be accessible to a wide audience, the programmes are also devised so they can be used by those in charge of training professional and community groups and teachers in schools and colleges. An advisory committee of trainers and educationalists, drawn from a range of ethnic minority communities, meets regularly to advise the production staff on content and treatment, and to monitor the development of the project.

➤*BIRTHRIGHTS* is a series of films dealing with culture, citizenship and identity from the point of view of minorities, highlighting the wealth of diversity in British society. An initial series of six programmes, broadcast in May 1991, showed that the formula was successful and won an award from the Royal Television Society. The principle behind the series is to have each programme made by a different black, independent, production company, in order to give black people a voice to speak about themselves and to counterbalance the white perspective. A second series was produced in 1992. Subjects covered include the image of black women – myths and stereotypes; ethnic minorities' relationship with the English countryside, an emblem of British traditions and social values; the history of the Arab community in the UK; and how ethnic minorities are represented in science fiction. In 1993 a third series was produced following the same principle and broadcast weekly on prime time during July and August. The themes were the development and role of the black press in Britain; the growing influence of black fashion, music and language in youth culture; the longstanding taboos, rooted in racist ideology, which affect relationships between black and white people; an in-depth portrait of a Chinese family running a takeaway food shop; and the experiences of West Indian women ATS volunteers brought to England in 1942 as part of the war effort.

BBC Education has also produced a number of programmes analysing how television portrays minorities and, often unconsciously, reinforcing prejudice against them. *The Black and White Media Show* produced by John Twichin, was the first series of three programmes which looked at the stereotypes created or repeated by television in various types of broadcast: comedy, drama, news and current affairs.

➤*BLACK AND WHITE IN COLOUR*, produced in 1992 with the British Film Institute (BFI), is a two-part documentary selecting images of black people from the history of British television. It is the result of five years of research carried out by the BFI and led to a book of the same name, edited by Jim Pines. The documentary, broadcast on BBC2 in June 1992, is the work of Isaac Julien and combines archive film with interviews with well-known figures from ethnic minorities: artists, actors, writers, film directors and producers, television critics, and so on.

But BBC Education decided to go further on, and started to develop a new programme entitled *Funky Black Shorts*.

➤*FUNKY BLACK SHORTS*, broadcast early in 1994, is the outcome of a new type of project initiated by the BBC Education Directorate, which commissioned the series from a black production company in order to encourage more black writers to work for television. The company asked black writers new to television to come up with ten-minute plays taking aspects of the lives of the black community in Britain and exploring them through drama. From the many contributions submitted, six were chosen and produced by the company Crucial Films (which also produces programmes for black comedian Lenny Henry).

Accompanying the series is a booklet that gives budding authors a guide as to how drama for television should be written. The idea is to encourage and equip more black people, from whatever background, to use television drama for cultural expression, exploring social issues and education.

BBC Community Programme Unit

This unit is responsible for two weekly programmes:

➤*OPEN SPACE*, in existence since 1973, gives members of the public access to television, especially those who feel that their interests are ignored or poorly represented by the media. Once a proposal has been accepted, the BBC provides all the technical and material support needed to actually make the programme, while editorial responsibility lies with the person who made the proposal. People from ethnic minorities were among those who had their proposals accepted.

➤*VIDEO DIARIES* is a project that was launched in the summer of 1990 and is broadcast on Saturday evenings by BBC2. It gives people the chance to describe their own lives, in their own way, without making any compromises, and to follow the project through from the planning stage to assembling the final film. Again, some people from ethnic minorities have been able to contribute to the programmes.

Mainstream programmes

The BBC regularly produces and broadcasts series and made-for-television films including characters from ethnic minorities as part of its mainstream schedules. This has become so common that it is impossible to mention all of them. In the soap *EastEnders*, for instance, broadcast three times a week at 7.30 pm on BBC1 for nearly ten years, several of the main characters are from the black and Asian communities and recent episodes have tackled the issue of racial violence. Other examples are the hospital drama series *Casualty*, shown on Saturday evenings on BBC1 for more than five years, the second series of Lenny Henry's sitcom *Chef!*, broadcast during the week at 9.30 pm, and the police drama series *Between the Lines*, shown on BBC1 on Friday evenings and repeated on BBC2 on Saturdays.

➤*THE BUDDHA OF SUBURBIA* is a drama series written by Hanif Kureishi, author of the film *My Beautiful Laundrette*. It describes the cultural conflicts of a young British Asian in the 1970s and 1980s and his search for an identity. Produced in-house by the BBC, the series was shown on BBC2 in November 1993.

➤*THE REAL MCCOY*, a series of Britain's black comedy sketches, has been broadcast weekly since 16 June 1994. It gives black and Asian comedians the chance to take a humorous look at their own worlds. The series won the the Commission for Racial Equality's Media Award in the drama category.

❷ Channel 4

Created in 1982, Channel 4's aim from the outset was to be the television of all minorities: ethnic groups, the disabled, the elderly, young people etc. Its schedules, which deliberately complement those of the other channels, set out to be innovative while working to develop the independent production sector. Channel 4 was the first to call on independent producers and workshops (in the 1980s, the channel was a major funder of the workshop sector) to produce a large proportion of its programmes and it now deals annually with more than 600 companies. When the channel started, willing to bring new voices to the screen and catering for tastes and needs not served by other television channels, the creation of a Multicultural Department was a logical decision; its brief was to give access to the screen to works about Black people, or made by them.The multicultural Department started to commission or purchase a wide range of programmes, including documentaries, soaps and sit-com, cultural and current affairs magazines, talk-shows, feature films and television films. These programmes are spread throughout the schedule, like any other programme.

Since 1 January 1993, Channel 4 has been reconstituted under the terms of the 1990 Broadcasting Act as the Channel 4 Television Corporation, a statutory corporation without shareholders, and has been charged with selling its own airtime to fund its operations. This put the channel in direct competition with ITV (it had previously sold airtime through ITV, which then financed it with subscription payments). Channel 4's success in selling its own airtime has surpassed the expectations of broadcasters and industry observers alike. But did this new situation have an influence on the channel's programming and commissionning? According Channel 4's 1993 report, the broadcaster spent 14 per cent less on multicultural programmes in 1993 (£5 million in 1992, £4.3 million in 1993). But in the same time, more hours have been commissioned, with 134 hours against 121 in 1992. This rise of almost 15 per cent indicates that the broadcaster is commissioning more programmes which cost less, such as talk-shows shot in studio, rather than financing fiction or documentary series.

However, even if Channel 4's commitment to fully reflecting Britain's ethnic diverstity can seem to occassionaly waver – in terms of hours broadcast or budgets allocated – its programme policy frequently contains reminders that despite such fluctuations doing so remains at the centre of its programming policy. This has been reflected in the channel's decision to theme its 1994 pre-Christmas and Christmas Day programming, as a Black Christmas. This special season contained plays, short films, comedies, documentaries, entertainment programmes and the pilot of a new youth magazine to be presented by controversial US rap star, Ice-T, from *Baad Asss TV*.

Equal opportunities are a high priority for the channel and the representation of people from ethnic minority backgrounds was 8.4 per cent at the end of 1993.

Magazines

Channel 4 started off with two News magazines, *Eastern Eye*, made by existing London Weekend Television staff and aimed at Indians and Pakistanis, and *Black on Black*, aimed at Afro-Caribbeans. A few years later Farrukh Dhondy, Channel 4's Commissioning Editor for multicultural programmes, decided to merge the two magazines into one called *Bandung File*. According TO Dondhy, 'programmes like the *Bandung File* abandoned ant-racism for a black view on world affairs'.

►*BANDUNG FILE* dealt with cultural and current affairs issues concerning non-white Britain and Western Europe as well as the Third World (India, Pakistan, Bangladesh, Africa and the Caribbean). This popular, provocative programme was also unpredictable - looking at politics from a different angle and reminding viewers that they have minds of their own. Produced by Tariq Ali, *Bandung File* was on the air from 1985 to 1991, when two new magazines, *Rear Window* and *The Black Bag*, were launched.

►*REAR WINDOW*, also produced by Tariq Ali and his company Bandung Production, is about international art and culture. In a creative documentary style, sometimes even incorporating fiction sequences, it adresses a wide variety of subjects. By way of example, in 1993 *Rear Window* presented the Khalili Collection, a unique collection of Islamic works of art, and asked whether a museum of Islamic art should be opened in London. Another programme traced the story of Sabu the Elephant Boy, a young Indian who became a Hollywood child star in the 1940s and 1950s. In another, Senegalese musician Youssou N'Dour took viewers on a 24-hour tour of his home town, Dakar, and yet another allowed them to discover the Istanbul opera house, which is totally subsidised by the Turkish state.

►*THE BLACK BAG*, a 30-minute weekly magazine shown at 8 pm, is devised by black and Asian journalists and produced by various different companies. It sets out to be radically different, tackling sensitive subjects that have previously been avoided by television. '*Black Bag Specials*' are commissioned regularly and are sometimes followed by studio debates, such as:

►*THE ROUNDHOUSE – A HOUSE DIVIDED*, made by Bacachaks Productions and presented by Darcus Howe (author, television personality and an important figure in the black community), investigates a project launched in the 1980s to set up a Black Art Centre in the Roundhouse in London. Despite substantial financial support from the authorities, the project never got off the ground. Darcus Howe looks into the reasons for the failure. The programme was broadcast on 11 August 1993.

►*RACE BUSTERS*, produced by Folio Productions and shown on 7 April 1994, followed a group of racial harassment victims in Bristol who set up their own support organisation, SARI (Support Against Racial Incidents). In the two subsequent weeks, Darcus Howe introduced films about the rise of nationalism and the extreme right in the United States and in Russia. These were followed by studio discussions.

►*STARS, TSARS AND SWASTIKAS* is the general title of two programmes produced by Yo Yo Films and broadcast on 14 and 21 April 1994. The first describes a gang of skinheads called Extreme Hatred as well as Tom Metzger, leader of the White Aryan Resistance (WAR), who owns a cable television channel in the United States devoted to his campaign for white separatism. The second programme follows the Russian heavy metal group Korosia Metallica on a train journey from Moscow to Ukraine, where a particularly virulent form of nationalism has emerged since the collapse of communism.

The diversity of contents tackled in the *Black Bag* series as well as in the other programmes commissioned by the Multicultural Department shows the openness of mind of the channel in dealing with multicultural programmes, which are taken with a wide meaning. Also, rather than giving priority to ethnic minorities's prgramme proposals, the Department has chosen to select them for their professional qualities, even if they are not produced by black production companies. This choice is often criticized by Black and Asian producers.[1]

According to a representative of the Multicultural Department, *Rear Window* will not be continued, but a new series of *The Black Bag* is currently in production. The slot devoted to arts is now being made up of two strands: the first on modern multi-art pieces, the second will be narrative-led investigations into any multicultural art area.

Documentaries

Every year the Multicultural Department commissions documentaries or documentary series. In 1994 the major ones were:

➤*KARACHI KOPS*, produced and directed by Faris Kermani, which featured a police station in the Pakistani capital and followed police officers as they went about their daily tasks of making arrests and investigations. The five 30-minute programmes were broadcast in January and February in the original version with English subtitles. The series was variously praised and attacked for its 'fly-on-the-wall' portrait of Karachi's police force. While many applauded the Multicultural Department's ambitious series and its broad audience interest some complained that it failed to contextualise the material that it contained or be sufficiently critical of the seemingly-brutal behaviour of some of the Karachi officers.

➤*ISLAMIC CONVERSATIONS*, which followed on from *Karachi Kops* in February and March was produced by Epicflow Films. The six documentaries showed a series of conversations with the most influential Moslem philosophers, providing an up-to-date view of Islam.

---

1   See Salim Salam article, earlier in this book.

Talk shows

Channel 4 broadcasts numerous talk shows, the best known of which in multicultural circles is *Devil's Advocate*. On the air for several years, it is presented by radical journalist Darcus Howe.

➤*DEVIL'S ADVOCATE*. Produced by Trevor Phillips at London Weekend Television, this studio-based programme takes an unconventional approach to people or current events, such as the publication of a book or a dispute in the press. The decor is of a courtroom and the guest is put 'on trial', undergoing cross-examination from Darcus Howe and members of the studio audience. Guests in August and September included Pakistani cricket captain Imran Khan and the BBC's South-East Asia correspondent for the 30 years, Mark Tully.

➤*DOING IT WITH YOU IS TABOO* is another talk show produced by SOI Film and Television and broadcast in October 1993. Three 50-minute programmes looked into how black men and women saw their white sexual partners. The first programme gathered various black women in the studio to talk about their experiences with white men, the second was devoted to black men and their relations with white women, and the third to black gays and lesbians and their white partners. Although some might say that Channel 4's commmissioning of the programme was audacious, the series has been heavily criticised for a variety of reasons from 'black racism against white people', sexism, to sensationalism.

Drama and comedy series

➤*DESMOND'S*, a sitcom started in 1989 by Trix Worrel, who is of Caribbean origin, is regarded as a major success story on British television. Produced by Humphrey Barclay, it is broadcast weekly over a period of about four months and takes a humorous look at life in a hair salon in Peckham. Desmond, the main character played by the late black actor Norman Beaton, takes viewers into his salon and all human life is there: family, friends, ambitions, jealousy and misunderstandings. A new series was in production in autumn 1994 and was due to be shown later in the year.

Channel 4's dramas are either commissioned or bought by the Multicultural Department. *A Girl's Fate*, a six-part series based on short stories by different authors, was commissioned from BV Videographic Private Ltd. The programmes, lasting 30 minutes, were shown in July and August 1994. Each concerned a slice of the life of a young woman in India, from childhood to marriage to early motherhood. The whole formed a sort of homage to Indian womanhood. *Little Napoleons*, a four-part series produced by Picture Palace Films, tells the story of two councillors and their political rivalries. The leading roles were taken by black actor Norman Beaton and Indian Saeed Jaffrey. The series was shown in June 1994.

➤*KASAK* and *THE GREAT MARATHA* are two examples of purchased series. The 21 x 30-minute episodes of *Kasak* were bought from Pakistani television and shown in the original version with English subtitles from 1 May to 18 September 1993. They trace the life of a widow, Sabrina, who works in a textile factory and is determined to succeed in life against all the odds. *The Great Maratha*, based on the life of 18th century Maratha warrior Madhadji Scindia, is an epic drama series which started on Channel 4 on 10 September and was due to run for 20 weeks.

Feature films

The Multicultural Department usually commissions or co-finances one or two films every year. Famous examples are *My Beautiful Laundrette*, *Salaam Bombay* and *Mississippi Masala*. It should be emphasized that discovering new talent is an important factor in looking for and selecting projects.

Alongside these initiatives, film seasons are scheduled which may be centred either on a country, a region, a theme, a director or an actor. Hindi Nights, a season that ran from 12 August to 17 March 1993 with an Indian film each week, featured superhits and blockbusters of the past and present. 'The Multicultural Season', shown from November 1993, presented films by Asian directors exploring contemporary issues: *Mississippi Masala* (directed by Mira Nair), *After Midnight* (written and directed by Shani Grewal) and *Electric Moon* (directed by Pradip Krishens).

The Independent Film and Video Department

The aim of this department is to propose programmes which are genuinely different from those on the rest of the channel, and from UK television programmes in general. They are expected to be radical and experimental in both form and content in order to give a new perception of the world and to offer a space to voices which cannot usually make themselves heard. Talents that never found their place in mainstream television have had a fresh opportunity in the department and many proposals from the workshop movement and from abroad, especially Third World countries, have been commissioned. Programmes made about immigration over the past year have included:

➤*THE TRUE LIES IN ROSTOCK*, produced by Spectacle and broadcast on 22 July 1993, which analysed the situation of new immigrants to reunited Germany, after the violent racist attacks in Rostock.

➤*SWEET FRANCE*, a coproduction by Migrant Media in the UK and IM'Media in France, which looked at racial tensions in France between 1980 and 1993, including the influence of President François Mitterrand's immigration and social policies and the start of the anti-racist movement 'Touche pas à mon pote' (Hands off my mate). Broadcast on Channel 4 on 12 November 1993, it is worth noting that this film has never been shown in France, apart from a few short extracts.

➤*MANY RIVERS TO CROSS*, part of the series *The Black Bag*, explores the plight of Somali and Ethiopian refugee groups and the underground escape route through Europe which offers help and shelter to people threatened by ever-stricter immigration rules. Produced by Moonlight Films, the programme was shown on 25 June 1994.

Cable channels

At the start of the 1980s, a new era opened up for cable television in the UK. The restrictions previously imposed on the installation and operation of cable networks gave way to new legislation, the 1984 Broadcasting Act, which established the Cable Authority, a public body made responsible for regulating cable operations on a national basis. The country is divided up into areas to be cabled. After a system of bids, franchises are granted to cable operators who are entrusted with the task of building and running networks in their area. The new regulations introduced in January 1991 specify that it is up to each channel to obtain permission to broadcast from the Independent Television Commission (ITC), which replaced the Cable Authority and the IBA. Cable operators are authorised to broadcast any channel that has received such permission, without having to seek permission from the ITC themselves.

Each cable network, which usually has more than 30 slots, is supposed to put together a selection of channels liable to interest prospective subscribers. Several possibilities are open: foreign channels, those originally meant for broadcasting by satellite, others run by private companies or cable operators and intended for broadcasting solely on cable. The technical opportunities available mean that a wide range of channels can be produced especially for cable: local channels, theme channels and those targeted at cultural, social or professional minorities.

❶ **TV ASIA**, a satellite channel based in London, is intended for Asians settled permanently in the UK. On the air since 1992, it broadcasts for 12 hours a day, from 6 pm to 6 am on weekdays and during the day at weekends. Its schedules are composed largely of Indian films, with some 750 shown every year. The language most often used is Hindi, followed by Urdu and English.

❷ **IDENTITY TELEVISION (IDTV)**, financed by the American cable channel Black Entertainment Channel, is targeted at Britain's black community. Launched in June 1993, it specialises in black entertainment programmes for all the family, including drama, documentaries, current affairs, sport, music, religious and children's programmes and talk shows. Transmitting 18 hours a day, seven days a week, IDTV does little of its own production at the moment and uses mainly programmes purchased from American, African and Caribbean television programmes. Currently broadcasting to the London area, IDTV plans to extend its service to other major cities in 1995.

❸ **JAPAN SATELLITE TELEVISION (JSTV)**, which is financed by a consortium of Japanese companies, broadcasts programmes in Japanese to all of Europe for Japanese people living abroad. The programmes on offer from 7 am to 6 pm are mostly current affairs magazines supplied by the Japanese channel NHK, since JSTV's prime objective is to maintain ties with the home country. Some drama, children's programmes and documentaries purchased from Japanese companies are also shown. The penetration rate for Japanese living in Europe (mainly in the UK, then in France and Germany) is about 25 per cent. It should be pointed out that most Japanese people living in Europe are only there on a temporary basis.

❹ **CHINESE NEWS AND ENTERTAINMENT (CNE)**, launched at the end of 1992, transmits a few hours a day from 1am onwards. Financed by a private company in Hong Kong, CNE buys its programmes from the Hong Kong channel ATV, China Central Television in the People's Republic of China, and Taiwanese television. There are plans to encode this channel and to extend its broadcasting time.

❺ **INDRA DHNUSH (Rainbow)**, a cable channel intended for the Indian and Pakistani community living in the UK, broadcasts in Indian languages (Hindi, Urdu, Gujarati, Bengali, Tamil and Marathi) without subtitles. It has about 14,000 subscribers and is available on 26 British cable networks, transmitting from 9.30 am to around midnight. The programmes (mainly films and series) are bought from independent producers and from television companies in India, Pakistan, Bangladesh and Sri Lanka. Some music programmes are also included, and at weekends a children's serial goes out at lunchtime. Indra Dhnush repeats its programmes in several time slots, using a no-frills style of presentation.

❻ **THE ARABIC CHANNEL** is an entertainment channel, broadcasting in Arabic without subtitles on the Westminster cable site, which has a high concentration of people of Arabic origin. It does not form part of the basic service but is available for a higher subscription fee. Its programmes come from Dubai television in the form of videocassettes, apart from the newscasts which are transmitted live by the Arabsat satellite at 7 pm daily. The Arabic Channel, which has about 2,000 subscribers, is on the air from 3 pm to 11 pm during the week and from midday to midnight at weekends.

❼ **MULTICULTURAL TELEVISION**, launched on 5 September 1992 by the leading Canadian cable operator Videotron, broadcasts to London at weekends between 6 pm and 11 pm. Programmes include films, talk shows, series, drama, music, children's programmes and local news.

Multicultural Television has five channels, each aimed at a different minority:

PTV (Persian Television) offers programmes for Farsi-speaking minorities and Iranians. Children's broadcasts, drama and traditional music programmes are purchased, but PTV is planning to broaden its schedules and offer local and national news, videoclips and series. It transmits 6–7 pm on Saturdays and Sundays.

Channel A aims to provide quality entertainment for Asians and other ethnic minorities. For instance, *Culture Beat*, a music and dance magazine broadcast from 7 pm to 7.30 pm on Saturdays with a repeat on Sundays, features performances never seen before in Britain. The channel has also featured a news, music and fashion magazine.

Hellenic TV, based in London, is the capital's first Greek television channel. On the air since December 1990, it has gradually broadened its schedules and shows Greek films, music shows, documentaries and series, as well as programmes purchased from Greek and Cypriot channels. Its in-house productions mainly concern the Greek community in the UK and current events there. Hellenic TV broadcasts on Saturdays from 7.30 pm to 9 pm.

BVTV (Better Vision Television) is aimed at the black community and transmits from 9 pm to 10 pm at weekends. Its own, English-language, programmes reflect the experiences of Afro-Caribbeans in London, featuring music (rap and reggae), documentaries, cooking, fashion and sport.

ART (Anadolu Radio Television) was London's first Turkish-language television channel. Its schedules include educational, cultural and religious programmes and accounts of the experiences of Turks in the UK, as well as traditional music, documentaries and cartoons. The channel also aims to broaden its range of news and discussion programmes. It broadcasts at weekends from 10 pm to 11 pm.

4

INITIATIVES

❶ **WORKSHOPS**, or regional collectives, are peculiar to the UK. Operating outside the usual circuits and frameworks, they attempt to provide a militant view of society, especially where minorities are concerned. The fruit of political activism and alternative culture, they reflect participants' desire to work outside established rules and standards, particularly on the financial level. The workshop movement has also given a voice to those who rarely have a say in society, dealing with political, social, cultural and ethnic issues. Financed by Channel 4, the British Film Institute and local organisations, workshops have sprung up all over the country.

The most important include the Black Audio Film Collective, started in 1983 by John Akomfrah, Reece Auguste and Avril Johnson and bringing together non-whites from Asia, Africa and the Caribbean, and Sankofa, started in 1983 by Isaac Julien, Robert Crusz and Nadine Marsh-Edwards[1]

Most programmes produced by workshops are politically committed documentaries: rather than harping back to the country of origin, they examine the upheavals of the present, loss of identity, exile and the generation gap.

Workshops are currently receiving less financial support than they did in the past.

❷ **THE COMMISSION FOR RACIAL EQUALITY (CRE)** set up a series of awards in 1992 for media contributions to better understanding of inter-ethnic relations in the UK. There are seven awards for different media and categories of programmes.

In April 1994, the award in the television drama category went to *The Real McCoy*, shown on BBC1, while the documentary *Crossing the Tracks*, commissioned for the BBC's *Birthright* series and broadcast on BBC2, won the current affairs and documentary category.

Meanwhile, in the summer of 1994 the CRE launched a campaign against racial prejudice with the advertising agency Saatchi & Saatchi. Spread over three years, it will take the form of radio and television spots as well as newspaper adverts. The campaign is being financed by companies and individual donations.

❸ **SPECTRUM** is a magazine produced by the British team behind the association Public Broadcasting for a Multicultural Europe. Launched in autumn 1993, its aim is to enhance the range and quality of multicultural broadcasting on radio and television. The magazine includes news about national and European actions on programme and programming strategy to tackle racism and xenophobia carried out by channels, independent producers, public bodies and private individuals, with the emphasis on the role of public television.

❹ **THIRD CINEMA FOCUS** is an event that takes place during the Birmingham International Film Festival in October each year. Its purpose is to present a selection of the best of world cinema and to promote current and future trends in black and Third World film culture. Screenings are complemented by discussions and workshops. In 1993, for instance, 'Adjusting the Picture: Black People on TV 1950-1990s', chaired by Jim Pines, author of *Black and White in Colour*, looked back at the construction of black identities through television portrayal. In 1994 the event was threatened by lack of financial support.

---

1   See Salim Salam's article (p. 50) earlier in this volume.

Part III
Appendices

Sources

Austria

Journals

– Fassman, Heinz and Müns, Rainer, Carrefour des migrations Est–Ouest, *Hommes et migrations* no. 1159, Paris, November 1992.

Articles, studies, reports

– *Almanach 1991/92*, rapport d'activités, ORF Osterreichischer Rundfunk, Vienna, November 1991.

– Baryli, Waltraud, 'L'opposition nationaliste lance une consultation populaire sur l'immigration', *Le Monde*, Paris, 24 November 1992.

– *Tendances des migrations internationales* Annual Report SOPEMI 1991, OECD, Paris, 1992.

– *Tendences des Migrations internationales*, Annual Report SOPEMI 1993, OECD, Paris 1994.

Belgium

Books

– Lapeyronnie, Didier (ed.) *Immigrés en Europe, politique locale d'intégration*. La Documentation française, Paris, 1992.

Journals

– 'Politique d'intégration et Islam en Belgique', *Revue européenne des migrations internationales*, vol. 6, n° 2, université de Poitiers, 1990.

– *Spectrum, The Magazine of Public Broadcasting for a Multicultural Europe*, no. 2 January 1994.

Articles, studies, reports

– *L'Integration, une politique de longue haleine, 1ᵉʳ rapport, vol. 1*. Commissariat Royal à la politique des immigrés, Bruxelles, 1989.

– *Les médias et les populations d'origine étrangère*, avis du CCPOE, Conseil consultatif pour les populations d'origine étrangère de la Communauté française de Belgique, Bruxelles, 25 juin 1991.

– *Rapport d'activités 1991*, RTBF, Bruxelles, 1991.

– *Rapport d'activités 1991*, BRTN, Bruxelles 1991.

Czech Republic and Slovakia

Books:

– *Cable and Satellite Yearbook*, London, 1993.

– *Television Business International (TBI) Yearbook*, London, 1993.

Articles, studies, reports:

– 'Bohême-Moravie: l'épouventail slovaque'. *Le Monde*. Espace européen, Paris, 3 November 1992.

– *Report for the Czech Republic*. Balkan Media, Sofia, March 1993.

– *Tendances des migrations internationales* Annual Report 1991 SOPEMI, OECD, Paris, 1992.

– *Tendences des Migrations Internationales*, Annual Report 1993, SOPEMI, OECD, Paris, 1994.

– Woodrow, Alain, 'La télévision Tchèque, inventaire avant divorce', *Le Monde* Radio TV, Paris, 14 December 1992.

Denmark

Journals:

– *Spectrum, The Magazine of Public Broadcasting for a Multicultural Europe*, January 1994 n° 2.

Articles, studies, reports:

– Mongaya-Hoegsholm, Filomenita, 'Danemark, la petite sirène qui fait peur' in: *l'Europe multicommunautaire* numéro spécial, *Plein droit, La revue du Gisti*, Gisti/IM'média, Paris, 1989–1990.

– *Migrants et médias au Danemark*, Council of Europe, Strasbourg, 1988.

– Sarin, Alexandre, 'L'esprit de tolérance malmené au Danemark', *Le Monde*, Espace Européen, Paris, 9 October 1993.

– *Tendences des Migrations Internationales* Annual Report 1993, SOPEMI, OECD, Paris, 1994.

France

Books

– Lapeyronnie, Didier (ed.) *Immigrés en Europe, Politiques locales d'intégration*. La Documentation française Paris, 1992.

– Noiriel, Gérard, *Le creuset français, histoire de l'immigration*. Le Seuil, Paris, 1988.

– Taguieff, Pierre-André (ed.) *Face au racisme, vol. 2, Analyses, hypothèses, perspectives*. La Découverte, Collection *Essais*, Paris, 1991.

– Weil, Patrick, *La France et ses étrangers, l'aventure d'une politique de l'immigration, 1938–1991*, préface by Marceau Long. Calmann-Lévy, Paris, 1991.

Journals

– *L'immigration, Centre d'information éducative*, Collection Ouverture sur la vie, FAS Boulogne-Billancourt, 1991.

– Perotti, Antonio, 'Pour une politique d'immigration', *Études*, Paris, September 1992.

Articles, studies, reports

– Abdi, Nidam, 'La parabole du pays natal', *Libération*. Paris, 27–28 November 1993.

– *Bilan de la société privé M6*, 1991. Conseil supérieur de l'audiovisuel, Paris, 1991.

– *Bilan de la société privée Canal Plus* 1991, Conseil Supérieur de l'Audiovisuel, Paris, 1991.

– *Bilan de la société privée TF1*, 1991. Conseil Supérieur de l'Audiovisuel, Paris, 1991.

– Duteil, Guy & Louart, Carina, 'Télévision et intégration'. *Le Monde* Radio TV, Paris 11–12 September 1994.

– Humblot, Catherine, 'Télévisions d'Europe et immigration: état des lieux et des discours'. *Le Monde* Radio TV, Paris, 31 May-1 June 1992.

– *Immigrés: réussir l'intégration*, rapport au Premier ministre, Secrétariat Général à l'Intégration, Paris, June 1990.

–Solé, Robert, Tincq, Henri and Bernard, Philippe (eds.) 'La France et l'Islam', *Le Monde*, Paris, 13 October 1994.

– *Tendances des migrations internationales*, Annual Report 1991, SOPEMI, OECD Paris, 1992.

– *Tendences des Migrations Internationales* Annual Report 1993, SOPEMI, OECD, Paris, 1994.

Germany

Books

– Falga, Bernard, Withol de Wenden, Catherine and Leggewie, Claus (eds.), *De l'immigration à l'intégration en France et en Allemagne*, Editions du Cerf, Paris, 1994.

– Hennebelle, Guy (ed.) *Le tribalisme planétaire*, Arléa-Corlet, Collection Panoramiques, Condé-sur-Noireau, 1992.

– Koschinski, Mickaël, *Fernsehprogramme als Mittel de Integration*, Essen, 1986.

– Schnapper, Dominique, *L'Europe des immigrés*. François Bourin, Paris, 1992.

– Wievorka, Michel (ed.) *Racisme et xénophobie en Europe, une comparaison internationale*, La Découverte, Paris, 1994.

Journals

– 'Cinemas Métis, de Hollywood aux films *beurs*', *CinemAction* no. 56, Condé-sur-Noireau, 1990.

– *La lettre du CIRAC*, Centre d'information et de recherche sur l'Allemagne contemporaine, Paris, 1992.

– *Spectrum, The Magazine of Public Broadcasting for a Multicultural Europe*, no. 2, January 1994.

– 'Une autre Allemagne', *Hommes et Migration* no. 1152, Paris, February–March 1992.

Articles, studies, reports

– *ARD Radio-TV*, Rapport d'activités, Hans Bredow Institut, Hamburg, 1991.

– Krüger, Udo Michael, 'Positionierung Offentlichrechlticher und privater Fernsehpro-gramme im dualen system, Programmanalyse, 1990'. *Mediaperspekitven*, Frankfurt, May 1991.

– *Tendance des migrations internationales*, Annual Report 1991, SOPEMI, OECD, Paris, 1992.

– *Tendences des migrations internationales*, Annual Report 1993, SOPEMI, OECD, Paris, 1994.

– *ZDF Jahrbuch 1991* Rapport d'activités, ARD, Mayence, May 1992.

Hungary

Books

– Brown, Charles (ed.) *Co-production International*, Television Business International (TBI), London, 1993.

– *Guide du cinema et de l'audiovisuel en Europe centrale et orientale*, Institut d'Études Slaves, IDATE/Eurocréation, Paris, March 1992.

– Hennebelle, Guy (ed.) *Le tribalisme planétaire*. Arléa-Corlet, Collection Panoramiques. Condé-sur-Noireau, 1992.

– *Television Business International yearbook*, London, 1993.

Journals

– Feldman, Ludovic, 'Le câble hongrois choisit la solution américaine'. *Angle droit*, Edicom, Paris. October-November 1990.

Articles, studies, reports

– 'Budapest lance une offensive contre la haine'. *Libération*, Paris, 26 October 1993.

– Riols, Yves-Michel, 'Brouillard Magyar', *Le Monde* Radio-TV. Paris, 22–33 March 1992.

– *Tendances des migrations internationales*, annual report 1991, SOPEMI, OECD, Paris 1992.

– *Tendances des migrations internationales*, Annual Report 1993, SOPEMI, OECD, Paris 1994.

Italy

Books

– Costa-Lascoux, Jacqueline & Weil, Patrick. (eds.) *Logiques d'États et Immigrations*. Kimé, Paris, 1992.

Journals

– Cruz, Antonio and Perotti, Antonio, *Bulletin Informations européennes* no. 16 & no. 17, CIEMI, Paris, December 1992 and January 1993.

– Forbin, Sylvie, 'Le paysage audiovisuel italien: la législature à l'épreuve', *Angle droit*, Edicom, Paris, August–September 1991.

– 'Free for all', *TV World*, London, March 1992.

– 'Les caractéristiques du débat sur l'immigration dans le contexte italien: revue de presse', *Migrations sociétés*, vol 2, no 11, CIEMI, Paris, September/October 1990.

– 'New world', *TV World*, London, April 1992.

Articles, studies, reports

– Belluati, Marinella, *Imagini di immigrazione. L'informazione giornalistica sui rapporti interetnici* (Thesis, Faculty of Political Science), University of Turin, 1990–1991.

– *Bilancio e consolidato di gruppo 1991*, Rapport d'activités, Radio Televizione Italiana, Milan, 1991.

– Decamps, Marie-Claude, 'Les quatre fronts de bataille de la RAI', *Le Monde*, 12 August 1994.

– 'L'Italie gagnée par la fureur xénophobe', *Le Monde Diplomatique*, Paris, January 1994.

– Rome, l'immigration dans l'arène politique, *Libération*, Paris, 25 June 1993.

– *Tendances des migrations internationales*, Annual Report 1991, SOPEMI, OECD, Paris, 1992.

– *Tendances des migrations internationales*, Annual Report 1993, SOPEMI, OECD, Paris, 1994.

The Netherlands

Books

– Costa-Lascoux, Jacqueline & Weil, Patrick. (eds.) *Logiques d'États et Immigrations*. Kimé, Paris, 1992.

– Hennebelle, Guy (ed.) *Le tribalisme planétaire*. Arléa-Corlet, Collection Panoramiques, Condé-sur-Noireau, 1992,

– Lapeyronnie, Didier (ed.) *Immigrés en Europe, politiques locales d'intégration*. La Documentation française, Paris, 1992.

– Schnapper, Dominique, *L'Europe des immigrés*. François Bourin, Paris 1992.

Articles, studies, reports

– Chartier, Christian, 'les Pays-Bas face aux sirènes de l'extrême-droite'. *Le Monde*, Espace Européen, Paris, 18 September 1993.

– *Jaarverslag, Rapport d'activités 1991*, NOS-Nederlandse Omroepprogramma Stichting, 1991.

– *Migrants et médias aux Pays-Bas.* Council of Europe, Strasbourg, 1988.

– *Tendances des migrations internationales*, Annual Report 1991 SOPEMI, OECD, Paris, 1992.

– *Tendances des migrations internationales*, Annual Report 1993, SOPEMI OECD, Paris 1994.

Norway

Books

– Hennebelle, Guy (ed.) *Le tribalisme planétaire*. Arléa-Corlet, Collection Panoramiques. Condé-sur-Noireau, 1992,

Articles, studies, reports

– *Tendances des migrations internationales*, Annual Report 1991 SOPEMI, OECD, Paris, 1992.

– *Tendances des Migrations Internationales* Annual Report 1993, SOPEMI, OECD, Paris, 1994.

Spain

Books

– Costa-Lascoux, Jacqueline & Weil, Patrick. (eds.) *Logiques d'États et Immigrations*. Kimé, Paris, 1992.

Journals

– *Migrations et Société*, n° 13, CIEMI, January/February 1991.

Articles, studies, reports

– *Bilan du colloque Migrant, médias et diversité culturelle*. Council of Europe, Strasbourg, 1988.

– *Bulletin d'informations culturelles et scientifiques de l'Ambassade de France en Espagne* n° 16, Madrid, October–December 1992.

– *Tendances des migrations internationales*, Annual Report 1991 SOPEMI, OECD, Paris, 1992.

– *Tendances des Migrations Internationales* Annual Report 1993, SOPEMI, OECD, Paris 1994.

Sweden

Books

– Hennebelle, Guy (ed.) *Le tribalisme planétaire*. Arléa-Corlet, Collection Panoramiques, Condé-sur-Noireau, 1992.

– Schnapper, Dominique, *L'Europe des immigrés*. François Bourin, Paris, 1992.

Articles, studies, reports

– *Les immigrés en Suède: feuillet de documentation sur la Suède*. Institut suédois, Stockholm, 1991.

–Lowänder, Birgitta & Hultén, Charly, *Immigrants information needs and minority, Language Broadcasting in Sweden*, SR, Stockholm, 1988.

– Routier, Airy, 'Le sang viking jaillira', *Le Nouvel Observateur*, Paris, 30 December 1993.

– *Tendences des migrations internationales* Annual Report 1991, SOPEMI, OECD, Paris, 1992.

– *Tendences des migrations internationales* Annual Report 1993, SOPEMI, OECD, Paris, 1994.

Switzerland

Books

– Hennebelle, Guy (ed.) *Le tribalisme planétaire*. Arléa-Corlet, Collection Panoramiques. Condé-sur-Noireau, 1992.

Articles, studies, reports

– *Conférence finale de l'étude collective relative au rôle de l'information dans la promotion des droits de l'homme des travailleurs migrants*. Bureau lausannois pour les immigrés, Lausanne, October 1988.

–Humblot, Catherine, 'Le service public dans l'oeil du cyclone', I-II. *Le Monde* Radio-TV, Paris, 10–11 March & 17–18 March 1992.

– *Rapport sur la conception et les priorités de la politique suisse des étrangers pour les années 1990*. Office fédéral des étrangers, Berne, April 1991.

– *SSR 1991/92: annuaire 1991/92 de la société suisse de radiodiffusion et télévision*, Annual Report, SSR, Berne, November 1991.

– *SSR 1993/94: Annual Report*, SSR, Berne, 1994.

– *Tendences des migrations internationales*, annual Report 1993, SOPEMI, OECD, Paris, 1994.

United Kingdom

Books

– Costa-Lascoux, Jacqueline and Weil, Patrick. (eds.) *Logiques d'États et Immigrations*. Kimé, Paris, 1992.

– Guimezanes, Nicole, *Les politiques d'immigration en Europe*. Probèmes politiques et sociaux n° 673. La Documentation française, Paris, February 1992.

– Hennebelle, Guy & Schneider, Roland, 'Cinémas métis: de Hollywood aux films beurs'. *CinémAction*. Corlet-Télérama, Paris, 1990.

–Lapeyronnie, Didier (ed.) *Immigrés en Europe, Politiques locales d'intégration*. La Documentation française Paris, 1992.

–Pines, Jim, *Black and White in Colour. Black People in British Television since 1936*, British Film

Institute, London, 1992.

Journals

– 'L'Europe multicommunautaire', *Plein droit, La revue du Gisti,* Numéro spécial, Gisti/IM'média, Paris, 1989–1990.

– Hivernat, Pierre,' La vente des concessions du troisième réseau, ou comment ITV devient Channel 3'. *Angle droit,* Edicom, Paris, 1991.

– Sergent, Jean Claude, 'Le remodelage du paysage audiovisuel britannique', *Médiaspouvoirs* no. 26, Paris, April–May–June 1992.

– Twichin John, *Black and White Media Show Book.* Trentham Books, Chester, 1988–1990.

Articles, studies, reports

– *1991, Report and Account, ITC.* Independent Television Commission, London, 1992.

– *BBC annual report and accounts 1991/92,* London, 1992.

– *BBC annual report and accounts 1993/94,* London, 1994.

– Bell, Nick, *Cultural exception,* TBI, London, June 1994.

– *Channel 4 Television Corporation: Report and Financial Statements,* London, 1993.

– Colonna d'Istria, Michel, 'La BBC rivale planétaire de CNN'. *Le Monde* Radio-TV, Paris, 20–21 September 1992.

– Fry, Andy, 'Out of the Ghetto', *Broadcast,* London, 7 October 1994.

– Lapeyronnie, Didier, *L'intégration des minorités immigrées, étude comparative France-Grande-Bretagne,* ADRI, December 1990.

– *Reports and accounts for the year ended 31st December 1991,* Channel 4 Television Company Ltd, London, 1992.

– *Revue de la presse britannique,* French Embassy, Cultural Service, London. November–December 1992.

– *Tendances des migrations internationales,* Annual Report 1991 SOPEMI, OECD, Paris, 1992.

– *Tendences des Migration Internationales,* Annual Report 1993, SOPEMI, OECD, Paris, 1994.

Festivals

Belgium

Filmer à tout prix (Filming at any cost)

Biennial, October. First held in 1977 (until 1984 it was called *Cinéma en marge, cinéma en marche*).

Aims to provide a window display for francophone Belgian cinema. Includes at least two major international categories, one for the best foreign documentary and the other – which may be documentary or fiction – on a specific theme.

Address:

Direction de l'audiovisuel du ministère de la Culture en Belgique francophone,
44 boulevard Léopold II,
1080 Brussels.
Tel: (32) 2 413 22 72 or 2 413 22 44, Fax: (32) 2 413 22 96.

Denmark

Dansk Kortfilm Festival

Biennial, August. First held in 1990.

Held in Odense. Aims to show the best Danish documentaries and includes a substantial proportion of films on refugees and immigration.

Address:
Statens Filmcentral, National Film Board of Denmark,
27 Vestergade,
DK 1456 Copenhagen,
Tel: (45) 33 13 2686, Fax: (45) 33 13 0203.

Balticum Film and TV Festival

Annual, May. First held in 1989.

A forum for television companies from around the Baltic. Encourages European coproductions, especially social documentaries.

Address:
Baltic Media Centre,
Ronnevej 1,
DK 3720 Aakirkeby,
Tel: (45) 56 97 37 37, Fax: (45) 56 97 37 36

Nordisk Panorama
Annual, September.

Aims to promote the best documentaries from Nordic countries. Filmkontakt Nord publishes a theme-based catalogue of fiction and documentary films on immigration and racism, produced by independent companies

Address:
Filmkontakt Nord,
29 A Skindergade,
DK 1159 Copenhagen K
Tel: (45) 33 11 51 52, Fax: (45) 33 11 21 52

France

Olympiades de la création vidéo et télévision locale
The second 'Olympiad' was being held in Norway in 1994; the third will be held in Atlanta, United States, in 1996.

Biennial, January. First held in 1992.

Forum for local and community television companies and video film makers from all over the world.

Address:
Association d'animation du Beaufortain,
Place de la Mairie,
73270 Beaufort sur Doron
Tel: (33) 79 38 33 90, Fax: (33) 79 38 16 70

Scènes de villes – Cinéma, télévision et monde urbain
Annual, January. First held in 1992

Selection of fiction films and documentaries of varying length on the theme of cities and suburbs. Aims to encourage encounters between the different types of urban area and cultures. Also includes lectures, debates and exhibitions, giving film makers, residents, local politicians and organizations the chance to exchange views.

Address:
15 rue Marteret,
69100 Villeurbanne,
Tel: (33) 72 43 90 59, Fax: (33) 78 93 56 35

Cinéma du Réel
Annual, March. First held in 1979.

Festival of ethnographic and sociological documentaries. It is followed by the *Bilan du film ethnographique* at the Musée de l'Homme in Paris.

Address: Cinéma du Réel,
Centre Georges Pompidou,
Bibliothèque publique d'information,
19 rue Beaubourg,
75197 Paris Cedex 04
Tel: (33) 1 44 78 44 21, Fax: (33) 1 44 78 12 24

Bilan du film ethnographique

Address:
Musée de l'Homme,
Place du Trocadéro,
75116 Paris,
Tel: (33) 1 47 04 38 22, Fax: (33) 1 45 53 52 82

Festival du Film de Strasbourg

Annual, March. First held in 1972.

Festival of full-length and short documentary and fiction films started by René Cassin, founder of the International Institute of Human Rights with a view of making the public more aware of human rights issues.

Address: Institut international des droits de l'homme,
1 quai Lezay-Marnésia,
67000 Strasbourg
Tel: (33) 88 35 05 50, Fax: (33) 88 36 38 55

Festival du Cinéma de Douarnenez

Annual, August. First held in 1978.

Festival of full-length and short documentary and fiction films aimed at making the films, history, culture and aspirations of minorities better known. A different group is featured each year. Also known for its annual overview of film and audiovisual production in Brittany.

Address:
BP 6/29,
rue du Rosmeur,
29172 Douarnenez CEDEX
Tel: (33) 98 92 09 21, Fax: (33) 98 92 28 10

Festival du film d'Amiens

Annual, November. First held in 1980.

Festival of full-length and short documentary and fiction films on cultural difference and identity, arranged in several categories with themes that change each year. The international category includes films from Africa and the black diaspora in general. Since 1983, the Amiens festival has been twinned with the Panafrican Film Festival (FESPACO) in Ouagadougou, Burkina Faso.

Address:
36 rue de Noyon,
80000 Amiens
Tel: (33) 22 91 01 44, Fax: (33) 22 92 53 04

Festival des trois continents de Nantes

Annual, November. First held in 1979.

Festival of full-length films, aimed at publicizing the more personal style of film from three continents (Africa, Latin America, Asia).

Address: 19A passage Pommeraye,
BP 33/06,
44033 Nantes CEDEX 01
Tel: (33) 40 69 74 14 or 40 69 09 73, Fax: (33) 40 73 55 22

Festival Images du Monde Arabe (FIMA)
Biennial, October. First held in 1993.

Aims to make known documentaries from Arab countries and to foster exchanges between film makers and producers on both sides of the Mediterranean.

Address:
Institut du Monde Arabe,
1 rue des Fossés Saint Bernard,
75005 Paris
Tel: (33) 1 40 51 39 15, Fax: (33) 1 43 54 76 45.

Italy

Festival Nonsolonero
Annual, June. First held in 1989.

Video festival made-up of programmes made for television and independent productions on themes concerning racism and immigration that change each year.

Address:
Coe Communicazione & Media,
Via Lazzaroni 8,
20124 Milan,
Tel: (39) 2 66 80 14 53 Or 2 66 71 20 77, Fax: (39) 2 65 71 43 38

Festival dei Popoli
Annual, November-December. First held in 1959

Selection of documentaries dealing with political, social and anthropological subjects presented in various categories. One that occurs every year is 'Cinema and Anthropology'.

Address:
Festival dei Popoli,
Via dei Castellani 8,
50122 Florence
Tel: (39) 55 29 43 53, Fax: (39) 55 21 36 98

The Netherlands

International Documentary Film Festival (IDFA)
Annual, December. First held in 1987.

International festival of documentaries on themes such as 'War and the Media' and 'Immigration and Minorities'.

Address:
Kleine Gartmanplantsoen 10,
1017 RR Amsterdam,
Tel: (31) 20 627 33 29, Fax: (31) 20 638 53 88

Switzerland

Rencontres médias Nord-Sud
Annual, April. First held in 1985.

International festival of television programmes about the Third World. Also includes seminars and debates on development and communication. Gives international bodies and non-governmental organizations stand space to present their work in the development field.

Address: Rencontres médias Nord-Sud,
c/o Télévision suisse romande,
20 quai Ernest Ansermet,
1205 Geneva.
Tel: (41) 22 708 81 93, Fax: (41) 22 328 94 10

Awards

Belgium

Media Prize for a Harmonious Society
Annual. First held in 1992

Aims to reward journalists from the press and broadcasting who give particularly impartial, balanced and sensitive coverage to the subjects of immigration and foreigners in Belgium.

There are two awards: one for the French-speaking community and one for the Flemish-speaking community. They go to journalists in the press and broadcasting in alternate years.

Each award is worth 200,000 Belgian francs.

Contact: Fondation Roi Baudouin
            rue Brederode 21
            1000 Brussels
            Tel: (32) 2 511 18 40
            Fax: (32) 2 511 52 21

Germany

Civis Prize
Annual. First held in 1988

Rewards radio and television broadcasts which encourage greater mutual understanding among Germans, foreigners and cultural minorities.

Four awards worth 5,000 Deutschmarks are made by the Freudenberg Foundation and the ARD.

Contact: Freudenberg Stiftung
            Freudenberg Strasse 2
            69469 Weinheim/Bergstrasse
            Tel: (49) 62 01/17 498
            Fax: (49) 62 01/13 262

The Netherlands

ADO (Anti Discriminatie Overleg) Media Prize
Annual. First held in 1987.

Rewards the press and broadcasting in alternate years. Only Dutch work qualifies. Another prize, for which foreigners are also eligible, rewards the first articles or films of promising young journalists or programme makers.
Each award is worth 10,000 guilders.

Contact: ADO
              Postbus 596
              3500 AN Utrecht
              Tel: (31) 30 341 264
              Fax: (31) 30 340 231

United Kingdom

The Commission for Racial Equality 'Race in the Media' awards
Annual. First held in 1992.

Aims to reward people working in the media who have contributed to a better understanding of interethnic relations in the United Kingdom.
There are seven categories: regional and local press, specialised press, radio drama, radio and press news, television fiction, news magazines, television documentaries.
Each award is worth £1,000.

Contact: The Commission for Racial Equality
              Race in the Media awards
              Elliot House
              10/12 Allington Street
              London SW1E 5EH
              Tel: +44 (0) 171 932 52 72
              Fax: +44 (0) 171 630 7605

Bibliography

Books and articles

–Batteguay, Alain and Boubeker, Ahmed, *Les images publiques de l'immigration*, CIEMI-L'Harmattan, Paris, 1993.

– Bonnafous, Simone, *L'Immigration prise aux mots*, préface by Gérard Noiriel. Kimé, Paris, 1991.

– Bourdon, Jerôme, 'Le Programme de télévision et l'identité nationale', *Médiaspouvoirs* No. 28, Paris, October 1992.

–Brown, Charles (ed.) *Co-Production International*, Television Business International, London, 1993.

– Costa-Lascoux, Jacqueline and Weil, Patrick (eds.) *Logiques d'états et immigrations*, Kimé, Paris, 1992.

– Daniels, Therese and Gerson, Jane (eds.) *The Colour black: Black Images in British television*, BFI, London, 1989.

– Eckhardt, Josef, 'Audiences reactions to television programmes about foreigners in West Germany', *Media Perspektiven*, Frankfurt, October 1990.

–Falga, Bernard, Withol De Wenden, Catherine and Leggewie, Claus (eds.) *De l'immigration à l'intégration en France et en Allemagne*, Editions du Cerf, Paris, 1994.

- Frachon, Claire and Vargaftig, Marion (eds.), *Télévisions d'Europe et Immigration*, INA/ADEC, La Documentation Française, Paris, 1993.

–Gilroy, Paul, *Small Acts: Thoughts on the politics of Black Culture*. Serpents Tail, London, 1994.

–Gilroy, Paul, *The Black Atlantic: Modernity and double consciousness*. Verso, London, 1993.

– Guimeza, Nicole, 'Les Politiques d'immigration en Europe', *Problèmes politiques et sociaux* No. 673, La Documentation Française, Paris, 1992.

–Hargreaves Alec, '*La Famille Ramdan*: un sitcom pur beur?' *Hommes et Migrations* No. 1147, Paris, October 1991.

– Hargreaves, Alec, 'L'Immigration au prisme de la télévision en France et en Grande-Bretagne'. *Migrations Société* No. 21, vol. 4, Paris, May–June 1992.

– Hargreaves, Alec, 'Ethnic minorities and the mass media in France' in *Popular culture and mass communication in twentieth century France*, Eds. Rosemary Chapman and Nicholas Hewitt, Mellen, Lewison.

–Hennebelle, Guy (ed.) *Le Tribalisme planétaire*, Arléa-Corlet, coll. Panoramiques, Condé-sur-Noireau, 1992.

297

– Husband, Charles (ed.) *A Richer Vision: The Development of Minority Media in Western Democracies*, UNESCO/John Libbey, London, 1994.

– James, Winston and Harris, Clive (eds.), *Inside Babylon: The Caribbean Diaspora in Britain*. Verso, London, 1993.

– Jelen, Christian, *Ils feront de bons Français, enquête sur l'assimilation des Maghrébins*, Robert Laffont, coll. *Notre époque*, Paris, 1991.

– Kaltenbach, Jeanne-Hélène and Pierre-Patrick, *La France, une chance pour l'Islam*, préfaces by Pierre Chaunu and Bruno Étienne. Les Editions du Félin, Paris, 1991.

– Karlin, Daniel and Lainé, Tony, *La Mal Vie...*, préface by Tahar Ben Jelloun. Editions Sociales, Paris, 1978.

– Koschinski, Mickaël, *Fernsehprogramme als Mittel der Intergration*. Die Blaue Eule, Essen, 1986.

– Lapeyronnie, Didier (ed.) *Immigrés en Europe, politiques locales d'intégration*, La Documentation Française, Paris, 1992.

– Lapeyronnie, Didier, *L'individu et les minorités, la France et la Grande-Bretagne face à leurs immigrés*. PUF, Paris, 1993.

– Marletti, Carlo, *Extracomunitari, Dall'immaginario collettivo al vissuto quotidiano del razzismo*, RAI-VPQT, ERI, Milan, 1991.

– Mermet, Gérard, *Euroscopie, Les Européens: qui sont-ils? Comment vivent-ils?* Larousse, Paris, 1991.

– Noiriel, Gérard, *Le Creuset français, histoire de l'immigration XIXe- XXe siècles*. Le Seuil, coll. L'Univers historique, Paris, 1988.

– Perotti, Antonio and Thépaut, France, 'Les Répercussions de la guerre du Golfe sur les Arabes et juifs de France'. *Migrations Société* No. 14, vol 3, CIEMI, Paris, March–April 1991.

– Pines, Jim, *Black and White in Colour, Black People in British Television since 1936*. British Film Institute, London, 1992.

– Regourd, Serge, *La Télévision des Européens*, Institut international d'administration publique, La Documentation française, coll. *Vivre en Europe*, Paris, 1992.

– Schlesinger, Philip, *Media, State and Nation*, Sage, London, 1991.

– Schnapper, Dominique, *L'Europe des immigrés*. François Bourin, Paris, 1992.

– Small, Stephen, *Racialised Barriers: The Black Experience in the United-States and England in the 1980s*, Routledge, London, 1994.

– Taguieff, Pierre-André (ed.) *Face au racisme: I Les Moyens d'agir, II Analyses, hypothèses, perspectives*, La Découverte, coll. Essais, Paris, 1991.

– Todd, Emmanuel, *Le destin des immigrés*, Le Seuil, Paris, 1994.

– Tribalat, Michèle (ed.) *Cent ans d'immigration, Étrangers d'hier, Français d'aujourd'hui*, préface by Michel-Louis Lévy. INED, PUF, coll. Travaux et documents, cahiers No. 131, Paris, 1991.

– Twitchin John, *The Black and White Media Show Book*, Trentham Books, Chester, 1988.

– Van Dijk, Teun A., *Communicating Racism*, Sage, London, 1987.

– Wangermee, Robert & Lhoest, Holde, *L'Après-télévision, une antimythologie de l'audiovisuel*, Hachette/Littérature, coll. Les Grands Rapports, Paris, 1973.

– Weil, Patrick, *La France et ses étrangers, l'aventure d'une politique de l'immigration 1938–1991*, preface by Marceau Long. Calmann-Lévy, Paris, 1991.

– Wieworka, Michel, *L'Espace du racisme*, Le Seuil, Paris, 1991.

– Wiewiorka, Michel (ed.) *Racisme et xénophobie en Europe, une comparaison internationale*, La Découverte, Paris, 1994.

Journals

– *Agenda interculturel, Centre bruxellois d'Action interculturelle*. Bruno Ducoli, Bruxelles.

– *Crosslines, Global Report*, Girardet, Ed (ed.), especially:

   – No. 5, vol. 1, *Co-production is good for you*, Geneva, October 1993.

   – No. 1, vol. 2, *European Television, Human Rights and Foreigners in Perspective*, Geneva, Jan/Feb, 1994.

– *Hommes et Migrations*. especially:

   – No. 1151–1152, *Une autre Allemagne*, Hommes et Migrations, Paris, February–March 1992.

   – No. 1154, *Le Poids des mots*, Paris, May 1992.

   – No. 1159, *Europe horizon 2000*, Paris, November 1992.

   – No. 1178, *Les lois Pasqua*, Paris, July 1994.

– *Le Courrier de l'UNESCO*, Paris, especially:

   June 1993, *La condition minoritaire*

   July-August 1994, *A la découverte de l'autre, étranges étrangers*.

– *Migrations Société*, especially:

   – No. 4, vol 1. *Médias et immigration*, CIEMI, Paris, August, 1989.

   – No. 11, vol 2, *Le Droit contre le racisme*, CIEMI, Paris, September–October 1990.

   – No. 13, vol 3, *Nouveaux flux migratoires*, CIEMI, Paris, January–February 1991.

   – No. 18, vol 3, *Immigrations et télévision*, CIEMI, Paris, November–December 1991.

   – No. 21, vol 4, *L'Immigration au prisme des télévisions*, CIEMI, Paris, May–June 1992.

– *M Scope Média*, especially no. 4, Paris, April 1993, dossier *Images de l'immigration dans les médias*.

– *Revue européenne des migrations internationales: URA, CNRS, Université de Poitiers*, Eds. Gildas Simon and Jacqueline Costa-Lascoux, especially:

   – No. 1/2, vol 4, *L'Immigration en France*, Poitiers, 1988.

   – No. 2, vol 6, *Politique d'intégration et Islam en Belgique*, Poitiers, 1990.

   – No. 2, vol 7, *L'Europe de l'Est, la communauté et les migrations*, Poitiers, 1991.

   – No. 1, vol 10, *Mobilisation des migrants en Europe, du national au transnational*, Poitiers, 1994.

– *Spectrum, The Magazine of Public Broadcasting for a Multicultural Europe*, January 1994, No 2.

– *The Black Film Bulletin* No. 2 & 3 British Film Institute, London, 1994.

Special issues

– *CinémAction*:

   – No. 14, *Cinémas du Maghreb*. Papyrus, Paris, 1981.

   – No. 56, *Cinémas métis de Hollywood aux films beurs*. Corlet, Condé-sur-Noireau, July 1990.

– No. 57, *Les Feuilletons télévisés européens*. Corlet, Condé-sur Noireau, August 1990.

– *TV1, Télévision française: la saison 1991*. Corlet, Condé-sur Noireau, February 1992.

– *Dossiers de l'audiovisuel:*

– No. 33, *La Télévision régionale en Europe*, Ed. Michel Trelluyer. INA/La Documentation française, Paris, September–October 1990.

– No. 35, *L' Europe audiovisuelle de l'après directive*. Ed. Guy Pineau, INA/La Documentation française, Paris, January–February 1991.

– *Eurodience* No 51, (lettre européene des programmes et des audiences), Dossier *Privées/Publiques: l'affrontement généralisé*, Médiamétrie/INA, Bry-sur-Marne, February 1992.

– *L'Événement Européen, Initiatives et Débats* No. 11, *L'Europe et ses immigrés*. Le Seuil, Paris, October 1990–1991.

– *Libération*, 'Migrations: la planète en courant', supplément du No. 3136, Paris, 22 June 1991.

– *Médiaspouvoirs*, 'Le Guide des télévisions en Europe', François Truffart (ed.), No. hors série, Paris, 1991.

– *Plein Droit*, 'L'Europe multicommunautaire', numéro spécial, Gisti/IM'media, Paris, 1989–1990.

– *Screen Digest*, 'World videorecorder market reaches maturity', London, June 1992.

Reports, studies, reference books

– Bardout, Jean-Claude and Farbiaz, Patrick, *Le Rôle des mass-media télévisés dans la production ou l'entretien des mécanismes d'exclusion sociale*, Paris, 1991.

– Beaud, Paul, *Médias communautaires? Radio et télévisions locales et expériences d'animation audiovisuelle en Europe*, Council of Europe, Strasbourg, 1980.

– *Conditions juridiques et culturelles de l'intégration*, Rapport au Premier ministre de mars 1992, Haut Conseil à l'intégration/La Documentation francaise, coll. *Official reports*, Paris, 1992.

– Corset, Pierre and Meissonnier, Anne-Marie, *L'Offre de programmes pour les jeunes*, étude réalisée par l'Institut national de l'audiovisuel pour le ministère de la Culture, de la Communication et des Grands travaux (Délégation au développement et aux formations), et le Service juridique et technique de l'information, Bry-sur-Marne, February 1991.

– Ducoli, Bruno and Martinow-Remiche, Anne, *Les Grands médias au service de l'identité culturelle des travailleurs migrants*, Council of Europe, Strasbourg, 1979.

– *Guide du cinéma et de l'audiovisuel en Europe centrale et orientale*, Institut d'études slaves Idate/Eurocréation, Paris, 1992.

– Hujanen, Taisto, *The Role of information in the realisation of the human rights of migrant workers*, Actes de la Conférence internationale de Tampere, June 1983, University of Tampere, Finland, 1984.

– *The Kagan Book of European Television Channels 1992*, Kagan World Media Ltd, London, 1992.

– *The Kagan Book of European Television, The Country Profiles 1992*, Kagan World Media Ltd, London, 1992.

– Lapeyronnie, Didier, *L'Intégration des minorités immigrées, étude comparative, France/Grande-Bretagne*, ADRI, Issy-les-Moulineaux, December1990.

– Lebon, André, *Immigration et présence étrangère en France, le bilan d'une année 1992–1993*,

Ministère des Affaires Sociales, Paris 1993.

– Masterman, Len, *Le Développement de l'éducation aux médias dans l'Europe des années 80*, Council of Europe, Education and Culture, Strasbourg, 1988.

– *Médias et minorités en Europe*, Ressources documentaires du CIEMI, Cahier No. 1, Paris, January 1991.

– *Migrants et médias: des travailleurs invités aux minorités linguistiques et culturelles*, Council of Europe, Strasbourg, 1987.

– *Pour un modèle francais d'intégration*, rapport au Premier ministre, premier rapport annuel, Haut Conseil à l'intégration/La Documentation française, coll. *Rapports officiels*, Paris, 1991.

– *Présence et représentation des immigrés et des minorités ethniques à la télévision française*, enquête ARA, CIEMI, Paris, October 1991.

– *Répertoire des associations immigrées dans la communauté européenne*, CIEMI, Paris, January 1991.

– Ross, Karen, *Television in Black and White: ethnic stereotypes and popular television*, Centre for Research in Ethnic Relations, Warwick University, 1992.

– Samuelson, Edward, *Les Jeux à la télévision française*, University of New York, 1993.

– *TBI Yearbook*, Television Business International, London, 1993.

– *Tendances des migrations internationales*, annual report 1991 SOPEMI, OECD, Paris, 1992.

– *Tendances des migrations internationales*, annual report 1993 SOPEMI, OECD, Paris, 1994.

– *The Portrayal of Ethnic Minorities on Television*, Broadcasting Standards Council, London, 1992.

Media titles available from John Libbey

Acamedia Research Monographs

Taxation and Representation: Media, Political Communication and the Poll Tax
David Deacon and Peter Golding
Hardback ISBN 0 86196 390 3

Satellite Television in Western Europe (revised edition 1992)
Richard Collins
Hardback ISBN 0 86196 203 6

Beyond the Berne Convention
Copyright, Broadcasting and the Single European Market
Vincent Porter
Hardback ISBN 0 86196 267 2

Nuclear Reactions: A Study in Public Issue Television
John Corner, Kay Richardson and Natalie Fenton
Hardback ISBN 0 86196 251 6

Transnationalization of Television in Western Europe
Preben Sepstrup
Hardback ISBN 0 86196 280 X

The People's Voice: Local Radio and Television in Europe
Nick Jankowski, Ole Prehn and James Stappers
Hardback ISBN 0 86196 322 9

Television and the Gulf War
David E. Morrison
Hardback ISBN 0 86196 341 5

Contra-Flow in Global News
Oliver Boyd Barrett and Daya Kishan Thussu
Hardback ISBN 0 86196 344 X

CNN World Report: Ted Turner's International News Coup
Don M. Flournoy
Hardback ISBN 0 86196 359 8

Small Nations: Big Neighbour
Roger de la Garde, William Gilsdorf and Ilja Wechselmann
Hardback ISBN 0 86196 343 1

European Media Research Series

The New Television in Europe
Edited by Alessandro Silj
Hardback ISBN 0 86196 361 X

Media Industry in Europe
Edited by Antonio Pilati
Paperback ISBN 0 86196 398 9

European Institute for the Media

Television and the Viewer Interest: Explorations in the responsiveness of European Broadcasters
Jeremy Mitchell and Jay G Blumler (eds)
Paperback ISBN 0 86196 440 3

Media titles available from John Libbey

Broadcasting and Audio-visual Policy in the European Single Market
Richard Collins
Hardback ISBN 0 86196 405 5

Aid for Cinematographic and Audio-visual Production In Europe
(published for the Council of Europe)
Jean-Noël Dibie
Hardback ISBN 0 86196 397 0

BBC World Service

Global Audiences: Research for Worldwide Broadcasting 1993
Edited by Graham Mytton
Paperback ISBN 0 86196 400 4

Broadcasting Standards Council Publications

A Measure of Uncertainty: The Effects of the Mass Media
Guy Cumberbatch and Dennis Howitt
Hardback ISBN 0 86196 231 1

Violence in Television Fiction: Public Opinion and Broadcasting Standards
David Docherty
Paperback ISBN 0 86196 284 2

Survivors and the Media
Ann Shearer
Paperback ISBN 0 86196 332 6

Taste and Decency in Broadcasting
Andrea Millwood Hargrave
Paperback ISBN 0 86196 331 8

A Matter of Manners? – The Limits of Broadcast Language
Edited by Andrea Millwood Hargrave
Paperback ISBN 0 86196 337 7

Sex and Sexuality in Broadcasting
Andrea Millwood Hargrave
Paperback ISBN 0 86196 393 8

Violence in Factual Television
Andrea Millwood Hargrave
Paperback ISBN 0 86196 441 1

Radio and Audience Attitudes
Andrea Millwood Hargrave
PAperback ISBN 0 86196 481 0

International Institute of Communications

Vision and Hindsight: The First 25 Years of the Internatuional Institute Of Communications
Rex Winsbury and Shehina Fazal (eds)
Hardback ISBN 0 86196 449 7
Paperback ISBN 0 86196 467 5

Acamedia Textbook

Political Marketing and Communication
Philippe J. Maarek
Paperback ISBN 0 86196 377 6

Media titles available from John Libbey

UNESCO Publications

A Richer Vision: The development of ethnic minority media in Western democracies
Charles Husband (ed)
Paperback ISBN 0 86196 450 0

Video World-Wide: An International Study
Manuel Alvarado (ed)
Paperback ISBN 0 86196 143 9

University of Manchester Broadcasting Symposium

And Now for the BBC ...
Nod Miller and Rod Allen (eds)
Paperback ISBN 0 86196 318 0

It's Live – But Is It Real?
Nod Miller and Rod Allen (eds)
Paperback ISBN 0 86196 370 9

Broadcasting Enters the Marketplace
Nod Miller and Rod Allen (eds)
Paperback ISBN 0 86196 434 9

ITC Television Research Monographs

Television in Schools
Robin Moss, Christopher Jones and Barrie Gunter
Hardback ISBN 0 86196 314 8

Television: The Public's View
Barrie Gunter and Carmel McLaughlin
Hardback ISBN 0 86196 348 2

The Reactive Viewer
Barrie Gunter and Mallory Wober
Hardback ISBN 0 86196 358 X

Television: The Public's View 1992
Barrie Gunter and Paul Winstone
Hardback ISBN 0 86196 399 7

Seeing is Believing: Religion and Television in the 1990s
Barrie Gunter and Rachel Viney
Hardback ISBN 0 86196 442 X

Published in association with The Arts Council

Picture This: Media Representations of Visual Art and Artists
Philip Hayward (ed)
Paperback ISBN 0 86196 126 9

Culture, Technology and Creativity
Philip Hayward (ed)
Paperback ISBN 0 86196 266 4

Parallel Lines: Media Representations of Dance
Stephanie Jordan & Dave Allen (eds)
Paperback ISBN 0 86196 371 7

Arts TV: A History of British Arts Television
John A Walker
Paperback ISBN 0 86196 435 7

Media titles available from John Libbey

A Night in at the Opera: Media Representation of Opera
Jeremy Tambling (ed)
ISBN 0 86196 466 7

IBA Television Research Monographs

Teachers and Television:
A History of the IBA's Educational Fellowship Scheme
Josephine Langham
Hardback ISBN 0 86196 264 8

Godwatching: Viewers, Religion and Television
Michael Svennevig, Ian Haldane, Sharon Spiers and Barrie Gunter
Hardback ISBN 0 86196 198 6
Paperback ISBN 0 86196 199 4

Violence on Television: What the Viewers Think
Barrie Gunter and Mallory Wober
Hardback ISBN 0 86196 171 4
Paperback ISBN 0 86196 172 2

Home Video and the Changing Nature of Television Audience
Mark Levy and Barrie Gunter
Hardback ISBN 0 86196 175 7
Paperback ISBN 0 86196 188 9

Patterns of Teletext Use in the UK
Bradley S. Greenberg and Carolyn A. Lin
Hardback ISBN 0 86196 174 9
Paperback ISBN 0 86196 187 0

Attitudes to Broadcasting Over the Years
Barrie Gunter and Michael Svennevig
Hardback ISBN 0 86196 173 0
Paperback ISBN 0 86196 184 6

Television and Sex Role Stereotyping
Barrie Gunter
Hardback ISBN 0 86196 095 5
Paperback ISBN 0 86196 098 X

Television and the Fear of Crime
Barrie Gunter
Hardback ISBN 0 86196 118 8
Paperback ISBN 0 86196 119 6

Behind and in Front of the Screen – Television's Involvement with Family Life
Barrie Gunter and Michael Svennevig
Hardback ISBN 0 86196 123 4
Paperback ISBN 0 86196 124 2

Institute of Local Television

Citizen Television: A Local Dimension to Public Service Broadcasting
Dave Rushton (ed)
Hardback ISBN 0 86196 433 0

Reporters Sans Frontières

1994 Report
Freedom of the Press Throughout the World
Paperback ISBN 0 86196 452 7